About the author

Aidan Ricketts is an experienced social and environmental activist as well as a prominent activism educator, academic and writer. Aidan has written for many academic journals and contributed to several books. He is also a lecturer with the School of Law and Justice at Southern Cross University, Lismore, Australia.

THE ACTIVISTS' HANDBOOK

A step-by-step guide to participatory democracy

Aidan Ricketts

Zed Books

LONDON | NEW YORK

The Activists' Handbook: A step-by-step guide to participatory democracy was first published in 2012 by Zed Books Ltd, 7 Cynthia Street, London N1 9JF, UK and Room 400, 175 Fifth Avenue, New York, NY 10010, USA

www.zedbooks.co.uk

The illustrations were drawn by Kudra Falla
Set in FFKievit and Monotype Plantin by Ewan Smith, London
Index: ed.emery@thefreeuniversity.net
Cover designed by Rogue Four Design
Printed and bound in Great Britain by the CPI Group (UK) Ltd, Croydon CRO 4YY

Distributed in the USA exclusively by Palgrave Macmillan, a division of St Martin's Press, LLC, 175 Fifth Avenue, New York, NY 10010, USA

A catalogue record for this book is available from the British Library
Library of Congress Cataloging in Publication Data available

ISBN 978 1 84813 593 2 hb
ISBN 978 1 84813 592 5 pb

CONTENTS

FIGURES

Introduction: cycles within cycles

Recently I provided a community activism consultancy for a group of residents threatened by the rising sea-level on Australia's east coast. It was different from my usual line of work; these were not environmentalists fighting some new damaging development, or local residents busting political corruption. This was a group of property owners, threatened by erosion and frustrated at the government's lack of compassion for their community's predicament. Most of these people had never been activists before; they had previously enjoyed a quiet life by the sea until the tide of history (and the tide itself) shocked them out of the complacent belief that the government could be relied upon to take care of their interests. Some of my activist colleagues queried why I was helping this group of people, whose concerns seemed largely proprietary and only partly communitarian in nature. While I was helping map their campaign, one of the residents also asked me, 'What is your interest in coming here and helping us? Why are you doing this?' It was as if he suspected I had another another motive. After explaining that I was actually receiving a small fee, I went on to explain the real reason why I was there.

I believe in real democracy, and I believe in the power of communities to organize to pursue their interests, and I am passionate about helping people take a stand and make a difference in the world.

To many of my activist colleagues, and even to many of the residents themselves, the issue looked like just another NIMBY (not in my backyard) issue, but to me it was so much more. This little community was faced with the loss of their homes owing to climate change; they were a test case for how society and government would respond to the impact of climate change, and more importantly they provided a human face to an issue which to many people had so far only been an abstract environmental problem.

I sincerely believe that when people wake one day to find an issue on their doorstep that they cannot just ignore, there is enormous potential for transformation. This is why I am supportive of many groups that others may label as NIMBY. What is important in all community campaigns is the potential to overcome passivity and unleash empowerment. My social change work has shown me time and again that when individuals first break the habit of political passivity they begin a journey from being a passive subject to an active citizen and beyond to being a lifelong activist. Taking a stand on a local issue, or even taking a small stand on a big global issue, may seem like a small step, but for so many people it unleashes a power that lies dormant in us all. In this book I discuss the life cycle of social movements, but underlying this is the life cycle of activists themselves.

When a person first takes a stand on an issue, they are transformed. The people around them start to see them differently; their neighbours and colleagues may see them as a potential leader, their opponents as a threat. Soon enough their first ordeal of awakening occurs, most often when they are attacked publicly for having dared to stand up. Possibly for the first time in their lives they encounter first-hand the stubbornness, lies, hypocrisy and embedded corruption that reinforce the vested interests they have dared to oppose or question. This is a critical stage for people; they may become despondent and defeated. But more often there is a great dissonance that ignites a fire in the belly far deeper and more powerful than the small issue that first awakened them; they begin to feel the need to make changes in the world around them, to change the values, attitudes and world views that caused the problems in the first place. From a NIMBY a much grander social change activist is frequently born.

There is also a tertiary stage in the life cycle of an activist, something like the metamorphosis of a larva to an adult insect, capable of multiplying its own kind many times over. This metaphor begins to explain why I have written this book.

After working long and hard on a campaign, and particularly after achieving success, we may ask: What next? Should I simply retire from the field and take all my experience and knowledge with me? Or should I choose another campaign and throw myself into it with the same passion and energy? Or is there a more effective path?

For me, the answer was obvious; as an educator, educational designer and experienced activist, the best contribution I could make for the future was to become an activism educator. I realized that as an activist I could really only work on one campaign at a time, but if I could help train up other activists then hundreds, possibly thousands, of campaigns might benefit. This in itself caused me to realize that my own world view had expanded remarkably, and instead of being issue-focused I had become focused upon the process of social change and participatory democracy itself.

Since then my passion has been to develop resources that can guide other activists and social change advocates to greater insight and success.

This book is not about the issues that people work on, it is about how to go about it. I am comfortable with the idea that some people may use this book to work on campaigns that I may not agree with. To me it's not about the issue, it's about empowering people to take a stand.

The ideas for this book began many years ago as a manual for activist training that accompanied face-to-face training camps for the North East Forest Alliance (NEFA). Later the opportunity arose to develop a university-accredited 'Public Interest Advocacy' course through Southern Cross University. The university course has been an ongoing success, but there was a need to reach out to the wider community, and so together with some colleagues I started running activism clinics at a major public festival at Woodford in Queensland from 2003. It was through these clinics that many opportunities for real-life consultancies arose and I was able to refine, field-test and further develop the techniques and tools contained in this book. But once again there was a limit to my ability to visit groups in person and conduct workshops to 'tune up' their campaigns, so I decided to develop a set of written materials.

I sincerely hope that this book inspires and empowers activists and campaigns and most importantly that it saves newly emergent activists from the ordeal of having to 'reinvent the wheel' of strategy, planning and implementation of successful campaigns. It is a practical book based on years of research, consultation and first-hand experience. I have endeavoured not to reinvent the wheel myself; where reliable texts or websites already provide useful information I have aimed to direct readers to these; otherwise I have aimed to encapsulate in as accessible a form as possible the essential tools, tips, skills and strategies for effective activism. I would like to acknowledge the contribution of my colleagues Simon Clough and John Corkill, who worked with me in some of the earliest phases of this slowly evolving project. In particular John made a significant contribution to the evolution of Chapters 3 and 5, and Simon made a significant contribution to the evolution of Chapters 2 and 11.

The book is arranged into twelve chapters that cover discrete aspects of the subject matter.

Chapter 1 explores the idea of participatory democracy itself and examines the fundamentally important concept of public interest activism and advocacy. Chapter 2 explores the nature, core values and life cycle of social movements as vehicles for social change. Together these chapters provide an essential framework for understanding all of the more detailed and practical chapters that follow.

Chapter 3 discusses the strategic environment within which public interest activists and social movements operate and examines various approaches to enhance the strategic effectiveness of campaigns. Chapter 4 helps put all of this strategic thinking into practice and is one of the most important and practical chapters in the book, providing a range of powerful field-tested tools and processes for envisioning, planning and implementing successful campaigns. Chapter 5 goes on to explore the practical skills needed for conducting public interest research, generating publicity, using the media, writing media releases and appropriate professional writing. Together these three chapters alert activists to the most important foundational tools and practices for effective campaigning.

Chapters 6 and 7 advise on the most effective ways to work for change in either the government or corporate sector, respectively.

Chapter 8 addresses the modern art of activism by exploring physical protest, including marches, rallies, blockades and provocative and theatrical direct action. Chapter 9, on the other hand, examines the way in which activists use new technologies and provides practical advice for people wanting to launch new digital campaigns or add a digital component to an existing campaign. Ideally the lessons in these two chapters will be combined to brew powerful campaigns that engage in both digital and robust real-world actions for change.

Chapter 10 looks at using litigation as a campaign tactic. It examines both practical issues, such as dealing with lawyers and going to court, and the important strategic, organizational, financial and political issues involved. Chapter 11, on the other hand, is concerned with non-litigious means of conflict resolution and offers some tools for conflict resolution, including strategic questioning, negotiation and mediation.

Chapter 12 travels into the realms of personal experience, psychology, philosophy and even spirituality to help activists find ways to avoid personal burnout and survive long campaigns; this chapter also explores ways to build sustainability into the functioning of activist groups.

Together, the twelve chapters provide the background, insight, analysis and big picture necessary to frame social change work, then go on to explore the actual tools and processes for getting the job done effectively.

Life cycles provide a good metaphor for the theme of this book. Within the body of the work there is much discussion of the life cycle of campaigns and social movements, and this introduction explores the process through which individuals metamorphose from subjects to citizens and onward to activists and change agents. Implicit in the art and practice of social change work, of course, is an ongoing process of envisioning a better world. Social development has no end point; human societies will always need activists to address injustice, to promote sustainability, to help us achieve our collective potential and to help the planet survive. I hope this book will play its own small part in helping move individuals, social movements and societies along that path.

Acknowledgements

My thanks to my family for the love, support and forbearance to allow this book to be written. My very special thanks and acknowledgement to John Corkill and Simon Clough for their support and significant contributions to this project, and to Bill Moyer and Katrina Shields for their inspirational works and for the wheels I did not need to re-invent. My thanks generally to all of the brave, ethical people who inhabit this beautiful planet, who play their part in improving the way we live as a species upon it and with each other.

ONE | **Activism, advocacy and the practice of democracy**

Introduction

Activism, social change advocacy and the practice of democracy are inextricably linked. It is the work of activists and social movements which pushes society along, prompts it to deal with its own failings and inequalities and helps to manifest a vision of a better world. In order to be able to be effective as social change agents we need the ability to articulate our message so that ordinary people can identify with the campaign and come to support its goals. This chapter provides the theoretical foundation for understanding the way in which public interest social activism works to bring about useful social change. It provides an essential framework for understanding all of the more detailed and practical chapters that follow.

1.0 Democracy 24/7

Democracy is an idea grounded in the premise that political power derives from the will, or at least the consent, of the people. This is the easiest way to summarize a political idea that has a very long history both intellectually and in practice. There is a wealth of literature available on the theory of democracy, ranging from Plato through to thinkers like Locke and Rousseau and Paine, whose writings helped inform European and American movements towards democracy from the seventeenth century onwards. More recently writers such as Bookchin, Chomsky and Foucault have contributed new perspectives and critiques on the subject. It is not the purpose of this book to become deeply engaged in theoretical debate about the nature of democracy. The way the word democracy is used in this book does, however, go beyond merely describing a system of governance or a set of institutional arrangements involving the election of lawmakers; it describes a wide range of practices in a lived community that influence the direction of the whole society.

Democratic practice involves any actions where individuals or groups of people engage in public activities designed to influence change or direct the way in which society functions. It is intentional that this description refers to public activities, simply to distinguish democratic practice from various covert or private actions that may be undertaken for the purpose of exerting influence.

Understood in this broad sense democracy is a process that is occurring every day throughout society, and only a small part of that process may directly involve elections, governments or institutions of state. When we understand democracy in this way, as processes taking place, then the concept of activism automatically assumes a central place in this community of practice.

Activism is also a very broad term which refers to actions and activities intentionally designed to exert influence within democratic processes. In this sense we could see democracy as the process and activism as the specific actions and activities taking place as part of that process.

A number of terms are used more or less interchangeably throughout this book, including activism and social change advocacy. Activism can be highly organized or it can be sporadic and non-organized. Social change advocacy is a form of activism in which individuals or groups have a clearly defined objective and methodology for promoting change. Frequently an organized process for pursuing change will also be referred to simply as a 'campaign'.

This chapter will examine some very important contextual issues that frame the work of activists and advocates for social change. It is important to adopt a bigger-picture view of social change work to understand how a particular campaign or issue fits into a broader vision about society and democracy.

1.1 I disagree with your argument but I support your right to make it

A distinction can be made between the immediate issue that a campaign is about and the context within which the campaign takes place. When we take a small-picture approach to a campaign we may simply ask ourselves whether we agree or don't agree with a particular position. But if we step back we may ask ourselves broader questions, such as whether we support the processes by which individuals and communities are able to exert influence to bring about change in their world. When we ask this question we are considering a deeper issue about our personal or collective commitment to democratic processes. This book examines analyses and provides practical advice for people engaged in democratic practice, irrespective of the cause or issue in which they are involved. It is this approach which exemplifies a deep commitment to democratic practice itself rather than simply an issues-based approach. But it is fair to also make it clear from the outset that this book is primarily about campaigns that are conducted in relation to public interest causes rather than private lobbying, although as we shall see the distinction is not always clear cut.

1.2 Public interest campaigns

Earlier it was observed that democratic actions should be of a public nature. It is important to be able to distinguish between public activity and activity that is purely of a personal nature, designed to secure the private vested interests of individuals, corporations or economic sectors. We could get sidetracked into discussing whether self-interested or corporate activity can ever be considered democratic practice, and it would be hard to define clear dividing lines. A lot of political lobbying, for example, is done by self-interested individuals, industry lobby groups and other vested interest groups. This book is about activism and social change work that has public interest values as core components of the campaign aim and purpose. This is not to say that there is anything wrong with individuals and groups using democratic processes to pursue their self-interest, provided it is done openly and honestly, but for the purposes of this book it is important to maintain some distinction between the kind of self-interested lobbying that big tobacco companies may invest in and genuine campaigns that promote public interest values. It is not an easy distinction to maintain; while we can be clear that the attempts by big companies to dominate and influence the political process of government are not public interest activism, it becomes less easy to define the precise boundaries of public interest work in a host of situations where there is an intermingling of self-interest and public interest motivations in a given campaign. For  example, campaigns by trade unions for better wages or conditions clearly have a private interest element for the workers concerned but they are also public interest campaigns because of their role in achieving and maintaining these standards for workers generally. So while we can never be prescriptive about what is and isn't a public interest campaign we can at least explore some indicia that will help determine whether a particular campaign or action has a public interest focus.

The ability to represent the public interest is a strategically important aspect that underlies almost all genuine community activism and social change work. It is important to develop a broad concept of the public interest and to be able to articulate the way in which your campaign promotes it as distinct from private and vested interests. This distinction is important in a number of ways:

- it can affect how people perceive a campaign;
- it can affect the way the media treat the campaign; and
- it can affect your ability to seek legal redress and other important legal rights.

This distinction between public interest issues and vested interest issues will be explored in more detail later in this chapter, but first it is useful to step back a little farther to explore how we came to have such a distinction.

2.0 Life in a liberalist society

We live in a society that is preoccupied with private concerns, particularly property and financial concerns. Our legal system and our society's political and economic structures have been deeply influenced by the liberal ideological tradition, which emphasizes individuality as the most fundamental and significant feature of human existence. Our legal system in particular is constructed in a way that sees humans as isolated individuals within a sea of other individuals rather than as a collective community. In a society which so routinely overemphasizes the individualist aspect of human life, the social or community side is often neglected.

To use an example: the law has no problem recognizing the legal rights of one person to the use and amenity of a parcel of land which that person holds (a private right), but much greater difficulty in recognizing the entitlement of people generally to take action to protect important environmental qualities such as clean air, clean water or open space.

One of the challenges faced by public interest advocates, quite apart from achieving a particular outcome on an issue, is to have the issue seen as a legitimate concern in the first place.

Within liberal theory the role of community is often assumed to be entirely encapsulated within the functions of the formal mechanisms of state. A consequence of this is that the idea of community can start to appear vague and intangible. When this occurs the centralized state becomes the only clearly recognizable expression of collective power.

Such a view leads to some significant anxiety about the power of the state. Traditionally, liberalist thinkers tended to view the centralized state with suspicion, as a necessary but dangerous aspect of human social relations. The primary task that liberalist legal thinkers set for themselves was to strike a balance between individual rights and authoritarian state power. While this preoccupation with the assumed dichotomy between individual rights and state power has supported a range of individual rights, it has also tended to marginalize concerns which arise on behalf of the community generally that cannot be linked to an identifiable individual.

A middle position and one that underlies much of the perspective presented in this book is a more community-based understanding of society. This vision of society accepts the outer points of focus of the state and the individual as real but emphasizes the vitally important role of organized communities in mediating the exercise of power within society.

This vision of community power and social organization sees community participation as a vital part of the process of democracy and the concept of the 'public interest' as the key focus of genuine social change activity. Looked at in this way, community empowerment and community activism are essential aspects of a healthy democracy and hold the key to protecting individuals, minorities and the environment from exploitation, and are vital for the process of identifying, promoting and even changing widely held social values.

In an age when corporate power is also overwhelming individuals and communities it is more important than ever that human communities become more effectively organized to be able to draw together the power of the human community and use it to resist authoritarian government, exploitative corporate practices and environmental destruction. This important task lies at the heart of the purpose of this book as whole.

2.1 Liberalism and democracy ... not the same thing

We often hear the term liberal-democracy expressed as a connected idea. There is a reason the two words need to be put together and that is that they are not one and the same. While liberalism does emphasize the rights of individuals, particularly their private property rights, it does not automatically sit well with a democratic view of the world which ultimately strives to see real power returned to 'the people'. 'The people' used in this sense implies a community of citizens.

Classical liberals feared that the people so assembled might well at times choose to interfere with property rights, particularly of the most well off; consequently they had a certain fear of true democracy. Liberal democracies are systems that take steps to bolster private property rights in ways that will make them immune to community control. This protection of private rights over communal rights can be found in various constitutional protections of private property, as well as in laws that limit the community's right to be heard in court and in numerous other ways in which the common law is structured.

You may not need to know all the details of common law history and theory to be an activist, but it is important to understand that as community activists you may well find yourselves wanting to resist the power of private wealth (for example, land developers, mining companies, etc.) to achieve some public good. When you are involved in such a campaign you are promoting the democratic aspects of our society over the property-centred aspects. You are advocating a 'public interest' concern, and you may be doing it at the expense of some wealthy property owner. It is important that you understand this point, so that you understand what you are up against and so that you can articulate the public interest nature of your campaign effectively. This may sound like words and theory, but it is very important to be able to identify and articulate the public interest perspective in any issue.

3.0 Public interest versus vested interest

What is meant by this idea of the public interest?

An issue that often leads to confusion is the question of whether the public has to agree with you for your cause to be described as a 'public interest concern', and the short answer is 'No, it does not'.

In describing yourself or another person as an advocate of the public interest you are not asserting that everyone or even the majority agrees with that cause, but simply that the cause being advocated is a public rather than a purely private concern. If, for example, you are campaigning to end discrimination against a minority group, you may well not have the support of a majority of the public at all, but you are still promoting a cause which by its nature is a public interest concern.

That is not to say that the two never overlap; frequently one person's private concerns also have significant public interest content. To use an example, a particular individual's right to compensation for injuries sustained in a car accident will usually be a purely private interest, with no great bearing upon the rest of the community except perhaps to re-emphasize the well-established legal principle of making good damage caused to one person by another. On the other hand the right of a person to receive damages for the costs, pain and suffering caused by industrial pollution in an urban area will have a strong public interest content, impacting as it does on the interests of a whole class of affected persons within the community.

To take another example, Australia, the United States and Canada have all witnessed a high degree of controversy over the logging of old-growth forests in recent years. The environmentalists' concern for biodiversity values, public access to undisturbed forests and the protection of nature generally are clearly of a public interest nature. The environmentalists have nothing to gain personally or financially from forest protection (other than a sense of achieving what they see as right).

The timber industries, on the other hand, are primarily concerned about their own investments and profits and so (quite validly) are asserting a vested interest perspective. It may appear from this description that the environmentalist argument is being privileged by being described as public interest, and from the moral perspective of this book that is true, but it needs to be remembered that the private property perspective is dominant in our society and that the public interest perspective is an important counterpoint.

The issue is never completely black and white, either; timber companies may clearly represent vested interests, but where groups of concerned citizens from towns that rely on logging for income become involved and argue that the town will suffer socially if its economic base is withdrawn, they can realistically lay some claim to presenting a public-interest-based counter-argument to the environmentalists.

Public interest advocates may be activists, trade unionists, media spokespeople or ordinary citizens emboldened to make a public stand on a particular

issue. It is not the qualifications, occupation or skills of the advocate which defines public interest advocacy, nor is it any question of how many people agree, or whether there are other sides to the story; it is the act of advocating a cause which has significant public interest content.

3.1 Conflicting public interest perspectives

Sometimes there can be a public debate in which both sides are promoting a public interest argument. For example, in public debates about stem cell research both sides are arguing on the basis of public interest.

Another example of conflicting public interest arguments could be where there is a controversy about whether to cull feral animals in a nature reserve; you could have environmentalists in favour of a cull and animal rights activists against a cull. Both sides of these arguments are running a public interest campaign. This is because both sides of the argument are articulating and promoting distinct and competing social values.

So if both sides of a given argument can both be coming from a public interest perspective, how do we distinguish those campaigns or activities that are not involved with public interest concerns? The best way is to ask whether they represent mostly vested interests.

3.2 Is my issue a public interest issue?

To make this theoretical discussion more practical we should go on to consider the criteria that you might use for establishing whether your issue is a public interest one. In the exercise below we suggest that issues can range from being purely private vested interest issues to being fully public interest issues. In between there are the overlap issues that involve an element of both.

A quick checklist

1 *Is this an issue that affects only my own personal interests, particularly financial or economic?* If so it is probably not a public interest issue at all – it's probably a private vested interest.

2 *Is this an issue that affects my own economic or property interests but also those of other people in my situation?* If so it is probably not a public interest issue but rather an issue in which you and others have common vested interests, e.g. shareholders in a company, co-owners in a block of units.

3 *Does this issue involving my personal interests also include a wider issue of social or economic justice that makes it an issue of more general public concern?* If so it may be a blended issue that has a significant public interest element.

For example: if you are seeking compensation for asbestos poisoning from a corporation along with other similarly affected people (class action issue) or you are a group of residents opposing a noisy or polluting industry in your suburb, this is a partly public interest issue. These are often referred to as NIMBY (not in my backyard) issues. Although the term is often used in a derogatory way, many of the more successful and important public interest campaigns start from a NIMBY base.

4 *Is this an issue in which I have no direct stake as an individual other than my heartfelt desire to help bring about a safer, cleaner, more peaceful or more sustainable world?* Clearly a public interest issue.

3.3 Public interest campaigning in the courts

The discussion so far reveals that the position taken by this book privileges public interest campaigns over vested interest campaigns and this is an intentional political perspective, but it is important to be aware that common law legal systems actually discriminate against public interest advocates, particularly in relation to litigation through the courts. Litigation will be examined in more detail in Chapter 10, but for now it is important to be aware of the way common law courts traditionally view public interest advocates. Common law judicial systems (the UK, the USA, Australia, New Zealand and Canada) are primarily concerned with enforcing the vested interests of individuals, in particular their private property interests. This is an important threshold concept that needs to be grasped in order to go on to understand the general body of common law as it applies to public interest campaigns.

The English case of *Boyce* v. *Paddington Borough Council* [1903] 1 Ch 109 established a restrictive approach to allowing public interest advocates to appear in court in cases where they lacked what the court described as 'special damage peculiar to himself'. This approach exemplified the common law concern for the enforcement of private property rights and its reluctance to embrace litigation that went beyond the litigants' personal interests. The case was relied upon by the Australian High Court in 1980 in a controversial case (*Australian Conservation Foundation* v. *The Commonwealth*) in which the nation's leading environmental advocacy organization was denied standing to appear in court to challenge the legality of a tourism development on environmentally sensitive lands.

The court ultimately ordered that the ACF were prevented from even bringing the action because the Foundation did not have a sufficient 'interest' in the subject matter of the proceedings.

The following statement by the Chief Justice exemplifies the strictness of the traditional common law approach to public interest litigation:

Australian Conservation Foundation v. *The Commonwealth* (1980) 146 CLR 493

Per Gibbs CJ, (at 525) for the reasons I have given, the action was not brought by the Foundation to assert a private right. It is brought to prevent what is alleged to be a public wrong. The wrong is not one that causes, or threatens to cause, damage to the Foundation, or that affects, or threatens to affect, the interests of the Foundation in any material way. The Foundation seeks to enforce the public law as a matter of principle, as part of an endeavour to achieve its objects and to uphold the values which it was formed to promote. The question is whether, in these circumstances, it has standing to sue. (at 526)

(at 530) I would not deny that a person might have a special interest in the preservation of a particular environment. However, an interest, for present purposes, does not mean a mere intellectual or emotional concern. A person is not interested within the meaning of the rule, unless he is likely to gain some advantage, other than the satisfaction of righting a wrong, upholding a principle or winning a contest, if his action succeeds, or to suffer some disadvantage, other than a sense of grievance or a debt for costs, if his action fails. A belief, however strongly felt, that the law generally, or a particular law, should be observed, or that conduct of a particular kind should be prevented, does not suffice to give its possessor locus standi. (at 531)

You can access this case online at www.austlii.edu.au/au/cases/cth/HCA/1979/1.html.

This case gives you an understanding of the traditional approach of the common law courts to public interest advocates who seek to use litigation to achieve their ends. Fortunately, the courts in most jurisdictions are slowly changing and public interest litigants are increasingly able to bring cases in the public interest. English and Canadian courts in particular have relaxed these strict rules significantly in recent decades, and this is discussed in more detail in Chapter 10, which deals with litigation as a tactic.

The laws of standing are of significant practical significance for public interest advocates, but for our purposes here, they serve to illustrate symbolically the way in which common law principles have been used to suppress public interest litigation. Even though the restrictive rules of standing are in the process of being opened up to allow more public interest litigation, the underlying structure of common law and the causes of action that it supports continue to reflect the clear pre-eminence of private property rights over public interest concerns.

3.4 Other ways in which the public interest/vested interest distinction is important

The distinction between public and private or vested interests is important in other ways. While it can be a problem to be representing the public interest in litigation, it can conversely be an advantage in other contexts. It is an important element of social change work and community activism because of the need to get other people to support your cause.

Articulating the public interest effectively will help to make people sympathetic to your cause, and motivate them to become involved. As a public interest advocate, your motives should not be viewed suspiciously as you have nothing personal to gain other than achieving a better outcome for your community or for the planet. For this reason you have every reason to be open and honest.

Despite the resistance the courts have to allowing public interest causes to be litigated, the law more generally may offer some support to public interest advocates and activists involved in public interest work. For example:

- In the law of defamation, it can be a defence to an action for defamation that a person's motivation for making a statement that they honestly believe to be true was based upon the public interest. (For an example see S 31 of Queensland's Defamation Act 2005: www.austlii.edu.au/au/legis/qld/consol_act/da200599/s31.html.)
- Similar rules also apply in other common law jurisdictions. (See more detailed discussion in the chapter on strategic litigation, Chapter 10.)
- In some cases public interest exceptions may also facilitate the release of information under freedom of information laws.
- The fact that you are a public interest litigant may relieve you of the normal liability to pay costs in an unsuccessful court action. See *Oshlack v. Richmond River Council* [1998] HCA (www.austlii.edu.au//cgi-bin/disp.pl/au/cases/cth/HCA/1998/11.html?query=oshlack).

By far the most significantly powerful advantage of being identified with a public interest issue is in regard to public debate and discussion. Many activists are accused of having various personal agendas and being able to articulate the public interest aspect of an issue can contest this allegation and serves as a major rhetorical advantage in general.

4.0 The practice of democracy

We have considered the way in which public interest work directly invokes the ideals of democracy. It is a good time to have a slightly deeper look at the idea of democracy. Democracy is a contested term; almost every regime on the planet, no matter how oppressive, claims to be some kind of democracy. The challenge in most countries is to determine how robust a democracy the country is or aspires to be. Australian High Court judge Justice Kirby observed that democracy means more than simply 'a ceremonial visit of electors to the ballot box each triennium' (Kirby 2002: 3–4).

The practice of democracy requires citizens to take an active role in the affairs of the community and of the nation, and to be prepared to make those concerns felt and heard.

An important question for developed nations is whether they aim to have a 'maximalist' or a 'minimalist' democracy. At its worst a representative democracy can simply amount to a system in which people choose their oppressors every three or four years; at its best it can be a system which incorporates a thriving culture of political participation.

The participatory view of democracy sees the role of citizens' participation as being ongoing, through protest, assembly, referendum, court action, lobbying, strikes and direct action throughout and even independently of the electoral cycle. While most of these things are partly tolerated in the political culture of developed nations, they continue to occupy a very precarious and ambiguous position.

Particularly in common law countries other than the USA, it was traditionally uncommon to have any entrenched Bills of Rights. This has begun to change with Canada, the United Kingdom and New Zealand all adopting Bills of Rights. Canada's Charter is more powerful in that it is constitutionally entrenched, as are the Bill of Rights provisions in the US Constitution. In the absence of Bill of Rights protections, the common law recognizes very little in terms of specific participatory rights. In Australia, where there is no national Bill of Rights, rights of protest are not broadly recognized and people are frequently arrested for involvement in various protest activities. In the state of Queensland in the 1980s, for example, there was no right of peaceful assembly, all political activists were subject to surveillance, and strikes became a criminal offence in some industries. In most jurisdictions there are laws to prevent unions striking in support of another union's claim, or indeed for any political cause outside the narrow confines of workplace disputes. In this way the role of unions and of striking in broader social justice (public interest) concerns has been restricted, and so a key plank of participatory rights has been eroded.

4.1 The right to break the law

Even within an overall respect for the rule of law, a participatory view of democracy insists that protesters have the *right to (conscientiously) break the law* to make a political statement. This does not necessarily mean that they do not expect any legal consequences to follow; it may simply mean that they assert a right to conscientiously break a law but are prepared to suffer the prescribed consequences. The environmental movement worldwide and particularly in Australia has been a leading proponent of this approach. Greenpeace is an international organization that has prominently practised this approach at a global level.

It is important to note that participatory democracy and representative democracy are not mutually exclusive; the two can and do coexist given enough social recognition of the right to meaningful dissent. While representative democracy (the election of parliamentary representatives) is a more minimal concept of democracy, it is by no means worthless. It provides important mechanisms of popular control, and where it becomes culturally entrenched in a nation is useful in resisting the slide into totalitarianism.

One of the reasons why the practice of democracy (political participation) is so important is that democracy is not just a set of institutions or rules, it is a daily cultural practice. The important democratic qualities of political life are located culturally in a nation's ethos, and this is probably more important than whether such aspirations are also legally or constitutionally guaranteed. For this reason robust debate about the nature and theory of democracy is essential for the health and maintenance of the culture of democracy. This is also why a healthy awareness of participatory democratic rights is needed if we are not to slide into majoritarian tyranny.

Recent legislation in most jurisdictions in response to fears about terrorism illustrates how vulnerable our democratic values are, and how easily the infrastructure of a totalitarian state can be constructed even under a seemingly democratic constitution.

4.2 State power and corporate bureaucracy

In examining the nature and context of public interest activism, it is also important to remember that although the matter involves the public interest, it is not necessarily confined to the public sphere. While frequently it is the actions or inactions of government which provoke a public response, the growth of corporate power in the last fifty years has meant that corporations too have an ever-increasing impact upon the lives of individuals, the community and the environment.

This is an area that will be explored in more detail in a later chapter on corporate activism (Chapter 7). Government bureaucracy is a far more familiar target for public interest advocates, and the level of public accountability expected of government instrumentalities (in theory at least) provides an important component of the context of such disputes. When a public interest dispute involves or is entirely located in the sphere of private bureaucracy (corporations), assumptions about public accountability no longer apply and activists or advocates are faced with a different set of challenges. At times corporations are more vulnerable because of their profit motive, but beyond this, and if their particular offending behaviour happens to be highly profitable, the means available to ensure public accountability are far more limited.

Conclusion

Social change advocacy and community activism can be practised in a variety of ways, from ordinary people writing letters to newspapers, or holding local meetings, through to the activities of international organizations like Amnesty International or Greenpeace, which are well-funded groups that conduct international campaigns.

The range of potential subject matter of public interest causes is unlimited. While environmental causes have been particularly prominent public interest campaigns of the past thirty years, issues such as human rights, fair trade, animal rights, gender issues, Third World debt and heritage protection, to name a few, are also all prominent public interest causes. Public interest advocacy is not confined to major causes either. Advocating on behalf of disabled people, abandoned animals, aged people or for more funding for cancer research are all examples of public interest advocacy as well.

This publication is not concerned with the content of any particular campaign, or even its rightness or wrongness, but with the skills that are needed to engage in public interest advocacy and activism successfully. As we have seen, the content can vary enormously, but what unites all public interest campaigns is that they embrace matters of broad concern, beyond the narrow personal interests of the participants, and that in general they require the same set of skills and practices to achieve success. For this reason this publication is skills based. The topics that follow will deal with a range of distinct but interrelated skills necessary for successful public interest advocacy.

Below are some links to some larger public interest advocacy organizations that you may be interested to explore:

* Public Interest Advocacy Centre NSW Australia: www.piac.asn.au/about/
* Public Interest Advocacy Centre (Canada): www.ic.gc.ca/eic/site/oca-bc. nsf/eng/cao1928.html
* Public Interest Advocacy Centre British Columbia: bcpiac.com/
* Public Interest Lawyers (UK): www.publicinterestlawyers.co.uk/.

TWO | **Building successful social movements**

Introduction

Individual activists can achieve a lot, but by far the most effective and proven way to bring about social change is through organized groups and social movements. Social movements are an immensely powerful political force because they can harness the collective will and agency of masses of people to steer the process of social change. This chapter explores the nature of social movements, their core values and the features needed to make social movements more effective at achieving social change. This theoretical analysis is an essential contextual tool for understanding broader social change dynamics in the chapters that follow.

> Never doubt that a small group of thoughtful committed citizens can change the world, indeed it is the only thing that ever has. (Margaret Mead, 1901–78)

1.0 What is a social movement?

The term social movement is deliberately wide. It is wide enough to include formal organizations as well as loose alliances and even extends to describing non-organized processes of cultural change within society.

There may in fact be a range of different agents within a social movement, including individuals and organized and non-organized groups of people. Usually a specific social movement is identified by its values and the issues that it is active in promoting. Some good examples of popular social movements would include the world peace movement, environmentalism, feminism and the animal rights movement. Each of these social movements is quite complex and consists of numerous groups that share some but not all of their values in common.

Social movements effectively fill the gap between the individual and the state by harnessing the collective will and agency of many people to steer the process of social change. Social movements have proved remarkably powerful in the past and they remain an essential means by which people can be organized at the grassroots level to help respond to the increasing power of governments and large corporations. In examining social movements we will look at the core values of these movements.

In *Doing Democracy*, Bill Moyer defines a social movement as 'collective actions in which the populace is alerted, educated and mobilised, sometimes over years and decades to challenge the powerholders and the whole society to redress social problems or grievances and restore critical social values'.

Such a definition is very broad and potentially could include a wide range of groups and methods, including violent and non-violent, as well as tolerant and non-tolerant, movements. There is no reason to deny violent or non-tolerant movements the status of social movements, but for the purposes of this publication it is important to be clear that we are concerned only with discussing and analysing the most effective way for non-violent and socially tolerant social movements to operate. This is a deliberate boundary for this book. In the first chapter the difference between public interest and vested interests was explored; in this chapter our focus is further refined by an insistence on non-violence as a core value for the kind of social movements that this book aims to assist. Setting this boundary does not necessarily mean that all or any groups that utilize violence are automatically wrong; there are numerous examples of freedom fighters throughout history with whom it is easy to share some sympathy, but this is not the point. This book is written for public interest campaigners in modern developed societies whose social change work requires a commitment to building wide-ranging public support; there are numerous reasons why non-violence should remain a core value for such groups. There are also a number of other less universal values which are also common and important for the kinds of social movements under consideration, such as tolerance of diversity, egalitarianism and inclusiveness.

1.1 Non-violence as a core value

There are a range of reasons that support a strong commitment to non-violence as a core value; these range from deeply philosophical to quite pragmatic reasons.

Some reasons for securing non-violence as a core value:

- Non-violence aligns with the type of society that many people in social movements wish to create; it is important to model the kind of world that we aim to bring into existence.
- In general a social movement needs to attract broad community support in order to be successful and this is unlikely to occur if that support is alienated through the use of violence.
- A commitment to non-violence allows a diversity of people to participate in the campaign – the young, the elderly and the infirm.

- Many people in social movements are committed to the principle of non-harming because of personal ethics or spiritual beliefs.
- Non-violent social movements can dramatically reveal the oppressive and often violent nature of the power-holders in society. Images of peaceful protesters being attacked by the police can be one of the few opportunities social movements have to use the overwhelming power of the system against itself.

- Strategically a social movement using violence will be confronted by the full might of the police/army, etc., and realistically will have little chance of achieving its goals. A fundamental element of the modern state is its insistence that it should hold a monopoly on violence. Any use of violence in political actions challenges this monopoly on violence and is met with overwhelming force.
- Under terrorism laws enacted over the last decade in all relevant jurisdictions, even the relatively minor use of violence in political actions could be defined and prosecuted as a terrorism offence.

The force of non-violence is infinitely more wonderful and subtle than the material forces of nature, like, for instance, electricity. (Gandhi 1951: 384)

1.2 Minimum necessary damage to property

It is easy to draw an absolute line in the sand to distinguish personal violence from non-violence and, as we have discussed, the vast majority of social movements in modern developed societies are committed to non-violence as a core value. Less clear is the issue of property damage and the circumstances in which it is considered acceptable in campaigns.

Certainly most of the philosophical and pragmatic arguments against personal violence outlined above also apply to property damage, albeit with less moral force.

Unnecessary and wanton destruction of property as part of a campaign tends to alienate potential supporters and invites repressive state responses. Scenes of black-clad youths smashing windows and setting fire to cars and dumpsters at anti-corporate globalization rallies are an unfortunate and counterproductive hazard for the more respectable social movements that organize and take part in such rallies. But there continues to be ongoing debate about the precise boundaries for acceptable property damage arising from non-violent protest activities.

There are some people who view any destruction of property as an unacceptable form of violence for a social movement, and certainly for most groups involved in public protest actions the question of acceptable property damage can generate a lot of debate. At one end of the spectrum is what is sometimes referred to as 'holy NVA' (non-violent action), which preaches an absolute avoidance of property damage, but most groups end up adopting a more moderate NVDA (non-violent direct action) position, which accepts minimal necessary damage as part of a non-violent protest strategy.

The idea of necessary minimal property damage is popular because it avoids pointless or wanton destructiveness but allows some room to be flexible in the design of direct action tactics. This approach recognizes the reality that it may sometimes be necessary to break a lock, establish a barricade, or even disable destructive machinery as part of a campaign of non-violent direct action. This is especially relevant where tactics such as blockading, sit-ins and occupations are concerned, or where graffiti is the main tactic of choice. Many of the celebrated actions of organizations such as Greenpeace and Sea Shepherd, and many less well-known but heroic direct actions, involve minor property damage to achieve effectiveness. It appears the public are generally tolerant of necessary minimal damage and it does not generally lead to a haemorrhage of public support for a campaign. On the contrary, if direct actions are carried out well, public support can grow in response to the dedication and heroism displayed by campaigners.

There is no intention to be prescriptive about the issue of property damage in this book; it is important for every protest group, individual and social movement to decide for themselves what level of property damage they consider acceptable within the overall context of a non-violent campaign. There is an abundance of literature available on the topic, including some of the classic work by Gene Sharp, an American author and academic who has spent many years writing about the categories of acceptable non-violent action. *New Internationalist* magazine recently featured a debate on this very topic in its issue of February 2011 (www.newint.org/argument/2011/03/01/is-property-damage-in-protest-justified/).

There is a discussion of direct action tactics in Chapter 8 that further explores the issues that individuals and groups should consider when selecting tactics.

1.3 Adopting a structure that reflects your values

Egalitarianism, reflected in non-hierarchical (or less hierarchical) structures, is another core value for many social movements. For this reason social movements need to carefully consider the way power is organized within their own movement, because it is contradictory to model authoritarian power structures internally (within the movement) if the aims and values of your movement are to create more egalitarian structures in society generally. Perhaps the Bolshevik idea of creating the 'dictatorship of the proletariat' as a means of liberating workers is an infamous example of a social movement (communism) modelling a power structure that was ultimately not liberating for those involved or for society more generally. To avoid such contradictions it is wise for social movements to establish power structures internally that mirror their aspirations for social change more generally. So movements that seek to foster equality, diversity, power-sharing or tolerance should ensure that these values are observed in their internal structure. This does not mean that groups should have no structure or no hierarchy, but merely that attention should be paid to how the internal structure of a group aligns with the values and vision of its members.

The traditional model of power in our society is sometimes called the 'power over' or 'power elite' (Moyer 2001: 13) model, in that it relies upon society being ruled by powerful elites (hopefully but not always elected) to make laws and rules for others to follow. Modern nation-states almost all subscribe to a system of centralized authority in which the centralized state asserts a monopoly on violence as well as upon law-making and enforcement. This model of a centralized state backed by military and police power evolved in ancient times when the first city-states emerged following improvements in agricultural practices. Reggae artist Bob Marley is perhaps not too far wrong historically in characterizing this centralized model as the 'Babylon system'.

Centralized states with powerful militaries had the capacity to conquer neighbouring societies, most of which operated on less centralized models, such as early Celtic societies, and many societies subsequently colonized in the Pacific and Africa. So the powerful city-states effectively exported a new form of governance through military superiority from the Middle East to Greece, from Greece to Rome and from Rome to Europe. The European powers in turn exported this form of governance to the New World during the colonial era. Some models of a customary society that is more decentralized still survive, particularly in a number of Pacific countries like Vanuatu and Papua New Guinea, but overwhelmingly the centralized and militarized model of statecraft has come to dominate the globe.

It may not be achievable to substantially change the nature of modern nation-states in fundamental ways, but social movements certainly aim to moderate the way in which power is exercised in society by increasing opportunities for community participation in decision-making. For this reason social movements can be very important in offering new models for governance that can help to promote more egalitarian structures and practices.

1.4 Egalitarian structures

Bill Moyer (2001: 14) proposes the 'people power' model as an alternative to the centralized model of power. The people power model is most often associated with popular uprisings such as those in Egypt and the Middle East in 2011, and eastern Europe following the collapse of the Soviet Union. These mass uprisings are certainly good examples of powerful participatory democracy but they are only one model of social change, and usually one that emerges only in fairly extreme circumstances. Social movements that are working within a relatively stable system of governance need to be able to utilize more subtle models of power distribution.

Joanna Macy (Macy and Young Brown 1998: 52–3) describes a systems approach to power as a 'power with model'. In this conception of power it is the quantity and quality of relationships between people which are the critical factors in generating power. Macy's 'power with' model is more apt to describe the tendency towards more horizontal decision-making structures that often characterizes power relations inside social movements.

These theories about power over, power with and people power are useful, but each organization and each social movement tends to develop and produce its own structures and processes. Formal organizations such as unincorporated and incorporated associations tend to replicate quite formal and bureaucratic structures, having constitutions, office-bearers and identifiable procedures such as voting and executive meetings. Less formal groups such as cooperatives, coalitions and alliances tend to be organized more organically and frequently share decision-making power in quite decentralized ways. This model is facilitated by modern social networking and other tools of digital activism, and these kinds of groups have multiplied rapidly as these technologies have come to support their structures through enhanced means of communication and outreach. As observed earlier, some social movements are not organizations at all but simply cultural movements that reflect significant shifts in values within society. Feminism and the countercultural movements since the 1970s are good examples of such non-organized but still extremely powerful social movements.

The value of egalitarianism influences social movement groups to adopt particular structural features, which often include:

- collaborative (or even consensus-based) decision-making, where the agreement of all participants is required to reach a decision;
- flexible roles for participants and less emphasis on the concept of leadership;
- inclusiveness of difference, whether it be age, gender, ability, etc.;
- collaboration with other groups with similar aims.

2.0 Believing in the power of social movements

> The greatest challenge of our time can also be our greatest joy – to join together in the healing of our world. (Macy and Young Brown 1998)

The sheer scale of the problems that face the earth and its living inhabitants (including humans) can be overwhelming. Oppression, terrorism, climate change, sexual violence and people trafficking, slavery, species extinction and corporate globalization all combine to give us a picture of a planet in terminal decline, characterized by oppressive power structures that cannot be changed. It is hard not to become despairing about how humans have adversely affected our planet. Joanna Macy, in her book *Coming Back to Life* (ibid.), offers some extraordinary tools for coming to terms with the world situation and empowering people to find ways to make a positive difference. What we need to remember is that while the problems may seem ubiquitous so too is the human spirit of love, optimism and resourcefulness. It is never about one person needing to take on the weight of the world's problems; it is about people and communities understanding their interconnectedness and working on the various problems in their own small and large ways in different contexts all over the planet. This is precisely why social movements hold the key.

Social movements represent the interconnectedness of life that characterizes nature, and they represent in many ways a partly conscious and partly unconscious response by humans and human cultures to the challenges that face them. Social movements grow and change in response to the challenges they face, much as species evolve to deal with the conditions of life. It is the ability of social movements to emerge, evolve and mutate over time which equips them with the flexibility to keep bringing people together in a productive and resourceful way. While established and formally structured organizations are part of the overall emergence of social movements, they are only a part of the overall picture and incorporated within it.

Social movements are arguably the most powerful tools available to those involved in activism and social change advocacy. It is inspiring to stop and think for a moment of the numerous successful social movements that have positively changed the world:

- movements for democracy in many nations over generations;
- the anti-slavery movement;
- the movement to end child labour;
- the women's suffrage movement;
- feminism;
- ban the bomb;
- the gay and lesbian rights movement;
- the anti-nuclear power movement;
- the anti-war movement;
- the anti-apartheid movement;
- the Aboriginal land rights movement;
- movements to protect rainforest and old-growth forests from logging.

Social movements are not a quick fix. Many people involved in social movements have dedicated a large part of their lives to a particular issue or issues; real change takes time. Some social movements have worked at issues for hundreds of years, such as the peace, democracy and anti-slavery movements, for example. This understanding dictates a number of things. First, if you are in a social movement for the long haul you must look after yourself and your comrades; burnout and disillusionment are major enemies of social change. Secondly, change takes time because power-holders in society, like everybody else, do not relinquish power easily. Closely related to this point is the fact that those undertaking public advocacy are often targets for many forms of abuse. In the final chapter of this book (Chapter 12) we discuss the issues of personal and organizational sustainability involved in looking after the health and well-being of participants in social movements. The skills of renewal and sustainability are at least as important as the outwardly focused strategic parts of any campaign.

A key part of building a strong and tenacious movement is also gaining some understanding of what we may call the life cycle of a social movement. One of the most detailed and in-depth analyses of this idea is to be found in Bill Moyer's book *Doing Democracy*, in which he develops a complex map of the life cycle of social movements.

2.1 Requirements for success of a social movement

It is important to be aware of the assumptions on which Moyer's work is based (Moyer 2001: 19). Of particular significance is Moyer's point that 'the powerholders only rule as long as they have the consent and acquiescence of the people'. From this assertion comes the idea that the central focus of the social movement is to educate, alert, inspire and eventually involve the majority of the public. This is a focus that can be aided by particular strategic activities, such as protests, direct action, blockades or litigation. However, the activity itself should not be seen as the main purpose; changing public opinion should be the aim. Getting confused about the aim has led many activists to believe that a whole campaign is dependent on them personally stopping some activity. This attitude puts the activist and sometimes the campaign under extreme pressure, which can lead to burnout, despair or violent action. It is critical to keep the focus on public opinion and how to positively affect it.

Moyer offers what he refers to as the MAP model of social change, in which he describes an eight-stage process. The model is, of course, a model, and to some extent it is generic and theoretical, but Moyer's research is based upon many years of experience in a great range of social movements and it does usefully draw together a lot of experiences that are common to many social movements. The value of his modelling is that it helps give participants a bigger picture of their own campaign and a means for assessing their progress from a perspective larger than their own immediate intuitions and impulses. Perhaps most powerfully, Moyer's model suggests that the time when many activists are most despondent about the chances of success (perceived failure of the movement) is actually a significant step in the process towards success.

Because the model described by Moyer can appear very theoretical it is described below in conjunction with a real-life case study. The study, of the NSW old-growth forest campaign, was actually developed as a way of ground-testing the accuracy of Moyer's modelling in a real-life scenario. What was amazing was how closely the real course of events mirrored Moyer's model.

2.2 Eight stages of a social movement

The following analysis explores the North East Forest Alliance (NEFA) experience with reference to Moyer's eight stages of social movement success.

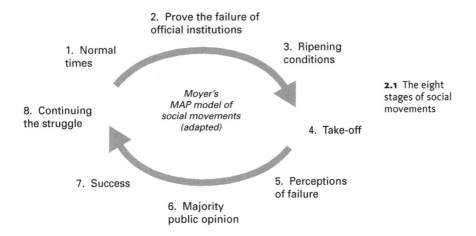

2. Prove the failure of official institutions

1. Normal times

3. Ripening conditions

Moyer's MAP model of social movements (adapted)

2.1 The eight stages of social movements

8. Continuing the struggle

4. Take-off

7. Success

5. Perceptions of failure

6. Majority public opinion

Stage 1: normal times

> Normal times are politically quiet times. The great majority of the population either does not know the problem exists or supports the institutional policies and practices that cause the problem. (Ibid.: 43)

The preconditions for NEFA's old-growth forest campaign were classical 'normal times'. There had been a largely successful rainforests campaign in the early 1980s which had followed on from protests in the late 1970s. The public's perception was that 'something had been done' about that problem, but otherwise all was quiet on the forests front. The power-holders (Forestry Commission, timber industry) operated more or less beyond public scrutiny, protected by their own official propaganda of sustainable forest industries. The public was unaware that, right under their noses, ancient forests with individual trees up to two thousand years old were being logged by an industry which was effectively old-growth-dependent.

Stage 2: prove the failure of official institutions

> The intensity of public feeling, opinion and upset required for social movements to take off can happen only when the public realizes that

governmental policies violate widely held beliefs, principles and values. (Ibid.: 48–9)

NEFA began as an alliance of numerous local groups that had begun to form, usually comprising people who lived in alternative communities close to old-growth areas being logged. NEFA was able to prove the failure of existing institutions in the first years (1989–90) by launching several successful challenges to the lawfulness of forestry operations in old growth, particularly the failure of the Forestry Commission to conduct Environmental Impact Statements (EISs) before logging. In order to be successful in these cases NEFA needed to engage scientific and legal experts and to undertake extensive research. Simply forcing the Forestry Commission to conduct EISs would never by itself have achieved NEFA's aim of ending old-growth logging, but it was an important way to achieve early victories, delay logging, embarrass the power-holders and build a reputation for the movement.

Stage 3: ripening conditions

Before a new social movement 'takes off' the appropriate conditions must build up over time, usually over many years. These conditions include the necessary context of historic developments, a growing, discontented population ... and a budding, autonomous grassroots opposition. (Ibid.: 51)

NEFA had won its court action to stop the logging without an EIS of an iconic old-growth forest area called 'Chaelundi' in 1990, but the response of the Forestry Commission was to rush through a quick EIS that would tick the formal boxes and allow logging to proceed. In 1991, Chaelundi was once again threatened, and this time the legal solution was not so readily available. At this stage NEFA was a small network that had begun to attract the attention of supporters and other organizations for its recent successes in other forest areas. NEFA instituted a blockade of Chaelundi at Easter 1991 with only a handful of activists, but moved quickly to build support from the existing network of environment centres and multiple-occupancy communities in the region.

Still confident that the movement was weak, the power-holders chose to 'wait out' the blockade rather than give it publicity by confronting it directly. What the power-holders did not expect, however, was the effective way in which NEFA would use its permanent camp as a base to build a large and powerful social movement. In Moyer's description he refers to the public seeing the victims' faces, which refers more to social justice campaigns. In this case the victims were trees, forests and ecological communities, and the fact that the camp was located in real old-growth forest meant that anyone visiting the camp saw the majesty and the tragedy at first hand. In this way visitors to the blockade site, including supporters, police, media and the curious public, had an experience to take away with them. Over the five months of occupation thousands of people had visited and connected with Chaelundi personally.

Stage 4: take-off

> New social movements surprise and shock everyone when they burst into the public spotlight ... Overnight a previously unrecognized social problem becomes a social issue that everyone is talking about. It starts with a highly publicized, shocking incident, a trigger event. (Ibid.: 54)

When the bulldozers, cherry-picker trucks and police wagons rolled into Chaelundi in the winter of 1991, the blockaders were more than prepared to withstand the initial onslaught. As the first media images of the power-holders' assault upon Chaelundi reached the news, hundreds prepared to rally to its defence. By the third day, the exhausted core group of NEFA activists was being reinforced by newcomers, and the blockade physically resisted police attempts to gain access to the forests for a full ten days.

Chaelundi became a nightly news event, and as a trigger event its repercussions were felt not only in the city, but also deeply within the ranks of the ruling state government. NEFA had launched legal action to stop the logging, and several days after the blockades had finally been cleared by police, it succeeded in obtaining a court injunction. For the power-holders, the campaign had been a major disaster. They had been weakened on every front, the blockade and NEFA appeared heroic, the terms Chaelundi and old-growth had become instantly recognizable, and the courts had found against the Forestry Commission for a second time.

Stage 5: perceptions of failure

> The perception of failure happens just when the movement is outrageously successful ... the high hopes of instant victory in the movement's take off stage inevitably turn to despair as some activists begin to believe that their movement is failing ... They come to believe that the powerholders are too strong. (Ibid.: 58)

In 1992 the power-holders responded to NEFA's successes in the previous year with special legislation to protect the forest industries from the outcomes of NEFA's successful court actions. This represented a significant setback for the movement.

Despite the setback, NEFA maintained its momentum throughout 1991 and 1992 in an almost non-stop campaign of direct action in the forests, culminating in its seizing of the headquarters of the Forestry Commission in November 1992.

Following the seizure, many people, particularly the power-holders, thought that NEFA was vulnerable or running out of steam. The Chaelundi campaign, and the year of non-stop direct action in 1992, had taken a toll on the participants; many people just couldn't take the time off from families, work and homes to maintain such high-energy, exhausting and unpaid work. Fortunately NEFA retained a small crew of highly motivated, mobile and committed activists, but increasingly the wide public support experienced during the Chaelundi campaign was draining away. The power-holders seized upon this in 1993 when they set a trap for NEFA and attempted to sue what they knew to be the core group of activists during the blockades at a site called Dingo State Forest. Despite the failure of the lawsuits against NEFA, blockades on their own were failing to save forests, and could be continued only as part of a broader political strategy.

By late 1994, with a state election approaching, NEFA changed its tactics, and instead of entrenching in large blockade sites in a defensive way, small bands of activists operated wildcat actions, in which individual logging operations would be stopped until such time as police resources could be mustered in response, at which point the activists would disband, before any arrest took place, only to re-emerge in another area, sometimes hundreds of miles away, to stop another logging operation. This wildcat technique was designed to highlight the scale and ubiquity of old-growth logging in the lead-up to the state election of 1995, as well as to exhaust the resources of the state to respond to constant and unpredictable forest actions.

Stage 6: majority public opinion

The movement's primary mission is transformed from protest in crisis to creating social change through a long term grassroots struggle with the powerholders ... Increasingly the movement wins the backing of a larger share of the public, which now opposes current policies and considers alternatives ... It is a slow process of imperceptible social transformation that creates new social climate and political consensus, reversing those that existed during normal times. (Ibid.: 64)

By the time of the 1995 state election, forest issues, blockades and counter-campaigns by the industry warning of job losses and mill closures were constantly in the media spotlight and on the political agenda. The public were clearly tired of the divisive conflict, and it was clear that government inaction would no longer be tolerated. There was a change of government, with the incoming administration narrowly winning office, promising to create a number of new national parks and more significantly to instigate a Comprehensive Regional Assessment of the state's forests with a view to finding a 'scientifically credible solution' to the forests conflict. What is most significant about this stage is that despite the increasing futility of blockades, NEFA had finally achieved a position where the majority of the public saw a 'problem' and wanted a 'solution'.

The scientific assessment was a great relief for NEFA, as its science had always been sound, yet it provided an acceptably neutral language in which the government could attempt conciliation of the issue.

Significantly, however, Stage 6 required NEFA to change its tactics and even its image as a social movement. Temporary blockades were suspended while there was a moratorium on old-growth logging during the assessment process. The stakes for NEFA were very high; the government could not be trusted to deliver a scientifically credible outcome, but the assessment offered the best chance yet for NEFA to actually achieve lasting protection of vast tracts of forest. Particularly by engaging with government and other stakeholders NEFA compromised some of its daring and romance as a radical social movement. At this stage it was subjected to severe criticism from within the activist community for 'selling out'; negative rebels were clearly disapproving of this new stage.

The scientific assessment produced new and reliable information about the forests which vindicated NEFA's campaign of the preceding years; the government proposed significant new forest reserves, but compromised the result to achieve political ends. Before the end of the process NEFA withdrew and threatened a return to protests in the remaining areas of old growth omitted from the reserves. The government countered with all the usual attacks about NEFA not accepting the 'umpire's' decision. Negative rebels seized upon the result to damn NEFA as a failure.

NEFA continued to be active throughout the late 1990s, in lobbying, blockading and in the media, and was able to add a string of further minor successes in those years. The new government was keen to be perceived as green, and NEFA's ongoing campaign was a constant irritation and threatened to derail the government's spin about its environmental record. During the late 1990s NEFA was no longer a burgeoning mass movement, but it continued to be influential on a government that knew that majority public opinion had long ago become set against continued old-growth logging. During this period NEFA's role returned to Stage 2 in some respects, by revealing at every point the gap between the government's rhetoric and reality.

Stage 7: success

Stage seven begins when the movement, after a long process of growing bigger and deeper, reaches a new plateau in which the social consensus turns the tide of power against the powerholders, launching an endgame process that eventually leads to the movement succeeding in reaching its goal. The endgame process usually takes one of three forms: dramatic showdown, quiet showdown, or attrition. (Ibid.: 75)

At the conclusion of the scientific assessment in the late 1990s NEFA had identified what was required to achieve a real end to the logging of high-conservation-value forest on public land. As the 2003 state election approached the government sensed that its record on the forests continued to be publicly viewed with suspicion, owing to the fact that blockades had not ceased, and forest conflict had not been resolved. Several weeks before that election the government announced that if re-elected it would place the remaining areas under dispute into reserve.

Social movement success seems very rare, and many of us are afraid to acknowledge it in case it causes people to drop their guard, but it is important to celebrate our successes, so we can find the hope and the empowerment that keep activism alive. The following is an e-mail from one of NEFA's founding and most persistent activists, Dailan Pugh, and these words, coming from a blockader and radical activist, are indeed significant.

Sender: Dailan Pugh
Subject: FOREST ICONS AND OLD GROWTH
Date: Thu, 3 Jul 2003 00:11:49

I asked people to cheer when I heard that [the government] had given a pretty strong commitment to protect NEFAs icons and all old growth on public land in north-east NSW. I was disappointed with the whimper in response. Now that the promise has been implemented will people cheer?

As a movement we do need to celebrate our victories when they warrant it; I think that, all else aside, the protection of all remaining old growth forest on public lands is a conservation milestone – in fact a bloody great victory – and the additional icon areas are pretty bloody good too ... The protection of old growth was one of NEFA's basic planks and our principal focus. To have now realised this dream, albeit only for public lands in north-east NSW, is a major victory. Let's hope that by us publicly celebrating this win we will entrench it in place and encourage the Government to extend it to private lands and other regions. I don't know about you, but I think it deserves a cheer or two.

In 2003 two of NEFA's most prominent activists were awarded Order of Australia Medals (the Australian equivalent of a British knighthood) for their contribution to forest conservation in NSW. For such an award to be given to people previously described as 'dangerous radicals' and 'extremists' is evidence of just how much a social movement can change public values.

Stage 8: continuing the struggle

The success achieved in stage seven is not the end of the struggle, but merely a landmark in a long term process of fundamental social change that moves the society closer to the ultimate goal of sustained citizen based democracy based on justice, ecological sustainability and the meeting of everyone's basic human needs ... In this period the movement has the opportunity to expand on its success, focus on other demands, promote new issues and most importantly move beyond reform to social change. (Ibid.: 80)

Having succeeded in its initial organizational objectives, NEFA needed to reflect and refocus in the new millennium. The victory in saving old-growth forests on public lands had not extended to saving them on private lands, so NEFA began a campaign to extend protection to private lands. This time, though, it was not operating as a large and explosive mass movement but as a smaller, very professional organization with a proven track record, aiming to further the outcomes of the awareness-raising it had so successfully achieved in the decade before. In addition to its attempt to extend its activities into private forestry, by 2010 NEFA had also begun revisiting state forests to monitor compliance with environmental laws in those areas that had remained available for forestry operations. New campaigns keep emerging, but the experience and the social change achieved during the earlier stages serve to support the ongoing work.

2.3 The possibility of re-emergent stages

While Moyer's model may appear quite linear, it is not quite that simple. For a start it is represented as a cycle rather than as a linear process, and secondly it is acknowledged that at times social movements will find that they need to re-engage in earlier stages of their campaigns to generate more momentum for overall change. The model is not meant to give any assurance of social movement success; rather it is meant to support the process of success by helping participants to gain a bigger picture of where in the cycle their movement may be at present, and hopefully this in itself will support strategic decision-making and avoid unnecessary despair. Obviously any theoretical model will be imperfect, or at least will need to be adjusted to the circumstances of a particular movement at a particular time.

Conclusion

The term social movement covers a wide range of organized and non-organized groups that work for changes in social values. Social movements by nature emerge and evolve in response to the social conditions that prevail, and for this very reason are the most powerful and flexible social tools for achieving change. In a sense social movements operate almost like the immune systems of complex organisms as a way of bringing malignant social policies under control. An understanding of social movements as largely organic, even where they contain formalized organizations within them, helps support the conceptualization of movements and campaigns having a life cycle. Moyer's descriptions of the typical life cycle of a social movement are clearly fairly generic and are at best only a model of what is likely, but they are not meant to be exhaustive of the possibilities. The great value in applying a model such as Moyer's MAP model is that it provides some perspective for agents within social movements which can enable them to evaluate success and failure and to strategically position themselves for the challenges ahead.

It is important that social movements model in their internal structures the values that they seek to promote in the wider society. It is also important that they operate in ways that promote an egalitarian vision of participatory democracy in order for them to be able to operate most effectively in the long term.

Given that social movements are a largely organic and ill-defined response to social conditions, there is usually no one person or agency able to ensure that the core values that are necessary for successful democratic social movements are properly enshrined or practised. For this reason it is the job of everyone involved in social movements to remain vigilant to ensure that values of non-violence, egalitarianism, inclusiveness and open decision-making are practised and promoted at every opportunity.

Social movements are the most effective response available to correct malignant social problems and policies. It is important to keep believing in their power.

THREE | **Strategy: the art of activism**

Introduction

Effective strategy lies at the very heart of successful activism. It is all very well to have a good cause, good information and good intentions, but to be effective, activists and social change advocates need to coordinate all of this into an effective strategy. Strategic thinking needs to saturate every aspect of campaign practice. This chapter will discuss the concept of strategy, and the strategic environment within which public interest activists and social movements operate, and will examine various approaches to enhancing the strategic effectiveness of campaigns. The need for strategic thinking will be re-emphasized in nearly every chapter of this book, so this chapter is a vitally important precursor to the more detailed discussions that follow.

1.0 Public interest strategy

To conceive and effectively implement a deliberate strategy requires considerable forethought and planning and necessitates a real understanding of what strategy entails.

The use of strategy in public interest campaigning is similar in some ways to its use in military and business contexts, for example, but there are key contextual differences that we must explore. Military and business applications of strategy explicitly focus on defeating, overwhelming or outmanoeuvring an enemy, business competitor or opponent. Dealing with an opponent, and more specifically an intelligent opponent, will often be a feature of a public interest campaign, but this will not always be the case, or there will be a more complex range of players than simply two sides. For this reason, four special aspects of public interest strategy will be explored:

- alignment of campaign goals or objectives with strategic focus;
- the need for articulation of the public interest;
- planning for flexibility: anticipating the knowable and the unknowable;
- timeline planning and persistence.

1.1 Alignment with strategic focus

It is essential that all aspects of strategic planning align with the campaign or organizational focus. Most often in a public campaign the immediate goal will be a change in the law or in the public policy or actions of government or of a corporation or industry sector. This immediate goal may be expressed in negative terms (to stop or oppose a position) but in reality most campaigns will be a combination of both negative and positive positions: 'don't do that, do this instead'.

The achievement of your public interest goals is likely to involve:

- mobilizing and influencing public opinion;
- tapping into or even modifying community attitudes or behaviour;
- advocating group action to support the cause being promoted;
- strategically engaging with power-holders;
- anticipating, considering and possibly countering opposing reactions.

To be successful, public interest strategies should also be designed to positively reflect and model the values that the campaign is designed to promote. For example: public interest campaign strategies for world peace should seek to inspire cooperation, accept diversity and eschew aggression.

1.2 Articulation of the public interest

Though it may seem an obvious point, an essential part of any public interest strategy must be the clear articulation of how the 'public interest' is being advanced by the campaign. This concept of the 'public interest' was discussed in detail in the first chapter and is an important rhetorical tool for constructing your arguments and strategies.

It is important to be able to explain the rationale behind the campaign and be prepared to argue it publicly. It is very important that the public, individually and collectively, understands why you are doing what you're doing. Reiteration of your public interest focus and restatement of your strategic rationale inform the public and also assist in maintaining focus and unity within your group, and help to attract further support for your cause.

Don't ever assume that it is not necessary to explain or even repeat the public interest rationale behind your campaign strategy simply because it appears obvious to you. Complacency, confusion or misinformation may be the result.

2.0 Planning for flexibility: plan for the unexpected

Effective strategy must deal with the unknowable, and in public interest campaigns this dimension of strategy is especially important since the wider public domain is inherently complex and can be unstable. This is partly because there are potentially a great number of stakeholders (many of whom may be presently unseen or unknown).

The possibility of a range of different stakeholders with different values or agendas creates a complex operating environment, since there may be many players operating and not all these players are necessarily opponents. The allies and foes mapping exercises in the next chapter are designed to help explore the issues that arise where there are multiple stakeholders. It is vital to get an overall picture of the cultural or political terrain within which your campaign is taking place, so conflict mapping exercises are vital tools for mapping out all of the stakeholders and anticipating their likely responses once your campaign starts to make an impact.

2.1 Anticipating backlash

Campaign gains will almost certainly create a reaction from other stakeholders, sometimes referred to as 'backlash'. While the number, nature, timing and extent of these reactions may be unknowable, the likelihood that there will be a backlash is knowable and needs to be kept in mind and planned for. It is not adequate to imagine your campaign as a linear progression from inception to success. Bringing about social change is a complex process that works on many different levels, generating unpredictable outcomes. You need to remember that the status quo has a certain cultural inertia and certainty that many people find comfortable, even if it is a less than optimal situation. Once your campaign begins to disturb the status quo you unleash many different responses. You need to expect some backlash from your opponents or from your target power-holders, but you should also expect some resistance to emerge from other stakeholders who have been disturbed by the impacts of your campaign so far.

Many public interest campaigners, finally seeing some of the fruits of their strategy being achieved, may fall into the trap of expecting that further progress can now be made easily and start to believe that the final realization of the strategy is very close. This is dangerous because when the inevitable backlash comes your group may be unprepared for it, and become dismayed or discouraged, which can lead to frustration and burnout and at worst abandonment of the campaign. Such circumstances can be avoided if the public interest strategy expects a backlash, recognizes it for what it is and has a flexibility that provides a capacity to respond. In the last chapter we explored Moyer's eight-stage life cycle of social movements. Moyer (2001) observed that in Stage 5 many activists fall prey to a perception of failure, partly as a result of the backlash from opponents and power-holders that they probably should have expected.

A useful mental attitude to adopt is to view backlash as a sign that your campaign has really had an impact. Usually the first response of power-holders to a new campaign is to simply ignore it. Backlash occurs when you have succeeded in proving that you cannot be safely ignored any longer.

Not only is backlash a sign of progress; if you are expecting it, it can offer strategic opportunities to your campaign. Your opponents may overplay their hand. (For example, where governments use undue force to defeat protesters and end up generating public sympathy for the cause.) Under these circumstances it is extremely important that public interest strategists analyse the backlash to recognize their opponents' errors in judgement, and be well positioned to exploit these errors.

There are times when the backlash from an intelligent opponent is well thought out, effective and quite damaging. In these situations sometimes you can do little more than wait, watch and attempt whatever level of damage control is possible. It may seem paradoxical, but good strategy is about forward planning, and it is also about remaining flexible and able to respond quickly to changed circumstances. A useful mantra for maintaining a strategic yet flexible approach is to 'accept the way things are but to find the most resourceful way to move forward'.

2.2 Anticipating internal organizational instability

Another key site where you should expect the unexpected is in your internal organizational dynamics. Public interest work is rarely financially supported by full-time employment. Campaign work often diverts campaigners from addressing other aspects of their lives. This situation can continue only for so long, and it's entirely likely therefore that at some time campaign workers' health, family or job commitments may intervene and force a reduction in their involvement, or even their withdrawal, possibly suddenly.

Alternatively, key people may suffer burnout and leave the campaign, or organizational conflict can cause internal tensions (discussed in Chapter 12), so it is important that the strategy does not become over-centralized and dependent on only one or two people who become indispensable.

Changes in personnel may create threats to the achievement of the campaign strategy or new opportunities. The departure of a member of the public interest campaign team is likely to require a reorganization or restructuring of the campaign, and may involve a major rethink. Acknowledging the unknowable and planning for flexibility implies a preparedness to make strategic changes quickly and relatively easily.

Being flexible and making appropriate choices in changing strategies involves careful analysis including risk assessment. There are several organizational approaches to planning that can provide for flexibility. These include:

- Leave gaps in your planned timelines so that programmed activities can be rescheduled when (not if) unforeseen events arise.
- Maintain some reserves/don't overcommit human, financial or campaign resources so that there is still a physical capacity to address new issues as they emerge, without withdrawing resources from somewhere else.
- Don't over-centralize strategic decision-making: delegate authority/ empower campaigners so that they have a capacity to be flexible and exercise their discretion within the strategic framework as events unfold.
- Wherever possible match key campaign personnel with a shadow person whom they are working with and mentoring or training.

2.3 Anticipating disruptive events and developments

So far we have discussed anticipating disruption from other stakeholders, from opponents or from within your own organization, but in addition completely unrelated outside events may have a major impact on your campaign. Major public events such as terrorist attacks, natural disasters, war, financial crises and royal weddings can have a major disruptive effect on your campaign. Some of these may only cause delay, but others may in themselves generate significant shifts in public sentiment that will require you to carefully reconsider your campaign approach.

So planning for the unexpected may sound a little odd, but it is exactly what you need to do to give your campaign the flexibility to ride through the tougher times. The following list helps bring together the major themes of this discussion:

Planning for the unexpected
- Expect that there will a range of stakeholders with divergent interests who will all respond differently to your campaign aims and activities.
- Expect resistance from some stakeholders.
- Expect backlash from your opponents or target power-holders, sometimes in the form of coordinated and intelligent backlash (counter-strategies).
- When backlash occurs, pause, understand the nature of it, then make your next strategic move.
- Expect internal instability in your organization and have practices in place to assist rapid redeployment of personnel.
- Expect external events to play a role in changing the overall context within which your campaign is unfolding and be ready to adapt.

3.0 Timelines and persistence

Having a great strategy on paper is next to useless if the timing of its implementation renders it ineffective or irrelevant. Taking action too soon can signal your intentions and alert your opponents, robbing you of the element of surprise; taking action too late can mean certain defeat.

In implementing a strategy some actions have fixed deadlines for completion while others may be more flexible. It is essential to develop planning frameworks that recognize this. Research into key dates and periods is essential since these factors will affect, if not govern, the delivery timelines for the overall strategy.

Such key dates and periods might include:

- The date submissions close for a government inquiry, development application or public consultation.
- When Parliament or Congress is sitting or in recess.
- When a key figure, such as minister or secretary, may visit an area.
- The date of a key meeting.
- When an election is scheduled or likely.
- School, university or public holidays.
- Annual public events that may create opportunities or obstacles.
- Media publication deadlines.
- Other advertised events such as festivals, conferences or lectures.
- Internal dates such as meetings, celebrations.

These inputs are part of the knowable, and because all relevant information needs to be factored in from the beginning, this preliminary research needs to be comprehensive. These knowable dates and timelines help provide a structure around which your planning for the unknowable can take place.

By plotting critical dates and periods and flexible events on a calendar, an understanding of the overlaps, sequences and opportunities becomes apparent. By using a countback technique, planning for proposed events can be conducted and the order and timing of preparatory actions can be defined. As new temporal information is gained, key dates and periods can be added to the calendar to inform the strategy's ongoing implementation.

3.1 Using a campaign calendar

Use of a calendar to develop campaign strategy gives a focus to strategy as a forward plan that takes expected future events into account. Updating a calendar as a tool for strategy can also be very useful in reconciling previously planned actions and proposed preparatory steps against actual dates and times. This is the forward planning part of using a campaign calendar.

Campaign calendars can also be a very useful reflective tool. Methodically noting all events and their outcomes afterwards allows later analysis from the point of view of strategy as pattern. This can be useful when analysing another stakeholder's or opponent's pattern of reactions.

Reviewing your group's own patterns in terms of how long it took last time to organize and implement an activity helps strategic planning because you can anticipate how much time may be required for a similar activity in the future. This can be especially useful where you are dealing with regular changes of key personnel.

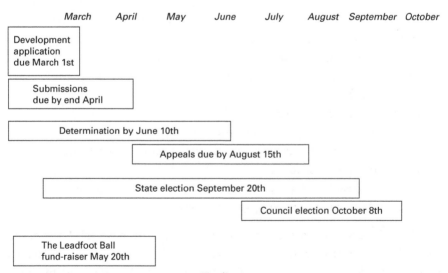

3.1 Timelines map

An example of a simple form of campaign calendar drawn from Chapter 4 is provided at the bottom of the page opposite.

3.2 Picking your moment

A function of flexible strategic planning is the ability to 'pick your moment' for a key action. Using the calendar will enable you to appreciate when that moment might be. Notwithstanding this planned approach, it is essential nonetheless that the action be delivered at an appropriate moment and the appropriateness of any moment may change depending on many external factors.

Factors you may consider in timing your event include:

- Key times when your supporters will be most able to take part (weekends, school or university holidays, or the best times for digital activities).
- Key times when your opponents will be vulnerable (prior to elections, corporate AGMs, or when they are distracted by other issues and less able to respond effectively).
- Key times when the public may be able to be reached or activated; coordinate your activities with or specifically avoid other large public events such as festivals, meetings, sporting events, religious holidays, etc.
- Coordinating your activities to tap into other issues currently arousing public interest or attention.
- Strategically delaying a news release when a major event is likely to swamp your coverage; choosing a slow news day.

3.3 Plan your campaign in stages

Many campaigns need considerable lengths of time to plan, prepare and implement. Rather than create a single event horizon, it may be useful to think in and talk about strategic phases of the campaign. This approach provides clarity and a coherent unifying concept for disparate actions over time, and may relieve the pressure of attempting to do too much all at once.

It also signals to other stakeholders such as your intelligent opponents that your strategy has durability and longevity. Such an approach says 'we know it will take time and we're not going away in a hurry'.

The stages may not simply correspond to a chronological timeline for the campaign, you may also integrate discrete aspects of the campaign into your plan. For example, you may consider that raising public awareness or establishing a robust digital presence is the first part of a campaign, which will be ongoing throughout, but that at a certain point (a point in time or after accomplishing an outcome) your campaign will move to a more active, combative or publicly visible stage. Later stages could entail strategic litigation, major public demonstrations, digital activist events, engagement in governmental lobbying or taking part in elections. The idea is that the campaign gathers momentum, broadens its range of activities and becomes more bold in its engagement with power-holders as it matures. It can be useful to set outcome-based triggers to moving to a new stage, rather than simply trying to arbitrarily assign chronological dates that may not reflect true campaign progress.

Ultimately the different phases or stages of the campaign may all be running simultaneously, but according to their own strategic planning timetables.

The advantages of identifying stages in a campaign plan are that such staged plans:

- Allow you to plan a long campaign from its infancy through its own stages of maturation.
- Allow you to plan for different aspects of the campaign to kick in at predetermined junctures based on achievement of earlier projected outcomes.
- Permit the development of parallel time frames for different parts of your campaign strategy to progress – for example, the community awareness strategy, the media strategy, the litigation strategy, the digital strategy and the fund-raising strategies.
- Provide a means to measure your success as you go along by assessing your achievement of campaign stages.
- Can help reveal useful times (between stages) to reflect upon the overall campaign progress.
- Can be used to counter perceptions of failure within the group when they arise.
- Provide useful occasions for celebration. Celebrating the achievement of

People united
Sometimes win

staged outcomes can be an important way of maintaining morale in long campaigns (discussed further in Chapter 12).

3.4 Persistence is its own reward

An old maxim, 'patience is its own reward', should probably substitute persistence for patience for activists who are a little more pushy than they are patient. Resourcefulness, persistence and perserverance are probably three of the most important qualities for activists and activist organizations to foster. By persisting in the face of significant opposition, the strategic objective will usually be achieved. This is because some stakeholders cannot continue to oppose your campaign indefinitely for a number of reasons:

- Owing to growing costs, internal dissent or burnout in their ranks.
- They may come to agree with your position after many years of considering your argument.
- Public opinion or political wisdom catches up.
- They are prepared to accede to your strategic objectives in order to resolve a prolonged conflict.
- You were right all along and history has caught up with them (climate change, old-growth logging, ozone-depleting substances).

In any of these events, the achievement of your strategic objective is realized because the campaign strategy persisted, and was flexible enough to change and adapt to external factors.

Having extolled the virtue of persistence in public interest strategy, it is important to note that this does not mean that it is necessarily relentless. Part of a strategy of persistence, flexibility and picking your moment includes being prepared to back off and take a well-earned break while other events transpire or other strategists assume responsibility, so that you can recuperate, attend to other life duties, gain perspective and insight and return reinvigorated. This falls within the idea of being able to balance acceptance of the way things are right now with a resourcefulness that enables you to take advantage of all opportunities to promote the kind of change you seek. Extolling resourcefulness and persistence does not mean encouraging you to bash your head against a brick wall; it may mean that you should go away and come back with a long ladder.

3.5 Valuing acquired campaign experience

Some public interest campaigns may take years to achieve their objectives. If your campaign group can manage to create effective files for information storage and retrieval, can manage the challenges of changes in campaign personnel and achieve a strategic profile in the community and media, then it is becoming a mature campaign, which brings with it some distinct advantages.

For a mature campaign, it is entirely possible that the knowledge base of the campaign group may exceed the corporate knowledge or institutional memory of the other stakeholders in government, authorities or corporations. This is a real strategic advantage since you will know things that other stakeholders have forgotten or never learned and will be able to see recent events in a broader historical and strategic context and to project a sense of inevitability into discussions of the strategic objective. The point here is to not see lengthy campaigns as inherently weak; they can have great strength because of their durability and persistence.

Some campaigns are possibly ongoing by their very nature; campaigns against war, poverty and oppression may never reach a point of conclusion when these things disappear from the planet for ever, but they still can and do achieve significant outcomes. It's scary to imagine what the world might look like if it had not been for widespread public opposition to nuclear arms, for example, or if organizations like Amnesty International did not exist to continuously campaign for human rights.

4.0 Strategy and community organizations

Community organizations differ inherently from other forms of organization, such as government and business, in that they usually involve some democratic process and rarely have a formal command and control structure enforced by strict discipline.

This creates a special context for public interest groups and requires special consideration of the following issues:

- strategic decision-making within the organization;
- the role of volunteers;
- a need for coherent understanding and acceptance of the strategy;
- strategic partnerships and alliances;
- the special role of survival and renewal strategies.

4.1 Strategic decision-making

Activist organizations and social movements are not usually run by CEOs (although Greenpeace is a notable exception). Strategic decision-making in public interest campaigns is almost always a product of group discussions and collective decision-making. Sometimes these decisions are taken at formal meetings and sometimes at specifically convened workshops or strategy sessions.

Community organizations are usually far more egalitarian and democratic than most other forms of organization. As such the process of arriving at a statement of strategic vision, goals and policy generally requires much clarification, discussion, debate and amendment before final adoption.

Along the way, during these discussions, a range of conceptual tools may be employed, which could include:

- The brainstorm: in a brainstorm anyone is invited to suggest any idea that may contribute to group vision or aim, no matter how crazy, without rebuke; all these ideas are then reviewed, grouped and prioritized.
- Drawing a power-holder map: this identifies the key players, their relationships and critical links. Once this is done the aim is to focus on weak points to break these links. In the next chapter you will be introduced to various mapping techniques including power-holder maps and allies and foes maps, each of which contributes to this process. (See Chapter 4.)
- Drawing a campaign calendar or 'road map': identifying the present situation and the intended final (conceptual) destination; sketching in steps and stages along the way, working both forwards and backwards in time to identify lead times and the action sequence. (This approach was described in section 3.3 above.)
- Drawing an integrated strategy map: in brief, the place to start is the immediate goal that galvanized the group into action ('the immediate goal'); the next step is to identify a deeper underlying objective that represents a unified vision for the group. Once these processes are complete it's possible to begin to move down the map to devise component strategies and in turn specific tactics for achieving the goal and objectives. (Chapter 4 provides detailed instructions on how to approach the making of an integrated strategy map.)
- SWOT analysis: strengths, weaknesses, opportunities and threats. SWOT is a popular method for undertaking strategic analysis. It is beyond the scope of this book to analyse it here. Nonetheless, many people find SWOT to be a very useful tool. A useful Internet site for an understanding of SWOT processes is www.marketingteacher.com/swot/history-of-swot.html.

4.2 Strategy on the run

Decisions about strategy may not always be part of a forward-looking initial planning phase of a campaign; they can also occur more urgently in response to reactions by an intelligent opponent or other changes of circumstance.

These more urgent strategic decisions are likely to require detailed briefings on the latest information and reiteration of the previously agreed strategic focus, before new strategic decisions can be made. This reiteration of previous strategic decision-making is often required in community organizations because of a lack of overlap between those present at the initial strategic planning session and those present later when strategic responses are to be made.

This turnover in attendance at meetings and the resultant diminished continuity is a marked feature of strategy in voluntary community organizations which has distinct advantages and disadvantages.

Advantages
- decision-making power is shared not centralized;
- a larger number of members are involved in important decisions;
- more people understand the strategy, its basis and elements;
- a wide range of views is considered in the decision-making process;
- the rationale for the strategy is regularly restated;
- the strategy is subject to regular 'reality testing' by latecomers;
- once made, the strategy is 'owned' by the group of people involved.

Disadvantages
- the decision-making processes can be unwieldy and inefficient;
- there is the potential to fall into 'analysis paralysis';
- there may be gaps in understanding the strategic rationale among those who participated early and those who came in later;
- delays in decision-making may prevent timely responses;
- the security of the strategic decisions may be easily compromised;
- an individual may frustrate and obstruct through obdurate dissent.

Not surprisingly, strategic decisions are best made in community organizations by a relatively small, close-knit group whose members know each other well and who have good continuity in understanding the campaign focus.

Often, when strategic decisions have to be made and the official decision-making processes are acknowledged by members to be slow, and/or unwieldy, community organizations will formally delegate these decisions to a small trusted group, such as the executive, to take on behalf of the organization. Sometimes a purposely created subcommittee may be formed, such as a campaign committee, a litigation steering committee, a task force or working group.

These subgroups may be conferred all relevant powers or may be delegated a specific authority with the scope of their activities defined and constrained.

4.3 Need for understanding and acceptance of the strategy

Because of the complexity of working within community organizations, it is important that all campaign workers understand and accept the group's strategy.

With this understanding and acceptance, campaign workers can gain a sense of context for their actions and comprehend how their involvement is contributing to the wider strategy. They may be able to see how they can advance the strategy themselves through their individual action.

Further, where the community organization agrees to devolve authority and power, the well-informed campaign worker may be able to exercise their discretion or initiative to promptly respond to new information, changed conditions or the actions of the intelligent opponent, sparing the need for the convening of a formal strategy session to make the relevant decisions.

The sense of empowerment that well-informed campaign workers can gain from being actively involved is a major reason why people persist in what can be long and difficult public interest strategies and campaigns. This sense of empowerment should be nurtured and encouraged wherever possible.

4.4 Strategic partnerships and alliances

While a single organization operating a public interest strategy can be effective and successful, it is more likely that success will be achieved through cooperation with other groups. Most individual campaign organizations are actually part of a broader social movement, such as movements for environmental sustainability, animal rights, social justice, peace or equality.

Other groups may operate with different internal rules, have a different perspective and strategic focus, or wish to maintain their own identity, creating challenges for cooperation and integration. Nonetheless, there are substantial benefits in working together, and the strategic advantages and disadvantages that may accrue need to be carefully considered.

Disadvantages could include:

- loss of independence in action;
- diversion of time and resources to alliance-building;
- disagreement or conflict over campaign direction or tactics;
- mismatch in decision-making styles and processes;
- loss of group identity and/or sense of empowerment.

Of course, it may not be advantageous to pursue an alliance, or the other party may not be willing to cooperate, in which case campaign strategy will need to take into account the other party's actions and the possible ramifications, such as competing for media coverage.

5.0 Framework for a strategic plan

There are no hard and fast rules to formalizing a strategy in writing. In most situations, writing down strategy is a valuable exercise and is often essential to achieve a group agreement for the adoption of a campaign strategy. While security issues may be a consideration for groups that have a genuine fear of leakage to opponents or police, written strategy nevertheless

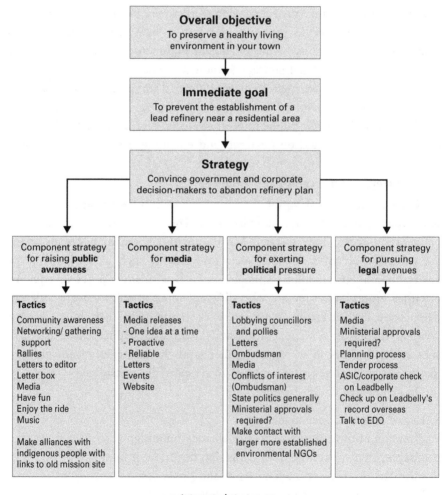

3.2 Integrated strategy map

can be a vital point of reference in the heat of the campaign, and can be especially useful to brief and enthuse newcomers to the group.

In the next chapter you will be introduced to practical processes for building a number of planning maps to help strategically plan public interest campaigns. The most central of all is the integrated strategy map itself. The example below shows an example of a strategy map for a campaign opposing the establishment of a lead refinery. Notice the way in which the overall objective and immediate goal sit above the more active parts of the map, such as component strategies and tactics. This hierarchy is very important because it helps all participants understand at every stage what the big picture is (goals and objectives) and how current activities (tactics) fit within that picture.

5.1 Accountable adaptable strategy

Public interest strategists must do more than devise and implement strategy if they are to succeed in their larger public interest goals. It is important to periodically monitor results and review performances to check that the strategy is appropriately focused, properly implemented and achieving the results intended.

The need for accountability in public interest strategy arises partly because the strategy is usually derived and adopted through group processes that are more or less democratic. Consequently it is important that those operating the strategy are accountable to the whole group and are prepared to explain and if necessary justify their choices of action. Volunteers, in-kind contributions, information, publicity and funds will be more likely to flow to the public interest campaign that is accountable.

It is important to strike a careful balance between implementing a strategy, evaluating its effectiveness and flexibly changing tack to abandon some tactics and include others. Expecting results too quickly and failing to persist may undermine the effectiveness of the strategy and may diminish confidence and support among campaigners and allies.

Such evaluations might be made annually to coincide with an Annual General Meeting or may be timed around predetermined events such as the conclusion of an identified phase or stage. Sometimes significant events, either internal or external, may provide the trigger for a broad evaluation of a strategy.

There are several levels to evaluating effectiveness:

- Operational: Checking how effectively the strategy is being operated by asking questions such as:

- Is the strategy's implementation consistent with the vision, goals, etc.?
- Are the strategists operating according to agreements made on time-lines, budget or internal consultation?
- Are the actions agreed upon being appropriately implemented?
- Do our campaigners and allies feel positive about working to implement the strategy?

• Outcome based: Checking how effectively the strategy is achieving the agreed objectives or desired outcomes by asking questions such as:
  - Have subsidiary goals been achieved?
  - Are we getting closer to achieving our objective?

• Fundamental: Checking on the strategic focus by asking questions such as:
  - Is the vision still appropriate?
  - Do the goals or objectives need updating?
  - Is the public interest rationale being properly served?

Periodic reviews help to revitalize campaigns and provide opportunities for new ideas and new personnel. On occasions they may be part of a process of winding up a campaign that has outlived its usefulness or better still has achieved its aims.

When this is the case it's important to take stock, thank people, satisfy outstanding accounts and archive materials for future campaigns to use.

Public interest campaigns provide excellent source materials for books, documentary films and exhibitions. Successful strategies warrant exposition, explanation and promotion, so don't be afraid to publicize your achievements and educate the next wave of public interest advocates.

Conclusion

In this chapter we have considered the essential elements of strategy in the context of public interest campaigns. We have explored the need to plan for the unexpected and to remain flexible. The careful planning of strategy and the setting up of staged campaign plans can contribute enormously to campaign success. This chapter provides an important theoretical basis for the practical processes and exercises provided in the next chapter and for all of the chapters to come. Strategy is a key consideration in all campaign work; it is the golden thread that can stitch together the elements of a public interest issue into an effective and successful campaign.

FOUR | Planning and mapping your campaign: practical tools and processes

Introduction

Mapping processes are the power tools of campaign planning. If you are embarking on a new campaign, or involved in an existing campaign that needs revitalizing, the mapping tools provided here are practical and field-tested processes that can powerfully transform your campaign. These tools have been developed in numerous real-life consultancies and workshops with activist groups and almost without exception can be employed to empower, focus and invigorate campaigns. In the previous chapter, we examined some theoretical aspects of strategy for public interest campaigns. In this chapter, we are going to provide practical processes, templates and exemplars for good practice that can be used in campaign planning.

1.0 Our working example: a story about you

For the purposes of this discussion, we are going to start with a hypothetical scenario to help frame the discussion and processes that follow. Pretend

that you are an ordinary citizen with little or no personal background in social movements. One day you wake to find that a lead refinery is being planned near your town (known as Corpvale). You are very worried about the health and the environmental implications of this, so you do something you have never done before – you decide to do something about it.

The first you know about the proposed lead refinery is when the story appears in your local newspaper (see overleaf).

Typically the story presents only the positive aspects of the development, and you may be left wondering whether you are the only one who has deep misgivings about it. Believe it or not, this is how most people become activists. They start as ordinary people who get pushed too far by something and they take a stand. You may not want to be a leader, you may never have considered yourself a political person, it is just that 'this is wrong and no one seems to be doing anything!' Congratulations, you are now in great company. Just think of Mahatma Gandhi, Emily Pankhurst,

Rosa Parkes, and read the quote below about how powerful each one of us is. You may end up looking at protesters and activists in a whole new light. All those activists were people who thought, 'It's wrong and no one seems to be doing anything, so I will.'

The following quote is regularly attributed to Nelson Mandela, but this

---

The Murdoch Rag

The news and views of the global elite
Saturday December 11 2011   *$1.20 freight extra*

2500 jobs in new industrial park: 'major boost for Corpvale'

Corpvale Lord Mayor councillor Burns has expressed his delight that Corpvale city has beaten international rivals to capture an historic deal with Leadbelly Pty Ltd for the development of a new heavy industrial park on the old mission site south of the city. The $2 billion development will include Leadbelly's proposed refinery together with infrastructure for a major new industrial park.

'This is great news for Corpvale,' Mr Burns said. 'This will secure our city's place as a major industrial port for the new millennium.'

CEO of Leadbelly, Ashton Black, said yesterday, 'Corpvale has been chosen because of the town's access to port facilites, and the co-operative attitude of the city's local authority.'

Local chamber of commerce president Ms Pixie Shrapnell welcomed the news, saying, 'It will provide a much needed and sustained boost for the region's economy. Now is a good time to be investing in Corpvale.'

The council's successful bid for the major employment-generating project involves commitments to provide key infrastructure and other incentives for the proposed new industrial park over the next twenty years.

Asked whether he expected any community opposition to the project, councillor Burns replied, 'Well we always expect there to be some hot air from the anti-everything crew – you know, the usual sudden discovery of the lesser spotted cabbage moth, or some ancient dog bones or something – but Corpvale is a forward-looking town and we're not going to put up with that sort of nonsense.'

4.1 The Murdoch Rag

appears to have been a popular misattribution. Nonetheless, it's a great inspirational passage for people embarking on the first step towards becoming a consciously active citizen and well worth repeating:

> Our deepest fear is not that we are inadequate.
> Our deepest fear is that we are powerful beyond measure.
> It is our light, not our darkness, that most frightens us …
> Your playing small doesn't serve the world.
> There's nothing enlightened about shrinking so
> that other people won't feel insecure around you.
> We are all meant to shine, as children do …
> And as we let our own light shine,
> we unconsciously give other
> people permission to do the same.
> As we are liberated from our own fear,
> our presence automatically liberates others. (Williamson 1996)

1.1 What happens next?

Every journey begins with the first step. From the moment you decide that you will 'do something' you are ready to take that first step. You may have taken a simple step such as writing a letter to the editor, and suddenly there are people ringing you and saying 'Good on you! I agree. This refinery must be stopped!' You may mention it to friends or colleagues and find some support and decide to take it farther, or you may go and visit a local environment or community centre and discuss it with people there. However you get started the important thing at this stage is to take a few practical steps towards involving other people. If you are unlucky you may find that no one you talk to seems to care; if this is the case, cast a little more widely for potential allies.

A letter to your local newspaper is a great way to put a flag up the flagpole about an issue and attract people who agree with you. Another way is to use social networking sites or the Internet to seek out people or organizations that may be supportive. An important qualification about your attitude here is that your central purpose should be to do something yourself (however small) rather than the more passive approach of looking for someone else who will do something. When you have this mental attitude you will draw others to you.

Suppose a friend suggests, 'Why don't you call a public meeting?' Why not indeed? If your issue is a very local one, like the scenario presented here, a local meeting is a very good start; it is one of the most basic forms of participatory democracy and a great way to begin face-to-face contact with other people. Social networking sites like Facebook and Twitter are also invaluable tools and can be used on their own or preferably in conjunction with face-to-face meetings.

There is a lot of enthusiasm currently for digital activism, and it does have enormous potential, but it is wise to see it as an adjunct to face-to-face activity, not as a replacement. Digital activism is discussed in detail in Chapter 9. There can be situations where a public meeting would not work so well, particularly if your issue is a much broader and geographically wide one and you really would not expect to attract many people to a face-to-face meeting. If this is the case you may be better off relying on digital-based activism tools in the initial stages, but you should never be too quick to dismiss the importance of the good old-fashioned public meeting.

So for now let's assume you book the local community centre meeting room, and you tell the newspaper about it (preferably by media release – see Chapter 5), put up some posters, create an event on Facebook, invite as many people as possible and alert all you can on Twitter. Next thing you know you are sitting there and wondering whether anyone will come. The doors are not knocked down, but slowly a small trickle of ordinary people come in and sit down (maybe only ten or twenty of them). You nervously get up and welcome them, introduce the topic, explain that you have no previous experience in things like this, and, most importantly, a friend collects everyone's names and contact details. This is the beginning of a great adventure.

1.2 The birth of a community-based campaign

You now have the beginning of your community activist group. Probably the first thing you will do is talk among yourselves. You will all be full of questions, such as 'Do we agree we want this refinery plan stopped, or at least modified?', 'Who makes the final decisions about this refinery?', 'What resources do we have?', 'How will we go about it?', 'Should we form a group?', 'What will we call ourselves?'

In the early stages it is great to just let these things happen by a brainstorming method. Brainstorming is where you just let everyone offer suggestions and you write them all down or record them all for later analysis and selection. Not all the ideas will be practical, but brainstorming sessions are very creative, they are very inclusive and democratic, and they can have surprising results.

You may want to create some categories for brainstorming and write them up on a board. For example:

- What is the issue/problem?
- What do we want to do about it?
- How will we achieve this?
- Who will do what?
- Whom do we need to convince?
- What more do we need to know?
- What skills and resources are available?
- Who can help us?
- How much time do we have?
- What could go wrong?

These are all good questions and are pretty much those everyone has at the start of a new campaign; they will get you a long way towards defining the boundaries of your campaign. Sooner or later, however, you will need to start coming up with a more integrated plan that coordinates these questions, and the answers you produce, in a coherent plan or strategy. This may not happen in your first meeting, but it needs to happen soon. This is where the process of campaign mapping becomes vital.

2.0 Planning a new campaign

We can now begin to bring all these ideas together into some practical methods of planning or 'mapping' your campaign. The documents you produce from these exercises can be called *campaign maps,* although they are sometimes also referred to as *conflict maps.* Conflict has its role, but not all campaigns need involve conflict.

The fairly intuitive list of questions that your group will have asked itself during the brainstorming session can now be broken down into some important categories, which bear a close resemblance to the strategic considerations considered in the previous chapter. In the grid on page 60 the middle column recasts these intuitive questions into more conscious strategic considerations; the right-hand column provides some suggested types of maps that can be drawn up. We will look at these maps in more detail shortly.

This grid gives us ten basic questions we want to answer. Just trying to answer these questions provides a very good structure for an initial workshop for your new group, but read on, because there are some very concrete planning processes you can use in such a workshop. If it is not possible or practical for your group to meet face to face then it is all the more important

Intuitive question	Strategic consideration	Type of map needed
1. What is the issue/problem?	What are our objectives?	Strategy map
2. What do we want to do about it?	What strategies will we use?	Strategy map
3. How will we achieve this?	What tactics can we use?	Strategy map
4. Who will do what?	Allocate tasks and responsibilities	Strategy map or task allocation map
5. Whom do we need to convince?	Who are the relevant power-holders?	Power-holders map
6. What more do we need to know?	What further research do we need to do?	Research strategy
7. What skills and resources are available?	What resources are available?	Research strategy Friends and foes map
8. Who can help us?	Whom can we form alliances with or seek assistance from?	Friends and foes map
9. How much time do we have?	What timelines should we set?	Timelines map
10. What could go wrong?	How do we plan for the unexpected?	Flexible planning diagram

4.2 Campaign questions grid

to adopt a structured approach to campaign planning. Digital tools, such as e-mail, Skype and wikis, can be used to conduct group discussions about campaign planning online. Drafts of various campaign maps can be uploaded and distributed so other people can help work up the documents. Wikis are useful for this purpose as you can upload documents and produce successive iterations of each plan or map. In the early stages of your campaign you are more likely to use popular and flexible tools like basic e-mail and Skype, but once your group is formed you may create various forms of open or closed online communities via e-mail lists, Facebook groups and other forms of networking to facilitate group coordination. These options are discussed in more detail in Chapter 9.

2.1 Step 1: setting objectives

The highest-order component of your plan is your overall objective, and under this is your immediate goal (different authors use different names; we will use these).

Objectives are statements about your values, about where your group wants to go and what changes you want to see in the world around you. Depending on the nature of your group, your overall objectives may be very broad and take a long time to achieve, such as 'world peace', or they may be more limited, such as 'maintaining healthy urban communities'. You need to be careful not to confuse an immediate goal for an overall objective. Frequently there will be a deep underlying issue such as industrial pollution, biodiversity or freedom from discrimination which really motivates your group, but your immediate focus is an impending issue right on your doorstep. Often the current issue is simply a concrete 'example' of the type of thing you want to stop. In this situation it is vital to distinguish between your immediate goal (dealing with the immediate threat) and your overall objective of bringing about changes in society, so that these things are less likely to happen in the future.

An example based on the Corpvale scenario is given in Figure 4.3 overleaf.

There are no fixed rules about how widely you draw these objectives and goals, but a good rule of thumb is that usually people will be sparked into taking action over an underlying value when an immediate (often local) crisis propels them into action. In such a situation it is a good idea to start by assuming that the immediate crisis represents an immediate goal, but that there is a deeper underlying value that motivates the people in your group.

There are very good reasons for taking this approach. To put it simply, if you do not articulate your underlying values you are unnecessarily narrowing

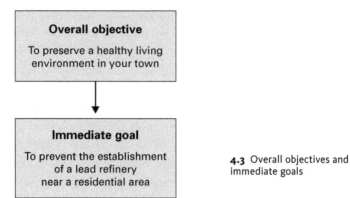

4.3 Overall objectives and immediate goals

the scope of your campaign, and too narrowly defining its real public significance. One consequence could be that you will be labelled as NIMBYs (Not In My Backyarders) because you have failed to articulate the underlying public interest issue, and secondly you will most likely shorten the life cycle of your campaign or movement.

Suppose the refinery goes ahead despite strident local opposition. If the only objective had been to defeat the refinery then your group is utterly defeated, but if your objective is to keep working for clean air, then your group has suffered a setback but continues to have a very real purpose (perhaps even more so now).

Suppose, on the other hand, you do defeat the refinery. Should your group just pack up and stop there, or are there other health and environmental threats in your town that you could do something about? Success breeds enthusiasm. Your group may go on to achieve many more positive outcomes yet.

This advice is based on the author's real-life experience of conducting

4.4 Overall objectives and immediate goals (SOF)

strategic mapping workshops for community groups. In 2004 I assisted a group of activists, Save Our Foreshores (SOF), from a coastal area in Australia. SOF had been galvanized into action because the local council was planning to give approval to a large consortium to construct a multi-storey hotel on the foreshore. The proposed development would have threatened public access to the foreshore and overshadowed an $8 million swimming lagoon that the state government had built for the people. In the strategic planning process the overall objectives and immediate goals were defined in Figure 4.4.

This description of the overall objective and immediate goal was important because it helped to uncover a deeper sense of commitment within the group, as well as expose the fact that the current 'crisis' was only symptomatic of a deeper problem in the area. Following the initial campaign the immediate goal was successfully achieved. SOF is now an effective and experienced community advocate on local planning issues and is now in a position to refocus its campaign on other public interest issues in the area. Since 2004 SOF has worked on three more successful campaigns, one of them in partnership with Greenpeace (opposing a shale oil mine), and is currently working to prevent a marina development in environmentally sensitive waters. This ongoing momentum of the group has been possible partly because of its commitment to the wider objective that motivated the people to take a stand on the first issue that they confronted. The truth is, if you really question people closely you will usually find a deeper, more heartfelt motivation for their activism than even they may be aware of at the time. The other advantage of adopting a broad and visionary objective is that activism can be fun and empowering and people might not want to stop after the first success.

Another aspect of envisioning a broader objective is that often your immediate goal will be reactive whereas your overall objective is more likely to be proactive. It is usually easier to gather public support for a positive and proactive vision. Activists and social change movements can easily be misrepresented as reactive, and as always opposed to something, but in reality most activists and social movements are pursuing a positive vision for a better world. It's vital to make sure that positive vision is articulated both within your network and to the general public.

2.2 Step 2: what strategies will we use?

After you are clear about your overall objective and immediate goal, you can start to devise strategies for getting there. Normally you need a range of strategies that relate to different aspects of the whole campaign, but it is a good idea to collect these 'component strategies' under the umbrella of one 'grand strategy'. This grand or overarching strategy is a statement of what is needed in order to achieve success. In many cases it will be something fairly obvious, such as 'convince the power-holders to change'. In the example of the lead refinery this grand strategy is expressed as: 'Convince government and corporate decision-makers to abandon refinery plan'. You can see how this statement tightens the strategic focus by identifying the particular outcome that your group is aiming for and by identifying the power-holders involved.

In designing the component strategies, there are some generic sub-categories that should be considered. These are of great practical importance. Most community groups should be considering what component strategies they will need in relation to factors like public awareness, media coverage, possible legal challenges, lobbying of politicians and other power-holders, and possible corporate strategies. It will also be necessary to have a fund-raising strategy (sometimes this is treated as an issue separate from the campaign as such, although often fund-raising and raising community aware-ness can be linked activities).

Your component strategies need to be tailor made for your campaign, but the categories of public awareness, media, political and legal are all quite common in most public interest campaigns.

Digital activism continues to be of growing strategic importance in cam-paigning, and it can contribute in a number of ways. Digital tools may be used as part of facilitating communication within your organization, and they can also be used as part of your public-awareness-raising functions. For these purposes digital activism tools can be incorporated within other more general component strategies related to awareness-raising and internal communications. In some situations, however, you may be intending to use digital activism as a key strategy in its own right. If this is the case then digital activism may form a component strategy in its own right and sit alongside other components like political, legal and media strategies.

So there is no limit to the range of possible component strategies that you may develop; this will depend on the nature of your campaign, but the following list provides a guide as to the most common categories of component strategy. Depending on your campaign some of these may be merged, adjusted, added to or left out completely.

Possible component strategies
- community awareness;
- networking;

- internal communications;
- media;
- digital activism;
- political;
- corporate;
- direct action;
- legal;
- fund-raising;
- research;
- economic;
- international.

So let's look at an example. Consider the Corpvale scenario again ...

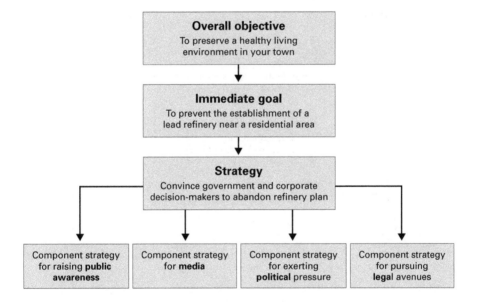

4.5 Corpvale strategic plan

2.3 Step 3: choosing tactics

Once you have determined your component strategy headings the next step is to identify specific tactics for making headway. Choosing tactics is something that will depend very much on your objectives, your strategy, the context of your campaign and also upon the resources and skills available to you. While it is always a good idea to have brainstorm tactics, you will later need to prioritize these in the light of what will be the most effective.

It is important to layer your plan so that you establish the correct hierarchy of objectives, strategies and tactics. This will help to prevent people mistaking a tactic for a strategy or, worse still, mistaking a mere tactic for the goal or even the objective. This kind of confusion is more common than you may realize. People are often inexperienced and can get carried away with a particular tactical step that they are working on. As an example, suppose you choose litigation as a tactic within your legal strategy. It is an easy mistake to start thinking that winning this court case is the whole campaign, and forget that at the same time you should also be keeping an eye on public awareness, political lobbying opportunities and media opportunities. Public interest campaigns are rarely won by a single knockout blow. Instead, you should expect that you will probably need to defeat your enemy by the death of a thousand cuts. Power-holders do not give up easily – they have too much to lose. You should not think that any one tactic is going to be the silver bullet.

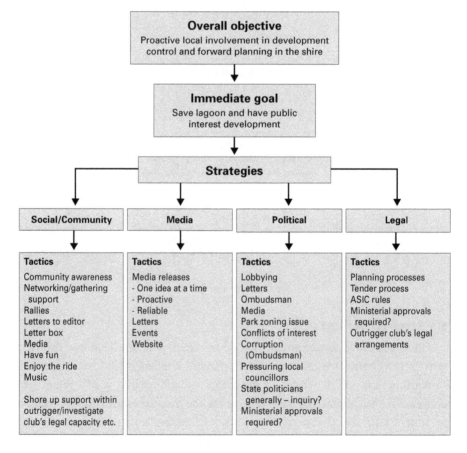

4.6 Full strategic plan

Having a well-set-out strategic plan has many advantages. It helps all members of the group understand the plan in a similar way and can help avoid damaging disagreements about the relative importance of each tactic or component strategy. It helps maintain a balanced and big-picture view of the campaign, and it is invaluable for briefing new members about the current state of progress.

Tactics will come from your circumstances. The workshop for SOF in 2004 generated a good example of tactics that may flow from a strategic plan of this nature. See the real-life example of the SOF strategy map in Figure 4.6:

2.3.1 The death of a thousand cuts: using multiple tactics to overwhelm your opponents This idea that you may have to defeat your opponent by the death of a thousand cuts is a recurring theme in activism. You should use your strategic planning stage to get a really broad-ranging grasp of all of the tactics that may be available to use in your campaign. You can still select the ones you think are most useful or appropriate and concentrate on these, but there's no harm in having a few extra tactics up your sleeve. Particularly when dealing with governmental or corporate institutional players.

Government and corporate institutions are usually quite resilient in the face of public pressure and sometimes quite experienced at trying to neutralize its effects. They may be ready for a predictable campaign in the media, for protest meetings and letters to the editor, but if you can suddenly confound them with a variety of surprise tactics you may be able to wrong-foot them. Once you know what your chosen strategies and tactics for achieving change will be, you may find it useful to also deploy a number of other nuisance or distracting tactics. I call this 'lighting spot fires under your opponent'. For government institutions these spot fires may take the form of formal complaint processes, inundating power-holders with requests for meetings, sending large numbers of submissions or formal requests for information, activating public participation processes, investigating and complaining about conflicts of interest, and any other tactics that will radically increase their workload, or put them under added scrutiny, while you concentrate on your main strategic attack.

For corporate players, the same spot fires can work but often need to take different forms. Going in through the back door and utilizing minority shareholder rights, initiating complaints to corporate investigative bodies or stock market regulators over irregularities you perceive in their corporate documentation, checking out potential conflicts of interest and again making formal complaints can be useful ways to harangue and distract them (see

Chapter 7). I call these tactics spot fires because on their own they may not be all that useful in achieving your main goal, but as a strategic tool for exhausting and hamstringing your opponent they can be very effective. Your opponent will be so busy trying to put out the spot fires you are starting that they will be distracted from the main blaze. I am not suggesting any dishonesty either; these tactics are genuine ways of seeking greater account-ability, and should be based on bona fide concerns – it's just that you may otherwise have discarded them as unlikely to yield positive results, but when you realize that simply by distracting your opponent you are gaining an advantage, they take on a whole new value.

The message here is to be very resourceful in taking stock of what tactics are available to you, and do not be too quick to discard possible options. Corporate players can sometimes be pushed to make a commercial decision to withdraw rather than face the escalating costs of fighting an unpredictable and damaging public interest battle on multiple fronts; politicians similarly may end up realizing that the fight is becoming too damaging for them. A golden rule for activists to remember is that power-holders are the ones who have everything to lose. This understanding helps turn your relative powerlessness into a form of power in itself. Usually the worst that can happen to you is that you lose your fight – pretty much where you'd be if you didn't start the fight in the first place.

Tactics are the fireworks of your campaign – they can be fun, attract a lot of attention, and if you are lucky they may make a sizeable bang.

2.4 Step 4: who will do what

Obviously, once you have generated a list of tactics that you can pursue it's important to make sure you have people who will take charge of each tactic. Depending on your organization you can divide tasks up in many ways. You may appoint a co-coordinator for each component strategy, for example, or go into more detail and assign particular tactics to particular persons to follow through. You will find that in the context of campaigning, official office titles such as president and secretary are not of much use. Campaign workers need to have designated roles that are relevant to your campaign plan. What is vital is connecting people to tasks effectively and giving them enough autonomy to complete their tasks. In some cases your group may not even be incorporated and may have no office-holders, only campaigners. Many groups operate as a large alliance with no incorporation, no constitution and no office-bearers, but a very efficient and organized system of campaign coordinators.

The following description of the North East Forest Alliance (NEFA) provides a good example of how relatively horizontal structures can work well for activist groups:

> Despite conducting a highly successful political campaign for well over a decade, maintaining a high level of recognition in local and state media, and being recognised formally by the New South Wales government on numerous occasions, NEFA never had a constitution, a secretary or president, any formal voting procedures, or any formal process for membership. That is not to say that it was not highly organised. (Ricketts 2003)

However you choose to organize your group's activities, it is vitally important to complete the strategic planning process by allocating responsibility for implementation to specific people. Without this vital final step the plan may be little more than a wish list. The process of allocating tasks will also be a good opportunity to assess your group's capacity and to delegate meaningful roles to people who may have been standing back at first. Many people have little experience in horizontally structured organizations and are more used to hierarchical structures which encourage passivity (see Chapter 12). The allocation of key tasks at a meeting can be very empowering for participants, and it can be surprising how much energy they will bring to the task once they take some ownership of it. Your strategic plan gives everyone the opportunity to see the campaign as a whole and to understand their own role within it.

2.5 Preparing your own strategy map

What we have constructed so far is a very basic initial strategy map. It is a document that can be used to focus your group; however, it is not meant to be rigid or unchanging, and it will need to be refined and revised many times in the light of new information and changing circumstances.

You have already seen the full version of the 'Corpvale' strategy map. Overleaf, in Figure 4.7, is an example of a generic version of a slightly differently structured map.

2.6 Step 5: whom do we need to convince? Making a power-holder map

Obviously, in public interest advocacy it is primarily the public whom you want to convince in the longer term, but in the shorter term you will need to convince particular power-holders to change what they are doing. Power-holders have a much more direct say over what happens in the short term than does public opinion. Public opinion is a complex and slow-changing

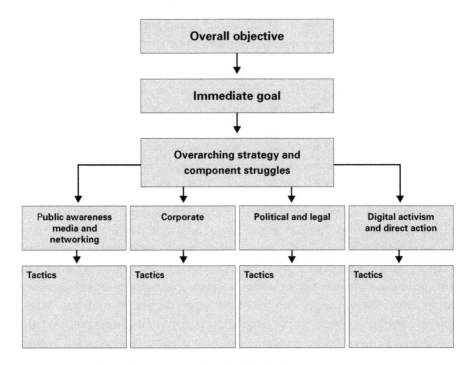

4.7 Generic strategic plan

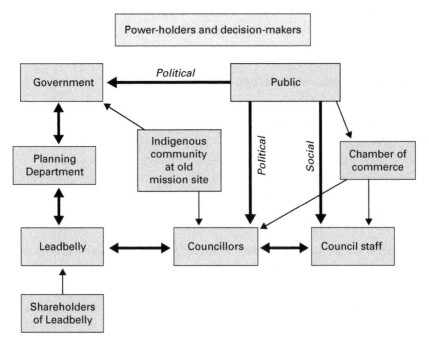

4.8 Power-holder map

business, and in any case power-holders are not always as responsive to public opinion as you may hope, particularly where there are other powerful vested interests at stake. You need only look at the campaigns against involvement in the Iraq war to see that power-holders will often ignore public opinion if they think they can get away with it. Your job as an advocate, then, is twofold: you must try to influence public opinion, but you must also convince the power-holders that they will not get away with ignoring you. The next thing we need to do is work out who the power-holders are in your campaign issue.

Opposite, in Figure 4.8, is a simple version of a power-holder map for the Corpvale campaign.

A power-holder map is a fairly simple flow-chart that helps you understand where power flows. Knowing where the power flows helps you understand where to exert pressure. You could copy the map and try to fill in the boxes as appropriate to your campaign, but the boxes change a lot from campaign to campaign, so it may be better to construct one of your own. The idea behind the map is that the arrows represent the direction in which influence flows, so in drawing your own map you need to start by identifying all the various stakeholders and power-holders and then draw in the arrows. You may find you end with intersecting arrows all over the page. This is common; it just means that you may need to go through several iterations until you produce a map that is easy to read.

A power-holder map is not just a descriptive tool, it is a strategic planning tool, and usually as you go about the process of completing the map your group will realize that there are more connections than you thought and more places where you can exert influence than you had previously appreciated.

2.7 What more do we need to know? Preparing a research strategy

It is important in any campaign to have a research strategy. This is discussed further in Chapter 5 along with other important aspects of research for public interest campaigns. For our current purposes, if your research needs are extensive it may be important to construct a research plan or research strategy. It is vital that in your mapping exercises you identify what you do know, what you don't know, what you need to find out, and how you will go about it. Remember always to leave some room for the unknowable. Overleaf is an example of a grid that sets out the varied research that would be needed for the Corpvale scenario.

The research strategy will be a constantly evolving document. As new information comes in, categories will change, new questions will emerge

What we know	What more we need to know	Who has this information?	Where/how can we find it?	What is unknown/unknowable	Who will do this?
The name of Leadbelly LTD	• Shareholders • Size • Related companies • Who are the directors	• Leadbelly itself • The corporate or stock exchange regulator or agency	• company searches • Stock exchange information • Become a minor shareholder	How important is this project to Leadbelly?	Mary
Who are our councillors	• Who supports the refinery • What conflicts of interest may exist	• The councillors • The assets register	• Meet each councillor and ask them • Check the assets register	Under-the-table deals and kickbacks	Apatia
Politicians	Where do they stand?	The pollies themselves	Meet and ask	Under-table deals and kickbacks	Apatia
Lead refinery	The health and environmental risks	• Scientists, lobbyists • Websites • Doctors	• Explore networks of academics and Drs who may be able to help • Look for NGOs that work on similar issues	The effectiveness of so-called 'safeguards'	Tina
Approvals will be required	• What approvals? • From which agencies? • What are the criteria/planning instruments • Can we object/participate? • Do we have standing to litigate? • What timelines?	• Council/government planning dept • Environmental and planning lawyers • Legal academics • Planners and civil engineers • EDO	• Make enquiries of council and state government • Look for law / planning people in our network • Check up the legislation ourselves	What backroom deals already exist	Jo

4.9 Corpvale research planning grid

and this will also have impacts upon your strategy maps. New tactics may begin to emerge once you have more information – for example, about your opponents. It is important that specific research tasks are allocated to specific people and that the outcomes are regularly reviewed and incorporated into overall strategic planning.

2.8 What skills and resources are available?

This question could well form another column of your research strategy map, or it could be included as a part of your friends and foes map, which we discuss below. You will often be surprised where help will come from. People with useful skills such as solicitors, engineers, scientists, doctors, planners and accountants may already be a part of your group or network, or may be able to be accessed from your network. The more you put your campaign out to the public, the more likely it is that you will 'call in' this kind of expertise. Campaigners should never assume they have to do everything themselves. It is surprising how often the skills that are needed are right there in the group, but nobody thought to ask. This is another big advantage of having an open, democratic type of organization. By constantly going back to your supporters for help and advice you also get the opportunity to ask for help with skills and networking.

2.9 Who can help us? An allies and foes map

You should never make the mistake of thinking you or your group are the only people who care about the issue. There may be many supporters, or potential supporters, out there, even among the ranks of those you assumed were your enemies (e.g. council staffers, ministerial staffers), who might lend a hand at times. A friends and foes map is a good way of taking another look at the whole issue, without making too many assumptions.

You should always make sure that you include in your map other (often larger), more established community organizations that may be able to help you. These groups often have experience from previous campaigns, resources or libraries, and they may be able to offer advice and assistance. Making use of these existing networks is an important part of your campaign planning and can save you from having to reinvent the wheel. On the other hand, you should not assume that such groups can solve your problems for you, or that they should take over the issue; just like your group, larger community organizations have limited resources and are usually fully engaged by the campaigns they are already running.

The idea of an allies and foes map is quite simple. You start with a page and list friends (people who are fully supportive) on the left and on the right-hand side people who you know (not just suspect) are working against you. Everyone else occupies some form of middle ground. In the middle of the page is the neutral/uncommitted line. In a meeting with your group, or as a collaborative online process, think of all the relevant players of any significance and begin to discuss among yourselves where they stand in relation to your issue. If you have no idea, leave them as neutral for now. This is not about strict categories of 'for' and 'against', and it is best to

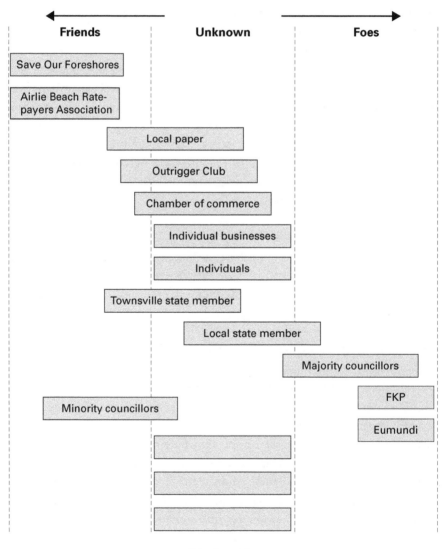

4.10 Friends and foes map

give people the benefit of the doubt. In this map you use a sliding scale from 'definitely friendly' through 'unknown' and 'neutral/uncommitted' to 'definitely foes'. An outcome of drawing a map of this kind is that frequently your group will discover that there is more help and support available than you had realized.

The terminology 'friends and foes' assumes that your issue involves some level of conflict or opposition, which is not always the case. Sometimes a campaign is entirely proactive and there is no opposition other than perhaps general apathy. This will be the case where, for example, your campaign is about improving facilities for people with disabilities. There is no one who would seriously oppose you, but you may need to overcome community apathy. In these kinds of campaigns a friends and foes map may be unsuitable, but you can adapt the same process to produce a mapping of 'stakeholders', which can include strong supporters and those who need activating.

An example of an early friends and foes map for the Save Our Foreshores campaign is shown in Figure 4.10, opposite.

2.9.1 Prepare your own allies and foes map A simple way to create a friends and foes map is to create a document on a computer that contains movable text boxes, place the name of each stakeholder in one of the boxes, and then in your group you can debate where on the scale from left to right to place the box. This is another process that should involve the whole group. It is often a surprisingly empowering exercise because many people begin their campaign feeling that it is them or their group against the world.

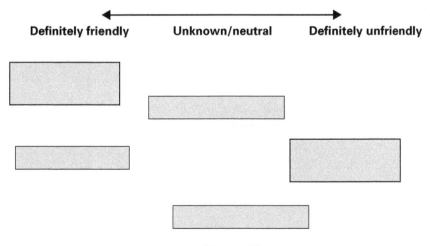

Definitely friendly   Unknown/neutral   Definitely unfriendly

4.11 Generic friends and foes map

The usual result of this mapping process is the realization that there are a lot of allies and potential allies out there and that your opponent may be relatively isolated, even though they may possess substantial economic or political power.

2.10 How much time do we have?

You will be able to draw up a timelines map only after you have completed some research about matters such as government approval processes, existing law, avenues for court action, available public consultation processes, legislative or policy timetables, elections, etc. You will then have some information to help you log the specific timelines. Timelines may also be affected by social events that may attract large numbers of people (networking/fund-raising opportunities) and your group's ability to raise finances or to source information.

Your timelines map will help make it explicit what tasks have to be done by when, what it is already too late to do, and where your efforts are best concentrated. This will feed back into ongoing revisions of your overall strategy maps.

Obviously, timeline mapping will also be constantly reviewed. The map can be configured in all kinds of ways; below is a simple version based on the Corpvale scenario. Notice that particular tactics or component strategies (planning processes, freedom of information [FOI], election campaigns, fundraising, etc.) each have timelines of their own. The right-hand side of the box is the deadline; the left-hand side represents the start of the preparation period.

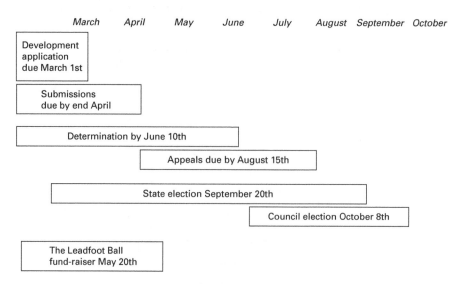

4.12 Timelines map

2.11 What could go wrong? Planning for the unexpected

The number-one rule in politics is 'don't stuff up'. The number-two rule is 'if you break rule one, then move on quickly'. Good planning will help you to see what's coming, but you should never get complacent or too rigid. Things change very quickly, and you have to remember that as your campaign gains strength the power-holders will abandon their first strategy of ignoring you and start to plan counter-strategies. When you start to be called names and they start saying terrible things about you in the media, don't panic; it means you've started to hurt them – it's a sign of success.

At times your opponents will launch counter-attacks that may be very aggressive or sustained. Try to keep clear. You must always be ready to adapt your strategy to take into account new circumstances, but you must never let your opponents bait you or force you on to a reactive agenda. You should always remember that as power-holders they have everything to lose; as change agents you have everything left to gain. An important rule for working with the media, for example, is never repeat your opponent's claims, no matter what they say about you. Use your precious media space to advance your own agenda, not to respond to theirs. For example, you should never write a press release in which you quote your opponent's claims in order to respond. Your best options are either to ignore the attacks or to respond to them by paraphrasing the attack then going on to the front foot quickly. For example, instead of 'They said ...' you can say, 'Despite recent attacks on our group ... we would like to reiterate our commitment to ...'. Where there is a real need to respond to public attacks, especially those appearing in newspapers, letters to the editor can be a better forum for responding to negative attacks than media releases because you get a better opportunity to explain yourself in full.

Many unexpected things will happen during a campaign, both fortunate and unfortunate. Always try to keep positively focused and remember that the more the power-holders attack you, the more successful you must have been. Stay on target and on message at all times.

Sometimes things do go wrong, and if they do your best response is to put a positive spin on it, and publicly apologize only as a last resort. It sounds awful but consider these real-life examples. A student union staged a sit-in at a university. While they were there they ordered pizzas. The opponents and media tried to make an embarrassing story out of this; apparently it suggested they were self-indulgent or uncommitted. The group apologized and as a result they were resoundingly ridiculed for it. The group would have done better just to have said, 'Our people were exercising their democratic rights of protest, and as hungry fee-paying students they have as much right as anyone to a good feed.'

In another, more challenging example, I was once doing media for a forest blockade, and against all of the rules of the movement, someone damaged a bulldozer. The damage control strategy went like this: I rang the police first and reported the event. Next, very quickly, a media release was issued reporting that the group had already contacted the police and offered every assistance, and that the group would never tolerate such acts of vandalism. The release then went back on to the front foot, arguing that the government was at fault for not resolving the issue of old-growth logging and that the wholesale felling of old-growth forest was an act of intergenerational vandalism that was unforgivable. Believe it or not, this worked, and the first story to hit the papers was our organization's own damage control story. Instead of apologizing, it's usually better to simply say, yes, that's happened, but the real issue here is the one we define it to be. There are of course times when public apologies are needed; if so they should be short, contrite and genuine, and you should also try to move on quickly. Private apologies are of course another matter, and these should be used as required.

There's not a lot more that can be said about expecting the unexpected. But whatever surprises are in store for you, a well-planned campaign with clear goals and a coherent and flexible strategy are the best insurance you can have.

Conclusion

This chapter has introduced some powerful techniques for building or refocusing a campaign. Naturally, advocacy and activism are ever-changing phenomena, and while a guide such as this helps you get started, you'll need to improvise and reinvent as you go along. The advice given here should be read in conjunction with the various other chapters in this book. Used in parallel with the processes described in other chapters, these mapping processes are a reliable practical tool for promoting ongoing campaign success.

FIVE | **Media, publicity and research**

Introduction

The most significant aim for any social movement or campaign is to progressively change public attitudes and perceptions about a particular issue. The process of winning hearts and minds underlies all of the strategic aims of a movement. Political solutions, if they can be achieved at all, will be short lived unless they are grounded in a significant groundswell of community support. For this reason the process of generating reliable information and data and being able to present these in a persuasive way to the public and to power-holders is of utmost importance in achieving long-term success. This chapter addresses the real practical life skills needed for conducting public interest research, generating publicity, using the media, and professional writing.

1.0 Information gathering

Information gathering is one of the most important tasks you will perform as a community activist. The success of your other strategies will often depend on how well you have performed this function. Good information produces informed strategies and accurate critiques, and is essential to effective public communication. Building a high-quality in-formation base for your campaign is like building strong foundations for a house.

Once you have sufficient reliable information, your next task obviously is to start to disseminate that information to the people who need to have access to it. Almost always this will include the public to some extent, but certain technical information may need to be communicated to particular power-holders or experts first.

1.1 A communications strategy

A communications strategy is one way of bringing all the elements of research and publicity together. It is very important for credibility in public interest activism that the key messages are accurate, clear and consistent, as well as being delivered positively and powerfully. You need to ensure that the efforts involved in research, in presenting information and in generating publicity are all working to support the agreed objectives of the campaign and aligned with the immediate goals and component strategies.

The diagram below illustrates the way in which research, strategy and publicity form part of an iterative cycle in a campaign.

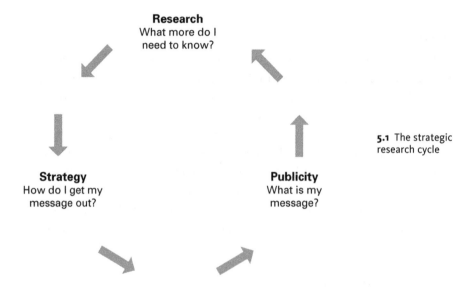

Research
What more do I
need to know?

Strategy
How do I get my
message out?

Publicity
What is my
message?

5.1 The strategic research cycle

2.0 Research

Your initial research will usually be an extensive process in which you need to gather information from a wide variety of sources covering a broad range of issues; you may need to answer very broad questions, such as:

• What are we responding to?
• Who makes the decisions?
• What facts are available?

Later on the research is more likely to become tightly focused. There may be discrete areas that require targeted and factual research. Some common key areas include:

• scientific information;
• applicable laws and procedures;
• economic data;
• history of the issue;
• background information about key players;
• evidence of particular allegations, claims, arguments that you want to make.

2.1 **Where to look for information**

The next step, then, is to know where you can go to find the information you need. Some good places to start include:

- public libraries;
- university libraries and academic databases;
- Internet sites;
- sources of local knowledge;
- public records, e.g. council, company, electoral, financial, reports and inquiries;
- freedom of information applications;
- fieldwork, surveys and questionnaires;
- networking with other community groups;
- expert opinion (there are 'expert registers').

The danger at this initial stage can be that your questions are too broad and there is too much information to sort through. If this is a problem you need to use a process similar to that needed to refine Internet searches; you need to narrow the search terms until you get a more digestible quantum of data.

Ways that can narrow the field of research include being more specific about what it is that you need to know – names? times? dates? – and also thinking about what the end purpose is; whom will you pass it on to? If the target is professional then it may have to be very detailed and well documented; if it is just for publicity it may be acceptable for it to be more general.

Recording the results of the research can save considerable time later. This means always noting the source of the information and the date it was accessed as you gather it; this is an important practice that avoids a lot of problems down the track. Finally you need to set a definite boundary for your research: when will you know you are finished or have enough material?

Later your research will be directed to very specific ends; often you will be seeking specific pieces of knowledge to complete the picture, prove a complaint or establish the facts for a legal challenge or other formal process. These key facts may be more elusive, but you will also have a clearer idea of what you are looking for.

You will often find that there is a lot of information circulating about your issue that is of dubious credibility. People in your network may be convinced that certain substances are poisonous, certain officials are corrupt or that certain motivations or unseen alliances are perverting the proper processes. It's important to deal with multiple sources of information intelligently. You need to be able to distinguish facts from mere theories, and to distinguish plausible theories from implausible ones. On the one hand you need to be open minded enough to take people's stories seriously and investigate them further where this is warranted, and on the other you need to be self-critical enough that you don't make the mistake of simply believing stories that support your point of view. People's stories can be signposts to where the important information lies, but you need to be rigorous before you treat them as facts so that you don't end up undermining the credibility of your campaign in the long term.

3.0 Presenting information

Information dissemination will involve either general dissemination (publicity) or targeted dissemination, where you are choosing to communicate certain information to key people. These could be key allies, advisers or experts, or specific power-holders such as government officers, or politicians.

Dissemination can take many forms, including:

- general publicity in mass or independent media or digital dissemination;
- targeted release, such as for formal submissions, reports, complaints, court cases or questions in Parliament or Congress;
- targeted leaks;
- public meetings;
- advertising;
- graffiti.

Different presentation skills are needed depending on the context. Before putting work into any presentation you should be clear about the intended message, the context and the target audience. The diagram below illustrates the important factors to consider in planning a presentation.

5.2 Plan your presentation

There are numerous ways of presenting information; the same information could be presented in several different ways to address different audiences and circumstances. Information that is meant for public dissemination needs to be presented in plain language in an interesting and attention-grabbing way. This is how media releases, public speeches, advertisements and media interviews need to be approached.

The same information being conveyed to a specialist audience, such as a court, parliamentary inquiry or complaint procedure, needs to be detailed, expressed in professional or discipline-specific language (law, science, economics jargon), factual rather than rhetorical, and well supported by documentation and quoted sources.

A key consideration, whether you are preparing general publicity or a formal communication, is whether you overtly include 'advocacy arguments' in your text. Advocacy arguments are your attempts to summarize the information in a way that persuades the reader to agree with your campaign aims. This is essential in campaign material such as brochures and posters, but it is usually avoided in formalized communications. Of course, it may still occur in formal documents, but it needs to be more subtle and not turn your factual presentation into a polemic.

Golden rules for information dissemination
- be specific and be clear about what the central message is;
- the information must convey the message you intend;
- avoid creating overload or allowing important points to be lost in detail;
- use introductions, summaries and headings to signpost the main message;
- the information needs to be relevant to the context of the presentation;
- tailor the information presentation to the audience;
- be clear about what outcomes you are seeking – requests for action should be direct and specific;
- anticipate the different ways in which your audience may respond and be ready for these.

4.0 Generating your own publicity

There are numerous ways of generating your own publicity that do not rely on the approval or cooperation of third parties such as newspaper editors or TV news directors. These alternative means of publicity are usually very important for new campaigns and can remain an ongoing part of grassroots campaigning.

These include:

- publishing a printed newsletter for supporters and other interested parties;
- creating a leaflet, handbill, brochure or flier, and distributing it at market stalls, railway stations, etc.;
- printing posters with a captivating image and a short, powerful message and pasting these up in key locations (shop windows, the passenger windows of your car);
- publishing a website and linking it to other sites and/or registering it with selected search engines;
- starting a Facebook group or at least publicizing Facebook 'events' associated with your campaign;
- printing your own stickers and choosing suitable locations for a 'stick-up': bus stops, behind doors in public toilets;
- producing other campaign publicity materials such as T-shirts, buttons, badges or caps and wearing them in the street and/or to events likely to attract a crowd;
- writing and performing street theatre;
- creating interesting, informative, attractive displays that communicate the key messages and report on campaign successes to date;

- hanging banners where they are unavoidably seen (but not stolen);
- organizing an interview spot on a community radio or TV station;
- running an art competition focused on your public interest theme;
- producing a short video that contains your key messages and images and distributing it via social media sites such as Facebook and YouTube;
- obtaining advertising rights to a strategically located billboard on which to display your message;
- organizing a community event such as a picnic day or working bee;
- utilizing web-based avenues for generating independent media (Indymedia);
- cross-linking all your digital outputs (e-mail alerts, videos, web links and Facebook pages) so that they can easily be shared by anyone who views them on Twitter, Facebook or YouTube (see Chapter 9);
- establishing an informal or formal SMS network through which to publicize and communicate (see Chapter 9).

4.1 Independent media

Independent media are by definition 'independent' of mainstream media groups. These independent media include local street magazines, student newspapers, community group newsletters, community radio and TV and computer bulletin boards. The Internet also offers great scope for independent media producers to create websites that display and attract material focused on public interest campaigns.

Independent media are more likely to carry stories or information about public interest campaigns because their editorial policy or their readership is potentially more interested and supportive. They are also less likely to have advertisers or subscribers to offend or alienate. The only disadvantage is that they may not have the reach of the mainstream media, or they may only be reaching people who are already sympathetic.

5.0 Accessing the mainstream news media

In theory the media serve the public interest by actively searching for breaking stories and fulfilling the public's 'right to know'. There are a number of factors which detract from the noble simplicity of this theory. Media owners often have their own agendas which are not necessarily aligned with the public interest, and they may exert significant editorial control to promote their own interests. The recent controversies surrounding the Murdoch media empire serve as a timely reminder of how extensive and dangerous the influence of media owners has become. Even if media outlets do not pursue overt political agendas, the fact remains that commercial media outlets are business corporations whose main purpose is to turn a profit. This means that commercial news outlets' primary function is to sell news rather than to publish good journalism for its own sake. This is not to deny that many outlets also take a pride in the quality of their journalism; it is to be hoped that they do. Finally, journalists who work in media businesses are under a lot of pressure to generate news stories quickly, and under various other pressures to respond to editorial policies and comply with in-house constraints, such as ideas about what is and isn't newsworthy, maintaining a range of stories and the need to appear to present balanced stories.

It's important to have your eyes open to the limitations of mainstream media so that your engagement is strategic and effective rather than naive and frustrating. It's important to understand that whether you agree with the way journalists and media outlets do things or not, you are going to have to learn to 'play the game' if you want to get good coverage. Once again the discipline for an activist in these situations is to accept the way things are, while finding resourceful ways to make a difference.

In terms of mainstream news media there are four main avenues: print, television, radio and online news services. The rules and tricks of the trade differ according to the type of medium being accessed.

5.1 How to get your story run (some more golden rules)

5.1.1 Make their job easy for them Every commercial media outlet is a business that sells news, and they need more news every day to keep their business running. So remember that you are not just begging them to run your story – you are providing them with free copy. The best way to get a good run in the media is to make it easy for them to feature your story. You do this by presenting your news story or media release in a style and format that fits easily into their output with little modification. Always remember: journalists work to tight deadlines and will respond well if you make their job easier for them.

5.1.2 Work with the publication deadlines of your media target You should find out the precise deadlines for each outlet. This will differ depending on the medium:

- for newspapers there is often a late afternoon deadline for the next day's edition;
- for evening television news it is usually early to mid-afternoon;

- for radio it can be more flexible, but if there's a particular time of day when you want it run, you should submit it close to that time;
- Internet news services tend to run 24/7 so the issue of deadlines is less important, but you should consider the best times for getting a fresh message out.

The idea is to target the deadline. Don't ever be late, but don't be too early either or the story may be considered old. Journalists and news media like to have the 'scoop', meaning they like to be the first to get the story. So often you should choose who you want to run your story or who you think is most likely to run it and target their deadline specifically. You can send it to other outlets afterwards, but make sure you hit your primary target at the right time.

5.1.3 Follow up by phone after you send your release Never assume that just because you e-mailed or faxed a media release it will necessarily be noticed. You should phone the news desk of the outlet soon after you send it and ask them whether they received it, do they think they will run it, do they need any more information. Be polite and be prepared to accept rejection; don't waste their time arguing with their decisions. The purpose of your call is to follow up, not to argue with them. If you know a particular journalist who has run your stories in the past, phone them personally and build a rapport.

5.1.4 Always use a written media release and e-mail or fax it A written media release is an essential first step. Partly because it's a deliberative process in which you are forced to clarify what the story is, what your message is and what approach you need to be using. A written release is absolutely essential for print media. Allowing yourself to be interviewed in shorthand by a print journalist then published in print is probably the single most dangerous thing you can do – the risk of being misquoted is extremely high. Written releases reduce this risk enormously. Even if you are going to be interviewed on radio or TV, the printed release gives you and the interviewer an idea of the script you want to adhere to.

5.1.5 Identify the news angle Make sure you can articulate why it is 'news' not just a rant. Always remember that your media release has to be a news story, it has to be about some event that happened or is about to happen or about some new and significant development in an ongoing issue, or about some conflict that is taking place. You use the news angle as a hook for getting your story featured and then deliver your important messages as part of your commentary on the story. For example, the fact that the residents of Corpvale have formed a group to oppose the proposed lead refinery is the event that is news, and then you can go on to say, 'the reason we oppose the refinery is because …'

5.1.6 Write your release in imitation of the 'house' style Your aim in writing a release (particularly for print media but also for other outlets) is to get the story reproduced unchanged or only slightly changed. Your best chance of achieving this is to copy the house style of the media outlet. This means, for example, that your release will include quotes from you, such as 'said Ms Walberger of the Clean Air Alliance' or 'according to Ms Walberger, spokesperson for the Alliance'. To do this effectively you need to be able to distinguish between paragraphs or lines that are factual background information (no quotation marks needed) and those that are claims, or advocacy arguments, that you are advancing, which need to be attributed to the spokesperson.

5.1.7 Cultivate your media contacts Your campaign is likely to be an ongoing affair so you need to carefully cultivate your relationship with the media outlets and journalists you use regularly.

The number-one rule is that your information *must always* be accurate. At first journalists will be wary of a new group with no track record and will hesitate to repeat your claims. If you embarrass them by causing them to write an inaccurate story you may not be given a further chance. If your release is about an upcoming future event, you must be able to deliver what you promise. Don't exaggerate massively about its size or again you will lose credibility.

Cultivate personal relationships with sympathetic, fair-minded or just plain important journalists. These personal relationships will really oil the wheels for you over time. Always be respectful of their professional boundaries, don't

expect favours, and remember to thank them for good stories. One way to reward a favourite journalist is by giving them a scoop on your biggest and best stories.

You must also make sure you write good releases with a real news angle. If your releases seem amateurish, naive or overly polemical they will be considered unreliable or simply too much hard work for the journalists to rewrite. Your releases should read like a news story on their own.

5.2 How to write a good media release

5.2.1 Be concise There is an art to writing a good media release. One of the keys is to be extremely concise and deliver a clear, punchy message. Releases should usually be written so that they do not exceed one page. They should usually start with a punchy lead paragraph that outlines the story, followed by a series of paragraphs where data, evidence, commentary or further explanation is provided. Usually you should also include some quotes from your group's spokesperson.

5.2.2 Have a clear news angle or story You need a hook, a news angle. Media outlets will resist running your release if you appear to be simply publicizing or worse still advertising an event, or if it simply appears to be commentary on an issue without having its own specific story. You need to be clear about what your story is, and make sure you lead with it. After that you can pack in your commentary. The story could be that a new group has been formed, or that a public event is proposed or has just happened, or that a complaint has been lodged, or that some unauthorized or damaging action has occurred; it can even be as simple as a story about some local people doing something. It doesn't really matter as long as there is a news event to hang the rest of the commentary on. You also need a good headline, and it should relate closely to your news angle. Your headline is only a suggestion for the journalists and is often changed by them.

Conflict and controversy are probably the most surefire angles with which to generate news stories, but you can also explore other news angles, such as:

- the unexpected;
- human interest;
- surprising revelations;
- famous people;
- action;
- humour;
- local interest.

5.2.3 Only cover one issue at a time One of the important disciplines is to only generate media interest in one story or issue at a time. There are a few reasons for this. For one it makes for clarity and easy understanding and reflects the way news stories are constructed. Secondly you should not waste potential future news angles by jamming several stories together as you should be aiming for another bite of the cherry farther down the line. A common mistake for new groups is to send out their first release in which they jam together all the various arguments on their chosen issue and all the things they plan to do about it. Apart from this being too busy and difficult to follow, it also means they have used up all their material in one go. A well-planned media campaign involves staged releases of information over time.

5.2.4 Never repeat opponents' claims Once your campaign gathers pace you will probably know you have stopped being ignored when you get attacked. A common response at this point is to issue a media release defending yourself from the attack. At times this is necessary and appropriate but in doing so you have to be very careful that you are not simply further publicizing your opponents' claims. You should never write a release that says 'our opponents say ..., but ...' because you are using precious media space repeating your opponents' claims. Instead, if you have to defend yourselves, use a style more along the lines of: 'Despite claims to the contrary, our position is ...', or at worst say, 'Local activists say they have been misrepresented by reports that they are opposed to job growth; in fact, they say, they have offered very detailed plans for job growth', and then outline your positive programme.

Negative media coverage about you is a great opportunity to grab attention and move your own agenda forward, but this is not achieved by repeating your opponents' claims. If an attack has been particularly sustained and damaging and does need a full explanation it is usually better to do this via a letter to the editor, rather than by way of a media story. The flipside of all this, however, is to be strategic; if you can trick your opponents into repeating your claims, go right ahead.

5.2.5 Always include a contact name and phone number Your media release is incomplete if it does not contain, usually at the end, the name and contact details of the person to whom enquiries should be directed, usually but not always the spokesperson named in the release. For example, it should say on the bottom line: 'For more information contact Ms Julia Walberger on 0402 567345 or by e-mail at walberger@amail.com'.

5.3 The format for a media release

The illustrations opposite provide an instructional example of how a typical media release should be structured.

5.4 Doing interviews

Doing interviews for print media is not recommended, but there are times when you will not be able to avoid them. The best way to protect

ORGANIZATIONAL NAME
and contact details

The headline is exciting

- The first paragraph is one that is punchy and articulates the news story and also delivers your core message. It is presented as a statement of fact.
- The second paragraph may provide some brief factual background information and need not be in quotation marks.
- 'The third paragraph may be a quote that introduces the author and re-states the core message together with some provocative quote or political statement,' said Ms Author, spokesperson for the organization.
- According to Ms Author, 'The third paragraph will develop the message further and will be most exciting if it contains a veiled threat of further confrontation if not taken seriously.'
- Then you will want to deliver basic information about where, when and how.

5.3 The format for a media release

CLEAN SKIES COALITION
e-mail: activist@cleanskies.org.au
tel: 0426 333292

New group vows to fight refinery plan

A new community group dedicated to fighting Corpvale council's plans for a lead refinery has been formed following a successful public meeting last night. The new group is called Clean Skies Coalition.

Spokesperson for the group, Ms Emily Activist, has said, 'We have the support and determination we need to bring this council to account to the residents of Corpvale. Our health and the health of our children is too important to bargain it away on some corporate get rich quick scheme.

'Lead is a highly toxic substance. It is not just residents who will suffer, there are nature-based industries at stake here as well.

'If the council thinks that they can force this destructive industry upon the residents of Corpvale without proper consideration of all stakeholders, then they are in for a nasty shock.'

For further information contact Emily Activist on 0426 333292

5.4 Example of a press release

yourself is to give short and very clear answers; this reduces the risk of being misinterpreted or paraphrased by the interviewer.

In all interviews it is a good idea to keep your printed media release in front of you; this should be your guide as to what the core message that you want to convey is. In all interviews, even if you don't have a printed release available, you should have a game plan of what you want to convey and stick to it. When doing interviews for TV or radio, deliver your most important points in short but unbroken sentences (so they can't be edited and must be used whole). They should be short because these are called a 'grab' by journalists, and each grab you provide should make sense and further your argument. This is also why you should talk in unbroken sentences, so that your whole sentence forms the grab.

An additional skill is to make sure you further your own agenda even if the interviewer is trying to take you somewhere else. For example, if the journalist says, 'Your opponents say your protests aren't legal', you can respond by saying, 'Well, the real question that needs to be asked is about the legality of our opponents' operation.'

5.5 Damage control

There are occasions where you need to go into media damage control mode. This may be when you have been unfairly attacked in a sustained way, or worse still when there has been some blunder on your own side. You should usually act quickly on negative or damaging stories, and it is essential to develop and use a 'damage control process'.

The first element of your damage control process is ongoing media monitoring. This way, if a negative situation arises, it should be detected as early as possible.

Damage in the media may take the form of untrue statements, misquoting by journalists or opponents, or simply negative stories put out by opponents or caused by public blunders on your own side; these can include spokespersons saying something stupid or damaging, or an event that is associated with your group which leads to adverse publicity, such as a violent demonstration.

The damage control process

- Check with anyone quoted that the statement reported was what they actually said.
- Assess the likely impact of the damaging story, how widely is it being reported or likely to be reported; is it localized, state-wide or national?

- Assess the urgency of developing a response.
- Identify any key people either in the group or outside who need to be contacted to be provided with information.
- Appoint spokespersons and prepare lines for response.
- Review subsequent media coverage and if necessary repeat all previous steps.

In most cases of damage control your responses are by necessity going to be reactive, but there are occasions where you have the chance to be proactive. An example of when you may be able to respond proactively is if there has been an event that has the potential to cause adverse publicity. You may be able to turn it to your advantage or at least minimize damage by being the one to break the story, but with your own spin.

In Chapter 4 I recounted a situation in which a bulldozer was vandalized at a forest blockade and I was responsible for the media damage control process. By getting in first and reporting the incident to the police, then going on the front foot by issuing a media release, breaking the story, expressing my organization's disapproval and then going on to explain that really this kind of thing was the fault of the government because of its irresponsible logging policies, I was able to turn a potential disaster into a positive story. Another good example would be a protest or march that turns violent; the best response would be to document and publicize any police brutality as effectively and quickly as possible in expectation of the almost inevitable backlash against protesters.

6.0 Researching your issue

We briefly considered research at the beginning of this chapter, but it is worth now taking a deeper look at this important function. Research is a constant activity in any campaign. It is best if your research strategy is well integrated with your more general campaign planning. When you have completed the campaign planning processes in Chapter 4, for example, you will have strategy maps, and friends and foes and power-holders maps. All of these processes then feed back into your research cycle because you will start to reveal gaps in your knowledge.

6.1 Background research

Background research includes the history of your issue, information about the various stakeholders involved and other salient facts. Researching the history of your issue is often done at the beginning of a campaign and it can throw up a lot of useful information. If you can find older campaigners or campaign groups that have tackled the same issue or a related issue in the past, you may find they have a treasure trove of information that could be useful to you.

Your power-holders and friends and foes maps usually help you see that there is a greater range of stakeholders than you may first have thought. Many campaigns begin with a very strong focus on governmental decision-makers, but you will find that there are a number of other stakeholders. Corporate players, for example, are often important stakeholders, and you may need to conduct some deeper research into their affairs, to uncover corporate and commercial links, shareholdings, investments and their history of involvement in similar issues. There is more information about tackling corporations in Chapter 7.

You may also want to research the personal and career histories of in-dividuals within governmental and corporate organizations. This can throw up interesting results, some of which could even help you understand their mindset better, or in some cases be suggestive of significant conflicts of interest, particularly in the case of public officials.

Research about other stakeholders can reveal opportunities for exerting influence and pressure, or simply inform you better as to how to fine-tune your strategies and tactics to best effect.

Resources for researching stakeholders include public sites that record corporate data such as stock exchanges, and corporate regulatory bodies, national registers of information such as census sites, electoral rolls, court reports and reports of legislative proceedings.

- Financial Reporting Council (UK): www.frc.org.uk/
- Financial Services Authority (UK): www.fsa.gov.uk/
- Industry Canada: corporationscanada.ic.gc.ca/eic/site/ic1.nsf/eng/home
- Securities Commission (NZ): www.sec-com.govt.nz/
- Australian Securities and Investments Commission: www.asic.gov.au
- US Securities and Exchange Commission: www.sec.gov/

There are also independent websites that monitor corporate behaviour which can be worth using to conduct searches on any companies you may be dealing with. See: www.corpwatch.org/.

6.2 Research to support your tactics

Once you start to develop particular strategies and tactics, you may find that the tactics themselves generate further research questions. In order to pursue a particular tactic some further facts may be needed. You may need to know, for example, what avenues of formal complaint or official appeal are available, and in turn these may require you to gather information to support your appeal process. If you choose litigation then obviously you will have to gather suitable evidence to bring before a court. If you are intending to use anti-corporate tactics you will need to gather as much information as you can about shareholders, directors, institutional investors and major customers and suppliers. If you choose to utilize direct action tactics, you may need to investigate the physical layout of the sites that you will target and their existing security arrangements, as well as investigate what the possible legal ramifications of your actions may be. Research is a constant function within campaigning because you keep revealing new research needs as you move along your campaign trajectory.

6.3 Research about salient facts

In a sense all the research outlined above is largely strategic and political in nature, but there is a very big area of substantive research that you may need to become involved in, and that is research about salient facts. This could entail scientific, social or economic data, physical processes, environmental or health risks – in fact information in any number of fields. Sometimes the information may be accessible by desk-based research, but often you will need to get out and find the information yourself. Sometimes data can be accessed from existing activist and public interest organizations or websites, or from experienced campaigners, or you may be able to find it in academic literature or government records. Factual research, especially where it involves field research, can be expensive and time consuming and requires specialist skills.

This will usually mean you need to employ professional expert consultants to help you generate reliable information and data about your issue. Some advice on obtaining expert assistance is provided in the following section.

7.0 Obtaining expert assistance

Experts are generally an expensive commodity, so before you reach for the telephone you need to be sure of what it is you are planning to do with the information. When you are engaged in litigation it is often essential to have expert evidence available. In some other contexts, such as when you are writing submissions to government, it may be highly desirable but not essential or affordable. For non-formal processes you can often solicit the assistance of friendly lawyers, doctors or academics who are known to people in your network, or known to be supportive of similar causes. Unfortunately, for very formal processes such as court cases you need to be able to show that the experts are independent of you, and this means you should be paying them at 'arm's length' commercial rates.

7.1 Finding relevant experts

Draft a list of possible experts in consultation with someone with contacts in the relevant fields; sometimes your more widely connected friendly experts may be the best people to advise you of which external experts to seek.

Fertile places in which to seek experts include universities, private consultancy firms, institutions such as museums, hospitals and professional associations. It is often advisable to try to contact the individual rather than the institution because the marketing arms of universities, for example, can triple the costs of engaging a professor.

Golden rules for dealing with experts

- You must be respectful and accept the fact that they decline to act for you.
- Don't ever attempt to coerce an unwilling expert; be as persuasive as possible, identify obstacles to their involvement and attempt to overcome them.
- Do *not* expect them to do what you want on demand; a very busy expert may work for you in the future if they're available and you have not already offended them; unless you're in a real hurry, make initial exploratory phone calls to seek 'an expression' of interest only.
- It's wise *not* to insist on an immediate answer; follow up positive expressions of interest with a letter referring to the phone call.
- Don't assume that they know about you, your group or your interests – provide background info and clear explanations.
- Answer their questions honestly; check that the expert has the relevant expertise and qualifications, not tangential interests.
- Investigate their 'personal' and 'political' views and attitudes beforehand.

7.2 Hiring experts

You need to be very explicit about your needs and expectations and ensure that you are communicating clearly with the expert about remuneration, deadlines and deliverable outputs before you go so far as formally engaging them. It is a good idea to begin by preparing a brief and seeking their feedback about the brief.

The brief that you prepare for your consultants should set out:

- the issue in general;
- the information requested;
- any relevant documents or information you wish the expert to consider;
- the questions to which the expert is asked to direct themselves in drafting their report;
- the preferred format for the statement report;
- your needs as regards confidentiality – in terms of documents supplied and evidence prepared;
- the timeline, including deadline, for completing the report or affidavit;
- what you undertake to do for them, such as supply documents, pay their out-of-pocket expenses, organize their travel, etc.;
- a clear and upfront statement about the financial obligations you can realistically meet.

Negotiate the terms of the brief with the expert before formally 'hiring' them or retaining their services.

8.0 Professional writing

Professional writing and communication involves being rigorous about recording, presenting and storing information. It is also important to know the various main forms of professional document that you may be using or required to prepare.

Effective packaging of information to a professional standard involves knowing what the title and purpose of a document is. There are, of course, innumerable different kinds of documents, but we will examine some of the more common ones below:

- memo;
- e-mail;
- letter;
- report;
- briefing note;
- background paper;
- submission.

8.1 Memoranda (memos!)

These are usually informal (often handwritten) documents used for passing on new, important or simple information to others: reminding someone of something; noting something on the file; or for quick notes or requests. Being informal documents, memos are not always labelled as such – it's a bit of a generic category. Sometimes in offices they are treated a little more formally to distinguish them from a scribbled note.

If you want to draw up a formal memo the format for headings could be:

From:
To: (including to file)
Date & time:
Re:

Frequently offices have tear-off pads that are presented in roughly this format for this purpose.

When is a memo not a memo? When it gets too long!

If you need to send someone a longer message you may choose to do it as a letter or more commonly these days as an e-mail.

8.2 E-mails

E-mails are playing a developing role in formal communication and one that we need to be a little wary of. They have taken over from much other written communication because of the speed of delivery, and the ease of response. E-mails are a form of written communication and as such they leave a record of what was communicated that cannot be easily erased. This is their big advantage, or disadvantage, depending on where you stand. The most important thing is to remember that e-mails are written and permanent. Use them deliberately where this is a desired outcome, practise the 'don't press send' rule, as outlined in Chapter 9, if you think you may later regret sending the e-mail in question.

The way in which e-mails are responded to continues to vary from office to office and person to person. Many people operate almost exclusively by e-mail, while others see them as a marginal and very informal form of communication. You can never be sure that an e-mail will be responded to, so it is often wise to follow up e-mails with personal phone calls or snail-mail letters if the communication is important to you.

8.3 Letters

Letters are a formal written document, although the degree of formality varies. They are used for passing on new, not-so-simple or personal information to others; requesting information; requesting actions; making an initial impression; or as a formal cover letter for a document such as an application or submission.

Culturally, letters are regarded as having a higher degree of formal significance than phone calls, e-mails or even personal conversations. For example, in mass lobbying campaigns, letters are still considered to count for much more than the same number of supportive e-mails. The big advantage of letters is that they take a while to prepare and send, so you have a lot more opportunity to think and reflect and amend than is often the case with e-mails.

Formal letters usually have specific purposes, such as notifying someone of something, requesting an action or response, or applying for something – a job or a government grant – or making a formal complaint. In these circumstances it is usual for the letter to be set out more formally, with the full contact details of the sender and the addressee, a formal subject line or reference, and a formal use of titles and greetings.

When sending letters as part of a campaign you should use the group's letterhead. If you don't have one – make one! A letterhead conveys a sense of formality and of organizational status.

When it is essential that a key decision-maker in a large organization actually sees your letter, include a bold or capitalized heading. For example:

FOR MR SMITH'S PERSONAL ATTENTION

Include under the addressee's name a bold or underlined heading which summarizes the letter's subject, e.g.:

Re: Complaint regarding Police Conduct

There are many styles for formal letters; these can be copied from letters you have received or downloaded from your computer. Most word-processing applications also provide templates for standard letters.

Wherever possible, address your letters to a named person, or use the office position, e.g. 'the Secretary' if you cannot find out who holds the position, and always include the date.

Don't underestimate the power of getting your message across in a good letter. For an important letter you should prepare a draft and show it to others for their comments and input. This makes for group accountability, increasing the chances that the letter represents the whole group, and ensures that all relevant points have been included.

Check your letter carefully to make sure that you have asked a question or made a definite request for action, because letters that do this must be responded to.

Sign off 'Yours Sincerely' unless you know the addressee well; type your name and position below where you intend to sign.

Avoid

- omitting the date!;
- forgetting to keep a copy;
- lengthy delays between signing and posting or delivery;
- misspellings of people's names;
- using incorrect or misleading titles;
- personal attacks or gratuitous remarks.

8.4 Reports

These are used for providing detailed information on fieldwork, research or committee or group activities to a particular audience, stating conclusions and recommendations, documenting the processes used in work or activities, or reporting progress on work presently under way.

Reports are often long documents that are clearly structured and divided under various section headings.

Suitable headings

- the report's name or title;
- abstract or executive summary;
- table of contents;
- list of figures;
- list of photographic plates;
- methodology;
- results;
- conclusions;
- commendations;
- recommendations;
- data records;
- references cited;
- index;
- annexures.

Content This depends on the subject of the report. In most cases, reports are reasonably narrowly focused and deal with one main subject. They are meant to be informative documents that are structured in a way that makes it easy to navigate to the relevant sections.

Avoid

- making unsubstantiated claims;

- use of unexplained acronyms, abbreviations or technical terms;
- advocacy arguments – leave these to letters, briefing notes, discussion or options papers;
- breaching confidentiality or copyright laws;
- including excessive annexures as padding.

Follow-up Know to whom the report is directed; ensure that key players have copies of the report and have read it; bring copies to relevant meetings; refer to and pursue action on any conclusions or recommendations; provide free copies to the media; organize a publicity launch; put the report on sale!

8.5 Briefing notes

These are used for encapsulating a complex issue in a short summary; updating progress on an ongoing issue; referring to other relevant information, including large documents such as submissions, reports, etc.; stating the current situation concisely; preparing a person for a public meeting or other function, where they may have to speak 'ad lib'.

They are commonly used by people who have no time to read very lengthy submissions, such as key decision-makers: ministers, ministerial staff, senior officials, journalists.

Suitable headings Ideally briefing notes should not exceed one A4 page, so headings and text will be limited. Include:

- name or title of issue;
- background;
- recent developments;
- the current situation;
- issues involved;
- action requested.

Content
- must be concise but not bland;
- use bullet points;
- limit use of long sentences;
- don't bury a problem; state it clearly.

Avoid
- exceeding one page;
- including too much detailed background info.

Follow-up
- check copy was seen by target;
- note decisions made or answers given.

8.6 Background papers

A background or briefing paper is like an expanded version of a briefing note. It too is used for bringing someone 'up to speed' but is more detailed than a briefing note, providing considerably more detailed information, outlining the players and their agendas, or introducing a new topic or concern. A background paper is still usually destined for someone with insufficient time to conduct further research into the topic, and it should be constructed in a way that makes it easy for them to speed-read it, as many professionals rarely ever read a document of this kind word for word. For this reason the way in which you construct the headings should be carefully designed to summarize the content of each section. A good way of knowing if you have done this is to read through the headings on their own. They should themselves tell the main story; the sections themselves should be the background to the story or the main supporting data. Important specific facts and findings can be highlighted in some way to also make it easier for the reader to scan the document and cherry-pick the most important parts quickly. Your role in preparing a briefing or background paper is to assist the reader to get a good grasp of the topic quickly.

Suitable headings
- name or title;
- introduction;
- affected parties;
- chronology or history of events;
- issues raised;
- opportunities available;
- risks involved;
- current state of play;
- bibliography and further reading.

Content
- cover or title page;
- headings and subheadings;
- explanations and arguments;
- summaries of other documents and events;
- quotations and acknowledged extracts;

- references to publications and media coverage;
- names and particulars of key contacts;
- anecdotes and examples;
- tables, graphs, lists, cartoons, sketches, maps, photos;
- suggested texts for further reading.

Avoid
- slanting a document overtly; its prime purpose is to inform, not convince;
- omitting key dates, events, info; it should be a 'stand alone' document;
- turning a backgrounder into a thesis.

8.7 Submissions

Submissions are used for formal input into public consultation processes, or requests for grants or other funding. Usually there has been some formal process involving a government agency calling for submissions, or there is a statutory process that requires a decision-maker to consider submissions. Submissions are intended to be factual statements addressing a particular issue. They can be slanted to represent the views of the person or organization making the submission but they are more powerful when they are factual rather than simply rhetorical. While a submission will usually advocate a position, it should be written in a calm and well-considered style; it should not be presented as a polemic.

Suitable headings
- submission's name or title;
- table of contents;
- executive summary;
- recommendations;
- introduction (to the group making the submission);
- comments on (draft document on public display);
- considerations omitted;
- options for consideration;
- references cited;
- index;
- annexures.

Content
The focus of the submission could be on the document on display, the guidelines for the grant application and/or information on the programme under which the funds are available.

Submissions are usually accompanied by:

- a signed covering letter;
- rational advocacy arguments;
- clear and constructive criticisms;
- recommendations;
- reasons to support arguments;
- references to other relevant published material;
- results or conclusions of original research.

Avoid

- commencing work on the 'due by' date;
- missing a deadline for submissions;
- concentrating on the negative;
- unwarranted claims of confidentiality;
- allowing copies of your submissions to be obtained by your opponents.

Follow-up

- know to whom the submission was made;
- ask for an opportunity to attend a hearing where you can expand on your submission and answer questions on it;
- lodge a copy with the local library and/or environment centre;
- expect and pursue a receipt or letter of acknowledgement;
- obtain a list of other people or groups that made submissions;
- attempt to obtain any summary of your submission that may have been prepared by the department or agency;
- attend the meeting where consideration will be given to public submissions and any decisions made.

Conclusion

Research, writing and publicity are core functions of any campaign or social movement. This chapter is long and detailed, but it covers an area of special day-to-day significance for campaigns and campaign workers. The nuts and bolts of how to conduct research, generate media interest and write formal communications are among the most basic functions that must be done well in a campaign, otherwise much of the strategic edge will be lost.

It is important to remember always that your publicity and communications are what the outside world sees of your campaign or social movement, and the quality of your research ultimately influences how seriously you will be taken by the public, media and decision-makers. The process of generating reliable information and data and being able to present these in a persuasive way to the public and to power-holders and decision-makers is of utmost importance in achieving long-term success.

SIX | Public sector activism: how to change the law and influence government policy

Introduction

Much of the work of social change activists will involve the public sector. The public sector includes: government at every level as well as the public service, departments and ministries, courts and semi-autonomous institutions such as various boards, tribunals and statutory corporations. This chapter explores the requirements for successful campaigns to change government policy, influence decision-makers or to bring about legislative change. It also begins by introducing the practical background to activism in the public sphere, by examining relevant aspects of constitutional law, and the process of democracy.

1.0 The public sector, the private sector and civil society

Modern legal systems, particularly common-law-based legal systems (those of most English-speaking nations), maintain a significant separation between the private and public realm and particularly between private and public law. Private law is concerned with relations between individuals, issues such as contract, marriage, personal civil actions for damages and compensation, for example, whereas public law is concerned with issues of broader social governance such as constitutional law, administrative law and criminal law.

While most institutions of governance are part of the overall machinery of the public sector, it is arguable that many large corporations have now evolved to a position where they are also de facto institutions of governance (Korten 1995: 54). A good example of this 'governance' power of corporations is the way in which insurance companies exert a major influence in controlling safety standards in buildings and industries through the terms of insurance policies.

So in a sense we can speak of the public sector as a form of public bureaucracy and the corporate sector as a form of private bureaucracy. Private bureaucracy consists of privately controlled profit-making entities that we call corporations, and there is also a third sector often referred to as civil society. Civil society includes a great range of organizations such as charities, political parties, social change organizations, trade unions, religions, not-for-profit associations, research institutes, public media and even less-organized groups such as social movements and cultural and ethnic groups.

Activism is conducted by individuals or by civil society organizations and their targets are usually public bureaucracies or private corporate bureaucracies. This chapter deals with the public sector; the next chapter with corporate activism.

1.1 Activism in the public sector

Most but not all community activism will involve public bureaucracy in some way, even if the issue is not solely located in the public sphere. Public bureaucracy may be involved as:

- a decision-maker;
- a legislator;
- an enforcement agency;
- a funding body;
- a strategic ally.

In order to understand how to make your campaign most effective it is important to understand the role that various elements of public bureaucracy play in your issue. This chapter provides a general introduction to the matters you need to take into account when planning your campaign. This is only a general guide as it needs to be broad enough to cover several different jurisdictions within its scope.

2.0 Understanding your national constitution

The constitution is a usual place to start for working out how the process of governance works in a particular country. For most English-speaking countries (excluding the UK and New Zealand) there is a written document known as the constitution which defines the powers and responsibilities of various governance institutions. In New Zealand and the UK, the constitution is usually said to be 'unwritten', although in practice the constitutional law of these two countries is made up of a complex assembly of written materials such as statutes, orders and court decisions, as well as a range of unwritten conventions.

The most significant difference between countries with written and those without a written constitution lies in the relationship between the constitution and other legislation. Countries with a single written constitutional document (Australia, the USA, Canada and many other Commonwealth and former Commonwealth countries) usually also provide that the constitution is 'supreme' over other types of law. This means that in those countries the power of the legislature is constrained by the constitution because any law that is passed that is inconsistent with the national constitution may be struck down by the highest court (usually called the High or Supreme Court).

This is a significant difference because in the UK and New Zealand legislation validly passed by the houses of parliament cannot be overturned by the judiciary, but in Australia, the USA and Canada and other countries with written and supreme constitutions, it is possible to mount challenges through the courts to overturn unconstitutional legislation. Constitutional challenge is a powerful tactic for activists to use where it is available because of the legal and moral force of a constitutional ruling. More recently, even in the UK, the home of parliamentary supremacy, judicial review of legislation is now permissible as part of the United Kingdom's obligations under European Community Law as enshrined in the Human Rights Act 1998 UK.

Another significant difference between the UK and New Zealand on the one hand and Australia, Canada and the USA on the other is that the latter three are all federal systems, which means that the constitution distributes power between the national legislatures (parliament or congress) and the state or provincial legislatures. The UK and New Zealand have what is known as a unitary system in which there is only one legislature for the country (although there may be two houses, as in the UK).

Some constitutions operate with two houses of parliament (bicameral); these include the USA, the UK, Australia and Canada, whereas New Zealand

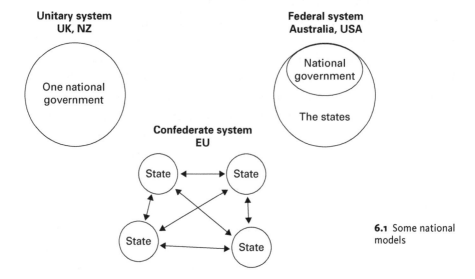

6.1 Some national models

has only one house (unicameral). Where there are two houses of parliament the legislative process is more complex, but this of itself usually means there are more opportunities for strategic intervention by social change activists.

The final and probably most significant difference between the constitutions in various English-speaking countries is whether they have a monarchist or a republican system. The most common monarchist model that you are likely to encounter is the Westminster model (the UK model), in which the monarch is the formal head of state, but the prime minister is the effective head of government. In the Westminster model the monarch's formal powers are constrained in practice by the need to act upon the advice of the prime minister (with the exception of some special reserve powers that are retained). The prime minister, then, is the more powerful figure in practice. In a Westminster system, the prime minister must be a member of the parliament and must enjoy the support (confidence) of the majority of the members of parliament at all times. In practice the Westminster system has been modified by the growth of party politics, because once a disciplined party gains more than half of the seats in the lower house, then they can safely expect the parliament to support them in confidence votes and to pass their legislation. It is only on those rare occasions when there is a 'hung' parliament (neither major political party commands a majority of seats) that the executive government (the prime minister and cabinet) needs to carefully negotiate its way through confidence votes and the passage of bills through the house.

A republican system such as that in the USA is significantly different. For a start there is no hereditary monarch; the supreme executive officer is the elected president. The president is both head of state and head of government, and exercises significant substantive power. The legislature (Congress) is responsible for law-making but does not have a direct role in choosing the president (Art II s1). The president does not need to obtain or maintain majority support in Congress to remain president. In practice this has meant that party unity is not as strictly required in the US Congress as it is in the Westminster countries, and so members of Congress in the USA are far more likely to vote other than on strict party lines.

These distinctions are relevant to activists in relation to lobbying politicians because in Westminster countries there is a greater emphasis on lobbying power brokers within established parties, whereas in the US system lobbyists need to pay a lot more attention to gaining the support of individual members.

On the US constitution, see topics.law.cornell.edu/constitution.

2.1 The importance of a bill of rights

Another important factor to consider is whether your country has an enforceable bill of rights included within its constitution. Some countries such as Canada and the USA have a constitutionally entrenched bill of rights, which means that governmental actions and even legislation can be overturned by the courts if it breaches the rights protected in the bill of rights. Australia has no such bill of rights and the UK and New Zealand have a bill of rights that has the status of ordinary legislation, which means it can be used to challenge administrative actions but does not have the power to override contrary legislation. Bills of rights can provide significant opportunities for social change activists, particularly those working on equal rights and anti-discrimination campaigns.

On the USA Bill of Rights: topics.law.cornell.edu/constitution/billofrights#amendmentx.

On the Canadian Charter of Rights and Freedoms: lois.justice.gc.ca/eng/charter/Charter_index.html.

2.2. The separation of powers

The concept of the separation of powers is a key concept in constitutional law in both Westminster and republican presidential systems. The idea of the separation of powers goes to the heart of the whole idea of constitutional governance in that it describes the way in which power is distributed as between the main institutions of governance so as to prevent all power being concentrated in the hands of one institution or person. If power were to be concentrated in the hands of a single individual it could be called an absolute monarchy or a totalitarian dictatorship, or where it is concentrated in the hands of a single institution such as a particular dominant political party then it can be described as a totalitarian system or a one-party state.

The separation of powers divides the overall governance power of the modern state into three basic components:

- legislative or law-making power;
- adjudicative or judicial power exercised by the courts; and
- executive power, which is the power to administer the affairs of state.

In a presidential republican system such as the US system these three powers are quite clearly separated, with the president holding the executive role of administering the affairs of state, the congress holding the power to make new law and repeal or amend old law, and the courts having the power to arbitrate in disputes between citizens, enforce the law and decide any constitutional challenges. While all three sites of power do interact significantly, they are meant to avoid interfering with each other's core functions.

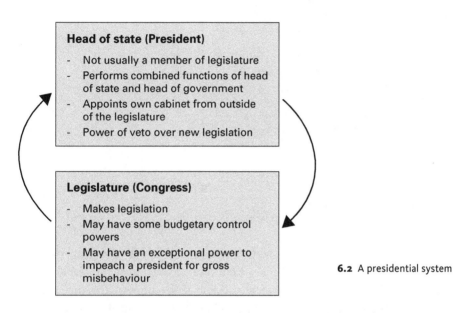

Head of state (President)

- Not usually a member of legislature
- Performs combined functions of head of state and head of government
- Appoints own cabinet from outside of the legislature
- Power of veto over new legislation

Legislature (Congress)

- Makes legislation
- May have some budgetary control powers
- May have an exceptional power to impeach a president for gross misbehaviour

6.2 A presidential system

In a Westminster system the separation between the executive and the legislature is not so clearly delineated. This is because the formal head of executive government is the monarch, but in reality the monarch is expected to act only in a ceremonial role in most situations and is usually confined to acting upon the advice of the prime minister in most substantive matters. The prime minister is the real head of government; the prime minister and cabinet exercise effective executive power.

The separation of powers between the legislature and the executive is not as distinct in Westminster systems as it is in presidential systems, because by design the prime minister and cabinet ministers must also be members of the parliament, and must rely on the support of the lower house to stay in government. This close relationship between the executive and the parliament is known as the doctrine of 'responsible government' and is intended to increase the accountability of executive government.

There are some countries that can be called Westminster republics because they have replaced the British monarch with their own civilian president, but they still continue to apply other features of the Westminster model, such as requiring the president to act upon the advice of the prime minister and

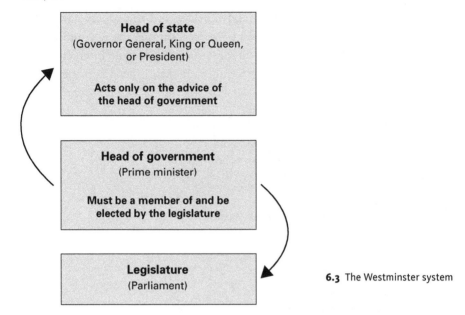

6.3 The Westminster system

requiring the prime minister to enjoy the support of the parliament. Vanuatu and Samoa in the South Pacific are examples of Westminster republics, and Australia is likely to become one of these at some time in the future.

On the Vanuatu constitution: www.paclii.org/vu/legis/consol_act/cotrov406/.

On the Samoan constitution: www.paclii.org/ws/legis/consol_act/cotisos 1960438/.

Understanding the precise nature of the system of governance in your country is an important first step in being able to design effective social change campaigns, especially where legislative or policy change is part of your agenda. There is, of course, a lot more detail that you will need before you commence strategic planning; you will need to understand how the process of governance is delegated to ministries and departments and how the decision-making and policy-making structures work within these departments. We will explore this in more detail later in this chapter, but first, while we are still examining bigger-picture issues, we should take some time to examine the idea of democracy from the perspective of a social change activist.

3.0 Representative democracy

Democracy to most people is a system designed to give the citizens of a country some say over who forms the government and how governance occurs. As such, democracy is an idea rather than any particular set of constitutional arrangements. Almost every country on the planet claims to be a democracy, and unfortunately even many oppressive or totalitarian regimes often continue to claim to be democracies, such as Zimbabwe, the former Soviet Union or at present Fiji. To say that a particular system is or claims to be a democracy does not tell us much about the precise way in which governance is arranged within that country, although popularly the occurrence of free and fair elections is widely accepted to be an important component of democratic governance.

There is also a useful publication produced by the US Department of State, *Principles of Democracy*, which sets out the indicia of free and fair elections. These include requirements such as:

- universal suffrage;
- one vote one value;
- freedom to register as a voter or run for public office;
- freedom of speech;
- freedom of assembly;
- an impartial or balanced system of conducting elections and verifying election results;
- accessible polling places;
- secret ballots: choice of party or candidate cannot be used against voter;
- legal prohibitions against election fraud;
- recount and contestation procedures (US Department of State 2008).

Without becoming too engaged in intellectual debate about different styles, there are several approaches we can take to the idea of democracy. The systems of governance in use in the USA, the UK, Australia, Canada and New Zealand are predominantly examples of 'representative' democracy. Representative democracy is a system in which the public at large vote to elect a relatively small group of law-makers and administrators, such as congressmen or members of parliament and popularly elected figures such as presidents. In theory these elected officials represent the views of the population at large. It's a simple theory and one that can be easily critiqued.

The advantages of representative democracy are that it is a practical and efficient way of converting the idea of popular consent into a workable process of law-making via parliament or congress. It provides a system in which the population at large has the ability to change governments, presidents or congressional majorities easily, without causing disruption to the overall system of governance, and it provides a substantial level of ongoing accountability.

But representative democracy on its own can have serious shortcomings. The voter's choice is interdicted by corporate sponsorship, concentrated media ownership and a range of other distorting factors. The outcome is often that much larger power plays dominate the political process and individual voters often end up feeling very marginalized from the process. Representative democracy can also have the effect of encouraging people to be politically passive and to allow their few minutes in a voting booth every few years to become the sole expression of personal political power. Politicians, political parties and media owners mostly benefit from the increased control that such passivity transfers to them.

Another serious flaw with many systems of representative democracy is that they represent a very majoritarian model in which the views of substantial minorities are often suppressed. Even at its simplest, a majoritarian system which allows a political party with 50.1 per cent of the vote to take power still has the implicit effect of disenfranchising the other 49.9 per cent.

Even for social change activists who are certainly not politically passive people, there can sometimes be too much attention given to doing politics via the representative institutions such as parliament and congress, and not enough to bringing politics back to the street or into the living rooms of ordinary people.

There is no doubt that representative democracy is an important and probably necessary form of democracy for nations with large populations, but it is also clear that it is not sufficient on its own to ensure a robust and healthy democratic process.

3.1 Participatory democracy

The representative style of democracy can be distinguished from the more active style of participatory democracy, but representative democracy and participatory democracy are not opposites. These two styles ideally exist side by side, and each reinforces the other. The term participatory democracy can be used to describe the whole range of activities in which citizens can and do engage in order to exert an influence on the political system over and above their bare entitlement to vote.

While representative democracy depends on the right to vote in free and fair elections, participatory democracy depends on a much greater range of civil rights that support civilian political actions, such as the freedom of political speech, freedom of association and to form organizations, the right to strike, march and protest, and the maintenance of reasonably permissive laws in relation to public order generally. Participatory democracy is a broader and deeper view of democracy which recognizes the danger of the tyranny of the majority and emphasizes the need for extensive rights of political participation outside of the more formal processes of elections and parliaments. Community activists are by nature proponents and practitioners of participatory democracy.

Unfortunately laws are made by elected representatives who may actually become hostile to public protests. In most English-speaking democracies there has been a steady winding back of some important civil and political liberties over the last fifty years. In Australia and the USA, for example, legislators responded to widespread protests about the Vietnam War during the 1970s by introducing more draconian forms of public order law (Ricketts 2002: 134). More recently, concerns over terrorism have provided a new rationale for winding back traditional civil liberties in relation to protest and organization (ibid.: 135). Laws that restrict the right to protest may in themselves become a target for activists, and in many cases activists may respond to unreasonable laws with civil disobedience and intentional lawbreaking. This is discussed in more detail in Chapter 8.

4.0 Exerting pressure on public bureaucracy

Most social change advocacy work will involve pressuring different parts of the public bureaucracy to take certain actions. In order to start planning your campaign properly you will need to know a number of things. The list below details some questions you may need to answer to get started ...

- What level of government is involved – national, local, federal, provincial?
- Are several layers of government involved?
- Does your campaign relate to legislative change or merely to administrative action by the government?
- Will there be any opportunities to use the courts to achieve your goals?

Each of these issues is considered below.

4.1 What level of government is involved?

This is where your knowledge of constitutional arrangements will come in useful, particularly if you are in a federation where the lines of demarcation between national and state or provincial government can be quite complex. The constitutions of each federation explain in detail what subject areas are covered respectively by national or state jurisdiction (Australia: s51; USA: Tenth Amendment; Canada: s91, s92 Constitution Acts, 1867–1982).

Local government is an additional layer of governance that is present in all jurisdictions, but it differs significantly from national and state government because it is usually not constitutionally established and does not have its own inherent legislative competence. Local government is established instead under relevant national, state or province legislation, and consequently it is not independent of the parliaments that establish it. In federations the power to establish and legislate for local government is mostly held at the state or provincial level. In Canada this is spelt out explicitly (s92 (8), Constitution Acts, 1867–1982). In Australia and the USA power to legislate for local government is part of the residual legislative power of the states (USA: Tenth Amendment; Australia: s107). In Britain and New Zealand the central parliament has legislative supremacy and as a result local government is established via national legislation.

The fact that local government is not an independently constituted layer of government can have important consequences for activists. One important consideration is that state or national governments will usually have the power to override decisions of local government. This means that if you win a concession from local government there is a risk that this could be overruled, or conversely that if you are not happy with the actions of local government you may be able to appeal directly to the responsible minister or to the state or national government. Another important conceptual difference between dealing with sovereign parliaments and dealing with local government is that local authorities are treated by the courts as 'delegated decision-making bodies' rather than as legislative bodies. In practice this means their decisions can be subjected to judicial review and consequently are capable of being quashed by the courts if they are not made in accordance with enabling legislation. This can be confusing for the public, for local government officers and for social change activists, because although local government representatives may be and usually are elected, this does not give them the status of legislators. In a formal legal sense they are merely administrative decision-makers exercising delegated power. The practical consequence can be that they are legally unable to deliver on a political mandate, if to do so would be in breach of the legislation under which the body is constituted (see *Wheeler* v. *Leicester City Council* (1985) UKHL 6).

Despite these limitations, local government can have significant power, and social change activists need to be aware of the powers and the limits upon those powers. Usually parliamentary power has been delegated to local government for a good reason, and so the overarching national or state governments may not be willing to override local government decisions. Local government, because it is more closely connected to communities, is an ideal place to get started with new ideas and establishing examples of new practices. For this reason, despite the limits to its legal powers, local government is usually an area in which public interest advocates remain very active.

4.2 Does your issue require legislative change?

If existing law has to be changed to achieve your goal (e.g. decriminalization of recreational drugs) your campaign needs a 'political solution', as you will need to convince the parliament (and the government of the day) to change the law. The courts cannot help you to bring about this type of change unless the legislation you object to is unconstitutional.

Bringing about legislative change does not usually begin at the parliamentary level; for most campaigns you need to start by building campaign momentum in the community by winning hearts and minds long before

you can push for a legislative political solution. Campaigns that promote law reform have a very specific end point, but campaigners must never lose sight of the fact that it is the political momentum that they build for change which will ensure not only effective change but also lasting change.

The most important lesson is to know that achieving a political win and legislative change is usually only the penultimate stage of a long-running campaign, and most of your attention, sometimes for years beforehand, should be focused upon building community support. Some of the digital activism host organizations discussed in Chapter 9 are expert at campaigning for legislative change. Groups such as GetUP, MoveOn and Avaaz are well worth investigating if you think your campaign will eventually move in this direction.

4.2.1 Law reform commissions At times your issue may be one where there already is a lot of community support for change, but where it is unclear exactly what form the changes will take. In this situation you may be able to contribute submissions to existing processes of law reform. Most of the Commonwealth countries have some form of law reform commission, which is a specialist body that deals with ongoing projects of law reform. The process is not so formally established in the United States.

• Parliamentary committee hearings or inquiries: www.aph.gov.au/committee/index.htm

- Australian Law Reform Commission: www.alrc.gov.au/
- NZ Law Commission: www.lawcom.govt.nz/
- Law Commission UK: www.lawcom.gov.uk/
- United Nations: www.un.org/law/ilc/
- Canlaw has useful links to law reform bodies in Canada: www.canlaw. com/reform/lawreform.htm

4.2.2 Lobbying political parties The other common route for legislative reform is via the policy processes of major political parties. The most fertile time for promoting law reform by this method is usually while parties are in opposition; this is when they tend to be most creative in adopting and working up new proposals. This strategy comes with some risks. The first obvious risk is that you are relying on the party to gain government and then to have the political will to implement the changes. Secondly, and perhaps more importantly in the long term, it is not advisable to have your campaign become too closely associated with any particular political party. As emphasized before, the real powerhouse of legislative reform work lies in building broad community support for change, and political parties are just part of the later stages of implementing that momentum for change. If you can build broad community support there is a chance that any political party will pick up your proposals, unless of course they go against some deep-seated article of faith for that party.

Political lobbying can take a number of forms. At its simplest it can be done by contacting local legislative representatives or by organizing campaign activities that target local members, such as e-mail or letter-writing campaigns, protests at their offices and, of course, using the media to publicize your message. This is especially useful in locally based campaigns.

If your campaign is a wider issue you can still utilize the techniques of local member lobbying, but network it using digital activism tools. This is often accomplished by having a 'day of action' in which you ask your supporters to contact their local members or organize synchronized local protests throughout the country.

If your organization is working on a broader issue of state or national significance your political lobbying should also extend beyond local member-based lobbying and include approaches to key power-holders within political parties, or key ministers, in relation to your issue. This kind of lobbying is more highly skilled and needs to be conducted by well-informed and presentable members of your organization. Many of the larger and more established advocacy organizations have permanent staff dedicated to this kind of lobbying work, and if there is a connection between your issue and the issues they work on it can be very useful to make contact with them beforehand for some advice and assistance.

A good way to gain experience as a parliamentary lobbyist if you have none is to start with the soft targets – members who you know are sympathetic. Meet up with them and during your meeting seek their further advice on who else to meet and how best to pitch your arguments. It is important not to become too intimidated by the process; if you start lobbying early in your campaign, you will acquire a lot of experience for the later stages when political lobbying is more likely to become a crucial deal-making tool.

4.3 The process of legislative change in parliaments: the committee systems

There are different processes you can select to promote law reform, and they do not always require overtly political styles of lobbying individual members. There is much behind-the-scenes work that goes on in and around the parliament. Most parliaments and legislatures establish either temporary (ad hoc) or permanent committees that report on law reform proposals and provide advice to the parliament. These committees are often constituted by members of government and non-government parties and often invite public submissions. Working on these committees constitutes a large part of the day-to-day work of elected representatives, and meeting various stakeholders to discuss change processes is a normal part of their workload. Knowing what committees exist and who is on them can be an important guide for your strategic thinking in relation to campaigning for change.

- For some interesting information about how laws are made, changed and repealed and how the committee systems work, go to the Australian parliamentary website: www.aph.gov.au/index.htm
- Parliamentary select committees NZ: www.parliament.nz/en-NZ/PB/SC/
- Parliamentary committees UK: www.parliament.uk/business/committees/
- Parliamentary committees Canada: www.parl.gc.ca/common/committee. asp?Language=E
- Congressional committees USA: www.house.gov/house/Committee-WWW.shtml

The committee systems in each of the national legislatures mentioned above are also replicated at the state and provincial levels in the USA, Australia and Canada.

5.0 Changing government policy: administrative change

As a general rule, if your campaign involves wanting existing law implemented in a better way, you are seeking administrative change. Administrative change occurs when you convince the government or other power-holders to adopt new policies, procedures, guidelines, safeguards or practices, or to change a particular decision, without the immediate need to change legislation.

This may involve lobbying politicians, bureaucrats, local councils or other state agencies. In some cases you may also be pursuing court actions against particular decisions or decision-makers.

Many campaigns will solely be seeking policy change at an administrative level, while in others legislative change may be an eventual aim, but in the meantime achieving administrative change is a more realistic target. Either way, it is important to be able to distinguish between the two modes of campaigning, as the methods and processes differ quite significantly. In some instances, for example, your campaign may be aiming to see existing legislation enforced and applied correctly, so changing the law is not a focus at all.

5.1 Building public support

The pressure you aim to exert on decision-makers must be supported by a public awareness campaign so that you are also building up public support for your position. As with legislative change campaigns, it is often a mistake for activists to assume the changes can be made from the top down; it is the building of public support which gives your campaign its real force and power in the long term. The material in the chapters dealing with planning and mapping (Chapter 4), research, media and publicity (Chapter 5) and direct action and protest (Chapter 8) deals with many of the techniques you will need to build public support. The next part of this discussion focuses upon the specific steps that are required to exert pressure on government agencies to alter their policy settings or practices. The

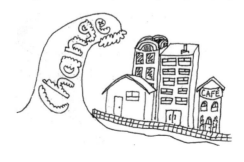

relative importance of pursuing avenues for changing government policy in your campaign will depend very much on your overall strategic plan and your goals and objectives.

5.2 Changing the policies or practices of departments or agencies

Even with significant public support, achieving change can still require extensive lobbying of ministers and key players in the government and in the ruling political party. At times, if you feel you are getting a sympathetic ear, especially where your case is evidence based, you may concentrate on lobbying efforts and hold off on overt public and political actions. This has the advantage of allowing you to work closely with power-holders, maintaining good communications and good faith. But you should always keep your powder dry and ready for use if you find you hit a brick wall in dealing with power-holders. It can't be said enough: the quality of your information and the public support you build are the real substantive tools in such campaigns.

Sometimes you don't need to change policy at a whole-of-government level, but merely within a particular department. Getting the decision you want from a minister, departmental secretary, department head or CEO will involve all the same strategies and tactics as for changing government policy, except that the issue is more confined and you need convince only specific power-holders. In this situation you need to be very strategic about how you build rapport, and on the other hand how you demonstrate that your organization is ready to go public with its information or campaign if no successful outcome is forthcoming.

5.3 Action by a regulatory agency

Sometimes your campaign does not actually require a change of governmental or departmental policy at all and may simply require you to propel a regulatory agency into taking a particular action. Examples of these kinds of actions could include where you are asking for stronger enforcement actions by bodies such as:

- anti-discrimination bodies;
- environmental protection agencies;
- local councils;
- investment industry watchdogs;
- ombudsmen.

The most important thing to do before you try to push an agency to take a particular position is to be well informed about the legislation that establishes the agency and what its powers are. You need to know what powers it has, when and how it can use them, on what grounds and according to what criteria it is required to make decisions. You should also inform yourself of what extra constraints, such as lack of resources, staff and/or information, may be hampering the body in question. Unless you know these things your attempts to persuade the body to make changes will appear very naive and poorly targeted and are not likely to meet with success.

Furthermore, if you are well informed about these matters, then you will also be able to develop further strategies for increasing the pressure on the agency if your initial front-door approach fails. It is always a good idea to have exhausted open and friendly communication processes before you resort to complaints and court actions, so the initial phase of dialogue is very strategically important, even if you have very strong doubts about whether the organization in question is ready to change. Once you've exhausted the channels for an agreed solution, you can begin to consider more confrontational approaches.

5.4 Complaints, reviews, appeals

Formal mechanisms exist for reviewing the practices of governmental decision-making bodies. Review and complaint procedures can range from relatively simple (and sometimes relatively superficial) internal complaints procedures within the agency itself, through to more independent procedures involving specialist review tribunals and ultimately to judicial review applications in the higher courts. It's not possible to give generic advice about how these all work in practice, but it is possible to describe these layers generally in order to help activists unravel the confusing details that may apply to their own circumstances.

The first place to start is always the legislation that establishes the decision-making body in question. Frequently the legislation will inform you of what rights you may have (as a member of the public) to object to decisions that you disagree with, or to seek review of decisions. Review procedures may take place within the organization's own structure or by reference to external independent bodies (such as the ombudsman's office, where these are established).

The legislation should always be your first point of reference to uncover the following:

• What are the specific decision-making powers in question?

- What particular matters is the body empowered to make decisions about?
- What prior processes need to have been followed for a valid decision to take place?
- What relevant matters is the body entitled to consider when making a decision?
- What matters, if any, is the body not entitled to consider?
- What specific actions is the body entitled to take to implement its decisions?
- What avenues of review are available for members of the public or aggrieved parties who disagree with a particular decision or action?
- Who is entitled to lodge a complaint, objection or appeal?
- In what form should objections, etc., be lodged?
- What time limits apply?
- What further avenues of appeal lie beyond the initial round of review, and upon what grounds?

Even if the legislation does not make any mention of review or appeal rights, this does not mean they are non-existent. The agency itself may have established its own internal procedures, or there may be some generic forms of review available through the government departments that oversee the particular agency. Ultimately every department will also have a government minister overseeing it, and complaints and requests for reviews can be directed to the minister. It is always worth exploring all of these opportunities.

Ultimately it is a well-established legal principle that governmental and public decision-making bodies are legally required to make all of their decisions strictly in accordance with the law, which means that they have to comply with the enabling legislation under which they are acting as well as with other more generic legal rules that apply to governmental and public decision-making.

There are basically two main types of review procedure: statutory review procedures, which are established by special legislation that applies to the body in question, or more generic judicial review rights, which were originally developed by the common-law courts.

5.5 Statutory review procedures

Statutory review processes can vary according to the particular decision-making body in question and the legislation that pertains to it, and may create rights for all persons (open standing) to seek review of decisions, or may restrict the right to seek review to particular persons or parties, or persons who can demonstrate a particular interest. Statutory review procedures sometimes establish a review body that has the power to reconsider the whole decision and substitute its own decision in place of that made by the original decision-maker. Where this is available it is called a 'merits review' because it allows the issue to be re-decided on its full merits.

Merits review is a creature of statute and is distinguished from the more general and well-established principles of judicial review, which have their origins in common law (judge-made law). Traditional judicial review in the common-law courts does not enable the court to substitute its own decision for that of the original decision-maker; instead the courts simply ask whether the decision-maker followed all applicable legal requirements in the process of making the decision. If the courts find a defect in the process, they can quash the original decision.

5.6 Judicial review

The superior courts in all jurisdictions (the UK, Canada, the USA, New Zealand, Australia) have inherent jurisdiction to enforce all of the laws of the nation. This means they automatically have a power to judicially review governmental and public decision-making bodies to ensure they have acted within the law, and the power to quash any decision that contravenes the law. This power is usually referred to as the power of judicial review. In addition the courts have over many years built up a body of principles that define the way in which such bodies should go about making decisions, and these are often called the principles of due process or of natural justice and fairness. Judicial review of administrative decisions is a complex area of the law. An excellent publication describing English administrative law in detail, entitled *The Judge over Your Shoulder*, is available online and provides a very good background to administrative law (www.tsol.gov.uk/ Publications/services.htm).

In some jurisdictions the older, more complex common-law rules have been replaced by more modern legislation that generically deals with the review of governmental decisions. See, for example:

- Australia: Administrative Decisions Judicial Review Act 1977 (www. austlii.edu.au/au/legis/cth/consol_act/adra1977396/)
- Canada: Judicial Review Procedure Act 1990 (www.canlii.org/en/on/laws/ stat/rso-1990-c-j1/latest/rso-1990-c-j1.html)
- United States: Administrative Procedure Act of 1946 (www.law.cornell. edu/uscode/5/usc_sup_01_5_10_I_30_5.html)

Because judicial review is only about reviewing the *way* in which the decision was made and not the *merits* of the decision itself, it has some disadvantages. In particular, the practical outcome of a successful judicial review application is that the decision in question is quashed by the court, which usually means that the decision-maker needs to have another go at making the decision properly. This is a great way for activists to buy time and to demonstrate the failings of the decision-maker, but there is a risk that sometimes the decision-maker will be able to arrive at a similar decision the second time around, provided they go about it the right way.

Judicial review has its limitations, but it is a powerful remedy because it applies across the board to all governmental and public decision-making bodies, whether there is specific legislation to provide for review or not,

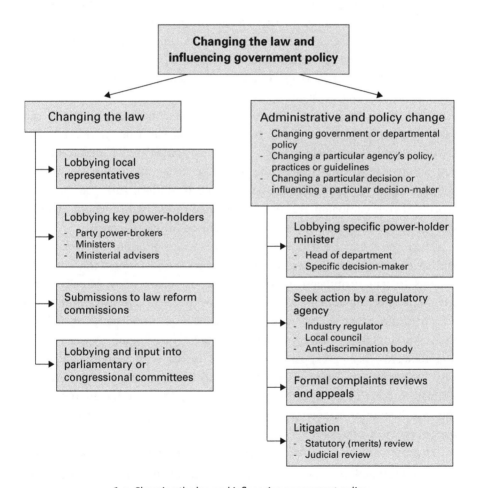

6.4 Changing the law and influencing government policy

and the courts are very reluctant to allow exemptions from this general supervisory jurisdiction that they possess.

This discussion serves only as a guide to the ways in which administrative decisions can be reviewed; in real-life situations there is no substitute for reading the legislation, and the policy documents of the decision-maker, and making sure you lodge any requests for review within the time limits specified and in the form specified. If you are considering bringing an action in the courts you will need to have the assistance of lawyers.

The diagram above sets out the range of processes that we have discussed for bringing about change to the law or to government policy.

6.0 Activism using the courts

Statutory review processes can but do not always involve the courts, but judicial review procedures, as their name suggests, will always involve the courts. Taking a case to court can be used at times as part of a strategy or tactic for achieving social change, but you have to be very careful to remember what you are trying to achieve and that the court case is merely one means of going about it.

Court cases can be very expensive and time consuming and they can easily take on a life of their own that can distract you from your campaign. If your organization decides to go down this road it's very important that you don't put all your eggs in one basket, so to speak, as the outcome of court cases is very unpredictable, and you need to make sure that the other aspects of your campaign are being maintained properly throughout and that you have a viable fallback plan in the event of losing in court.

Court cases can be a powerful way to attract attention to your cause and to expose the failings of decision-makers, and at times the collateral benefits to your campaign of bringing a court action may actually apply whether or not you actually win the case. For the vast majority of individuals who institute court action, winning the case is all important; for activists there are sometimes other strategic advantages of bringing the case (such as publicity, delay or exposing weaknesses in the legal system), and so it may be strategic to bring a case even when there is little or no chance of ultimate success in the courtroom. This is called strategic litigation because the case is part of a larger political strategy, and legal victory may be unnecessary, even undesirable.

Litigation will be a useful strategy in a social change campaign where:

- a law or an action you are challenging is unconstitutional (constitutional challenge);

- an administrative action breaches existing statute law or common law (judicial review);
- an administrative action has been taken in breach of a required procedure (judicial review);
- you have specific legal rights to challenge a particular decision on its merits (statutory rights);
- a class of people have had their legal rights infringed (class action);
- you are simply bringing the case to make a point or publicize an issue (test case).

6.1 Pitfalls of litigation as a strategic tool

Litigation can be expensive and distracting, and the courts tend to define the specifically 'legal' issue in the case much more narrowly than your group does. Sometimes the 'legal' issue will bear almost no relation to the real political or social issue you are concerned about. For example, in the Tasmanian Dam case ([1983] HCA 21; (1983)158 CLR 1) in Australia, environmentalists brought the case to prevent the construction of a dam in an important wilderness area, but the specific legal issue in the case was not about whether the dam should be built but purely about the constitutional power of the Australian government to override the legislation of one of its state governments.

The danger of this kind of litigation is that a loss in court may send a message to the public that the court has somehow legitimized the development; fortunately in that case the environmentalists succeeded in their legal challenge.

Litigation is a specialist area and is discussed in more detail in Chapter 10.

7.0 Corporate, media and other outside influences on government decision-making

So far we have looked at various ways the public sector may be involved in your campaign. We have looked at situations where you are seeking legislative change and situations where you are seeking to change decisions or place pressure on governmental or public decision-making bodies. Hitherto we have dealt with the public sector as a separate entity in this chapter, but you should remember that the public sector operates in a political, social, economic and international context, and that there may be many ways to exert pressure other than by direct lobbying or by seeking review of decisions. You should also be aware of who or what else is exerting pressure, possibly in an opposite direction to your campaign.

In addition to the influence exerted by social change activists, governmental action is continually being influenced by economics, corporate power, media ownership and international relations. These forces constrain national governments and government decision-makers to act in particular ways. Your campaign planning maps need to be complex enough to encompass all of the various formal and informal sites of power that impact upon your issue; the power-holders map (Chapter 4) is a good way to start mapping these influences, as is the friends and foes map.

Corporate power is growing steadily in relation to formal governmental power in almost all nations, and activists need to include strategies for influencing corporate power as well. This aspect is dealt with in more detail in Chapter 7. Corporate power has become so pervasive that even the usually conservative superior courts in both Australia and the United States have had occasion to warn about its capacity to exert influence on processes of public governance.

> Freedom of political discussion is essential to the democratic process ... but the salutary effect of freedom of political discussion ... can be neutralised by covert influences, particularly by the influences that flow from financial dependence. The financial dependence of a political party on those whose interests can be served by the favours of government could cynically turn public debate into a cloak for bartering away the public interest. (Per Brennan J in *Australian Capital Television Pty Ltd* v. *Commonwealth* (1992) 177 CLR 106 at 159)

> It has long been recognized ... that the special status of corporations has placed them in a position to control vast amounts of economic power which may, if not regulated, dominate not only the economy but also the very heart of our democracy, the electoral process. The State need not permit its own creation to consume it. (Per Justice White in *First National Bank of Boston* v. *Bellotti* (1978) 435 U.S. 765)

You may not be in a position to have a lot of effect upon the international, corporate or entrenched mass media ownership models that exert influence on governments, but it is still important to include your awareness of them in your strategic planning. Your public interest campaign by its nature will pit the power of public opinion against vested interests (see Chapter 1) and you need to remain clear that your central purpose is to raise awareness and to mobilize public opinion in favour of your cause. In all situations the best you can do is adopt a strategic approach that optimizes your use of all available avenues for promoting change.

Conclusion

Public governance is an aspect of almost every social change campaign, but the cardinal rule for activists to remember is that the public comes first. The success of social movements depends on their ability to build public support and momentum for the changes that they seek. The key is to then translate this growing public support into political, administrative or even legislative change. You should always keep your campaign objectives at the forefront and remember that influencing power-holders is a strategy or tactic to help facilitate campaign success, not the whole campaign itself.

In order to successfully engage with institutions of public governance you need to establish a sound institutional knowledge; this requires an understanding of constitutional arrangements and the distribution of power between levels of government. It also requires knowledge of the various power-holders and decision-makers involved in your campaign and the ways in which the legislation both empowers and constrains them.

Knowing these institutional constraints informs your strategy for bringing about change, whether you are proceeding by way of proactive lobbying or more confrontational means, such as complaints reviews and litigation.

Successful activism involves mapping and planning your campaign carefully, doing the research to gain knowledge of the institutional arrangements, mapping the way power is distributed among power-holders, mapping the formal and informal influences on power-holders, and always looking for the most strategic opportunities to exert your influence.

Successful use of the campaign mapping and planning processes discussed in Chapter 4 is an essential part of orchestrating a strategic engagement with public governance institutions. Implementing your plans by activating some or all of the processes discussed in this chapter will build a more successful campaign. In the next chapter we consider activism in relation to corporate targets; at times a combination of public sector and private sector activism will be needed to achieve success.

SEVEN | **Corporate activism**

Introduction

Activism in the corporate sphere is an exciting and rapidly changing field. Conventional anti-corporate activist techniques are being combined with new and more sophisticated tactics that use the corporations law itself and the rights of small shareholders as a means to pressure large corporations to adopt more socially or environmentally responsible policies and practices.

This chapter begins with a theoretical examination of the nature of the modern business corporation as a form of private bureaucracy as a necessary primer for activists working in this area. What follows is an examination of anti-corporate activism generally, followed by a guide to the most effective strategies that are currently emerging in the struggle with corporate power-holders and the skills and knowledge needed to successfully engage the corporate sector.

1.0 Why would we call corporations private bureaucracy?

Traditionally the word bureaucracy has been used to describe governmental institutions. Its use here to describe private corporations is both intentional and instructive. Nearly thirty years ago business ethics author Thomas Donaldson (1982: 110) referred to the tendency of corporations to develop into bureaucracies. What is implicit in the idea of corporations as bureaucracies is not only that they are large, impersonal and complex organizations, but that they actually do resemble (and sometimes usurp) government in terms of the power they have over the lives of citizens and even the kinds of functions they perform.

The increasing trend of privatization of former government utilities as well as the corporatization of government services has meant that private and public service providers have come to resemble each other more closely. From the citizen's perspective, there may seem to be little difference between a semi-autonomous government organization that controls municipal water and a private corporation providing the same service. Carl Mayer makes this point when he observes that corporations have a 'state-like' impact upon people's lives:

As privatisation proceeds apace, corporations are increasingly assuming functions traditionally reserved for states – running prisons, providing security, collecting trash, handling mail and information and even supplying education. The actions of large modern corporations have a state-like impact on the lives of individuals. (Mayer 1990: 162)

David Korten, in his book *When Corporations Rule the World*, describes corporations as institutions of governance, arguing that: 'Corporations have emerged as the dominant governance institutions on the planet, with the largest among them reaching into virtually every country of the world and exceeding most governments in size and power' (Korten 1995: 117).

In describing corporations as institutions of governance, Korten refers to the observable political and economic power in the hands of very large corporations, rather than simply defining governance in formal constitutional terms. Korten justifies his claim by reference to statistics concerning the relative power of corporations over national governments, and points to the influential role of large corporations in multilateral trade organizations (such as the International Monetary Fund, the World Bank and the World Trade Organization), as evidence of the corporate role in global economic and political governance.

The problem with presenting the corporation as state-like, however, is that it fails to take into account the nature of corporations as profit-driven institutions and the way in which this differs from the traditional role of the state, particularly in democratic systems of government. The unfortunate truth is that corporations may have a state-like impact but they do not have the accountability of democratic institutions.

The purpose of this chapter is to explore how working for social change in a corporatized environment differs from working in an environment dominated by public institutions. This is a very important issue because there are significant differences, and in most cases greater challenges, facing public interest advocates advocating for change through the private sector.

Public interest advocates of the future will increasingly find themselves confronted by the institutional power and inertia of private bureaucracy, and it is vital that advocates develop effective strategies for advocating for change in the modern corporate-dominated world.

1.1 Corporatization or globalization?

Media reports often refer to protests against WTO meetings and the like as anti-globalization protests, but a closer look at the debate reveals that it is not globalization itself but global corporatization which attracts so much criticism from communities.

The growth of the power of large transnational corporations during the last 100 years has challenged the sovereignty of many of the states in which they operate – particularly the less economically powerful nations. The ability to invest or withdraw capital has given multinational companies significant political power over governments. According to Joseph Karliner, author of *The Corporate Planet*, by the close of the last century fifty-one of the largest 100 economies in the world were corporations (Karliner 1997: 5). There is every reason to expect that the relative economic power of corporations compared to governments will have continued to grow since that time.

2.0 What are corporations?

It is very important for social change activists to be aware of the nature of business corporations. The modern business corporation is characterized by its formal status as a separate incorporated entity together with limited liability and the ability to function in complex corporate groups. This can be difficult for lay people to understand, but some digression into the history of corporations helps provide some insight. The corporate form was originally devised to provide a means by which existing institutions such as universities, hospitals and monasteries could own property and be recognized in the courts as separate entities in their own right. Later, the Crown adapted the idea of incorporation to create chartered business corporations such as the British East India Company to conduct lucrative colonial trade. At this stage incorporation was seen to be an exceptional privilege bestowed by specific legislation. Eventually, however, legislation was passed (English Companies Act 1846) that allowed the privilege of incorporation to be available to any business organization which complied with manner and form requirements established in the legislation. Corporations are creatures of statute, but over time the privilege of incorporation has become largely a formality. The result is that corporations can be created on paper and yet instantly acquire legal rights equivalent to and in some respects greater than those enjoyed by people. Unlike people they have no body, nor any emotional connectedness to other people, nature or the cosmos, and no capacity to be imprisoned or to feel pain.

2.1 The corporation as a 'legal person'

Particularly in the English-speaking legal systems, the principles of corporations law developed alongside a legal metaphor which explained the nature of the corporations as being the equivalent of a 'legal person'. One of the key misunderstandings fostered by this metaphor is the idea that because corporations have a single legal identity, they are therefore (legally and politically) a kind of individual. The only thing that is individual about a corporation is precisely that formally it is a single legal entity – but one that is by nature a collective enterprise, a bureaucracy. Corporations have successfully used this 'artificial personhood' over the years to gain a great many constitutional, common-law and human rights originally intended only for human beings. This is one reason why it is so important to reconceptualize them simply as private bureaucracies.

Describing corporations as bureaucratic formal organizations, rather than as persons, is much more accurate than describing them as legal persons because corporations encompass a number of shareholders as well as an array of decision-makers in the form of directors and managers. The precise nature of such organizations is defined by their structure, which integrates these different aspects into a unified, but separate, legal entity.

2.2 The mandatory self-centredness of corporations

There are some very important consequences of the way in which decision-making is structured inside corporations. Corporations operate according to a strict and formal process of internal decision-making, which mandates that all decisions will be made in the best interests of the corporation itself. This is markedly different to the decision-making capacities of both individuals and governments, as individuals have an unlimited moral capacity to act for the benefit of others (the public good) and government departments are constrained, in theory at least, to address the public good in all their actions. Corporations have no innate mechanism that can orient them towards the public good, other than their own pursuit of profit.

It is useful at this point to analyse the way in which the mandatory self-centredness of corporations is legally constructed.

2.3 The profit motive

The primary function of most major business corporations is the pursuit of profit or the holding of property. Unlike with persons, this orientation is predetermined by virtue of their internal company constitution.

2.4 The directors' fiduciary duty

The decision-making structures of corporations involve a split between ownership and control which mandates that directors should act only in the best interests of the corporation itself. At law this duty is known as the directors' fiduciary duty to the corporation, and it is enshrined in legislation.

The fiduciary duty which directors owe to act in the interests of the company provides a powerful obstacle to the entertainment of other-regarding considerations (such as social responsibility) by corporate decision-makers.

Historically, the legal model of corporate governance has excluded all outside interests; other groups may only be benefited to the extent that this furthers the interests of the company. Thus, the interests of employees, customers or the local community may be served only as a means of increasing shareholder wealth and may not be treated as ends in their own right (Parkinson 2002: 81).

While this constraint does not necessarily *prohibit* acts that are beneficial to others, outside benefit cannot be the main purpose. Company directors must be able to point to some resulting benefit accruing to the company. In *Dodge* v. *Ford Motor Company* 170 NW 683, Ford's management proposed to limit dividends in order to lower the price of cars and increase employment, so as to 'spread the benefits of this industrial system to help [employees] build up their lives and their homes'.

The court held that this was an improper purpose, finding that 'a business corporation is organised and carried on primarily for the profit of the stockholders. The powers of the directors are to be employed to that end' (ibid.: 684).

Far from permitting general philanthropic motivations, the directors' fiduciary duty even specifically excludes benefits to persons with whom the company has a direct relationship, such as employees. In *Hutton* v. *West Cork Railway* (1883) 23 ch. 654, for example, a company had transferred its undertakings to another company and was going to be wound up. After completion of the transfer, the transferor company passed a resolution to apply a sum of money to the benefit of certain officials who had lost their employment, even though they had no enforceable legal right to such a payment. In a now famous judgment, Bowen LJ even alluded to the idea that what was proposed may have been morally desirable, but legally invalid: '[T]he law does not say that there may be no cakes and ale, but there shall be no cakes and ale except such as are required for the benefit of the company' (ibid.: 654).

Corporations can and often do engage in socially responsible activities to improve their public image, and this is allowable to some extent, as expressed in the time-honoured passage below: 'Charity has no business to sit at boards of directors qua charity. There is, however, a kind of charitable dealing which is for the interest of those who practise it, and to that extent and in that garb (I admit not a very philanthropic garb) charity may sit at the board, but for no other purpose' (ibid.: 673).

A cautious description of corporations that can be drawn from this analysis is that modern business corporations are 'legally recognised collective organisations, which are primarily directed to the pursuit of profit and characterised by formal structures and rules that limit the moral autonomy of decision-makers' (Ricketts 2001).

2.5 Shareholder control?

So much for the duties of directors. A question which often arises is the extent to which shareholders are empowered to control the activities of corporations. In small private companies, shareholders may have significant control, but in large public companies shareholder power is usually widely dispersed, and frequently held by other corporations, especially banks, superannuation funds and insurance companies. These corporate shareholders are often referred to as 'institutional investors'.

Peter French, one of the authors of *Corporations in the Moral Community*, writes:

> With the wide dispersion of stock ownership, the relation between management and shareholders has become more abstract and formalised ... the shareholder becomes less of an individual human being and more an occupier of a relatively narrow, formalised position, that of investor. The scope of his or her interaction with the corporation shifts from a range of critical perspectives to a single demand: profit. (French et al. 1992: 39)

The mandatory nature of corporate self-interest is certainly problematic from a public interest perspective, but surprisingly there may yet be opportunities for well-organized public interest advocates to strategically use corporations law and principles to achieve public interest outcomes. The key to successful corporate activism lies in engineering a situation in which the directors will see responding to a public interest campaign as being in the best interests of the company.

3.0 The dangers of unrestrained corporate power

Corporations have evolved alongside the liberal/capitalist legal and economic system. An aspect of that mode of production is a faith that the choices made by individual humans in the marketplace will automatically orient production towards the satisfaction of human desires (and hopefully human needs).

Even if we were to accept the premise that human self-interest will ultimately produce human welfare, it may well be that human self-interest will not by itself produce the welfare of the environment, other species or even future generations. Nonetheless, if humans were the only ones making the market choices at least the outcomes of the market process would be reflective of human choices and desires. The advent of global corporate power, however, threatens to compromise the free market model in a far more sinister way.

Corporations, as we have seen, are institutionally incapable of pursuing an interest unrelated to their own self-interest. We cannot just hope that they will use their political and economic power in a way that will be beneficial to humans and the natural environment, for there is no reason why they would. Given that they are increasingly important participants in both the market and in politics, it becomes important to consider whether the kind of world that corporate self-interest would produce would be a tolerable world for humans.

Where humans need food, clean air and clean water, shelter, emotional closeness to other humans and functioning communities to survive, corporations' needs are very different. Corporations need:

1 a legal system that recognizes their existence;
2 a stock exchange to facilitate investment and takeover;
3 a monetary system;
4 resources;
5 humans to function as labour, management and consumers.

The fundamental juxtaposition which occurs in a society and economy dominated by corporations is that humans cease to be an end in themselves (which was envisaged in the liberalist world-view) and are converted into a means to corporations achieving their ends.

Certainly corporations could not survive if there were no humans, but the quality of human life is not a direct concern to them. Corporations do not have a direct stake in clean air or water, for example. Where human self-interest would eventually place a value on these things as fundamental to quality of life, the quality of humans' lives is not of direct interest to corporations. In fact if clean air were to become more scarce, it would only open up more markets for corporations to sell manufactured air to well-off consumers. This is not a far-fetched example; it already happens with clean water and anti-AIDS drugs. There is a very real advantage to corporations if the necessities of human life become scarce; not only does it create a market, it makes humans ever more dependent upon corporations and the monetary system for survival.

There is no conspiracy issue here. What is being suggested is not that there is a secret group which meets to plan this future, but rather that this is a future that is the logical (economically rational) outcome of a society dominated by corporate self-interest.

This is all a very chilling scenario, and an important perspective for social change activists to understand. Corporations have no inbuilt mechanisms that will deliver public interest outcomes. What is clear is that if corporations can act only in their own self-interest, the job of public interest advocates will be to convince the boards of directors that social responsibility will bring benefits to the corporation as a whole.

The foregoing theoretical discussion is meant to establish a fundamentally important awareness. The underlying basis of any campaign that aims to influence corporate decision-making is to target the corporation's interests and specifically its economic interests if it is to have any lasting impact. Activists have to be clear that the purpose is not to create corporate guilt, shame or remorse (there is no such thing), nor is it to hope that corporations and their decision-makers will embrace the public good as an end in itself; this cannot happen while corporations are structured in the way that they currently are. There may be some utility in appealing to the moral faculty of the individual humans who act as directors, but this is inherently limited. These people occupy positions in which they are strictly required to act only in the interests of the corporation and deliver financial returns to its investors, and as professionals this is what they will do. The point of corporate campaigning strategy is to convince corporate decision-makers that responding positively to public interest campaigns will be in their company's best interests. This is best achieved by activists targeting the economic interests of businesses, their commercial reputation, their market share and their investors. Additionally, campaigning to increase externally imposed state supervision and regulation of corporations is a valuable approach.

4.0 Public interest advocacy within the corporate sphere

For a number of years now human rights and environmental advocates have struggled with finding ways to influence corporations to act in more socially responsible ways.

There are several common ways in which social change activists attempt to influence corporate decision-making and activity; these include:

- public awareness campaigns;
- consumer boycotts;
- ethical consumerism;
- ethical investing.

We will also discuss various ways in which corporations law can be used to promote public interest outcomes through the use of shareholder rights and remedies.

4.1 Public awareness campaigns

Public awareness campaigns are, of course, the most basic and ubiquitous activity carried out by activists and social movements. Nonetheless, in the context of corporate activism they form the starting point of all of the processes described below. Unlike public bureaucracy, corporations do not have any inbuilt accountability mechanisms in the way that governmental institutions do. Public bureaucracies are administered by or under the supervision of departments and ministries and are ultimately responsible to the government of the day. Corporations, as explained earlier, have most of the privileges of individual citizens and consequently are not routinely required to be accountable either to government or to citizens.

This is not to say that there are not processes of accountability that may apply to them under various legislation. Corporations are, of course, subject to the general law, and usually also to various forms of regulation in relation to financial dealings, stock exchange activity and to some extent consumer law and labour relations laws. Certainly, if they can be shown to be in breach of any of these laws then there are avenues for activists to make them accountable.

In the absence of provable breaches of the law activists have to rely on corporations' and businesses' sensitivity to adverse publicity as a primary tool in promoting socially responsible behaviour.

The good name of a business and the reputation of its brand are considered to be important commercial assets, so understandably businesses and corporations are keen to protect their public image. Numerous substantial campaigns have been run over many years that have targeted corporations in this way. Some notable examples include campaigns highlighting unhealthy aspects of Nestlé marketing of milk products and more recently chocolates; long-running campaigns targeting Nike over poor working conditions in offshore factories; campaigns highlighting human rights issues in Shell's activities in Nigeria; and a range of concerns over the worldwide activities of the fast-food giant McDonald's.

Certainly corporations do respond to criticism, although their first response is not always constructive. Public relations consultants are often employed to market the image better as an alternative to making real changes to controversial practices, and in some cases corporations may turn and attack their critics and use legal suits to try to silence criticism. Fortunately such lawsuits against public interest advocates run a high risk of backfiring against the plaintiff corporation. See for example the Gunn's 20 litigation in Australia, where a logging company sought to sue twenty prominent environmentalists (*Gunn's Limited* v. *Marr* [2005] VSC 251, 18 July 2005, www.austlii.edu.au/au/cases/  vic/VSC/2005/251.html) and the famous Mclibel trial, where McDonald's sued activists (*McDonald's Corporation* v. *Steel & Morris* [1997] EWHC QB 366).

In both of these cases the litigation eventually backfired on the plaintiff corporations, but not before a lot of fear was successfully sown among the wider activist community.

It is very difficult to measure the success of publicity campaigns against corporations and businesses but the sheer scale of the publicity that can now be generated using web-based resources, and the amount of resources that corporations employ to counteract such campaigns, or more positively to respond to them, suggests that such campaigns are a powerful tool.

Perhaps some of the most encouraging analysis of the effectiveness of such campaigns comes from those who oppose them. Pro-corporate author Jarol Manheim (2001: 3) describes anti-corporate campaigns as follows:

> An anti-corporate campaign is a co-ordinated, often long-term and wide-ranging programme of economic, political, legal and psychological warfare designed to attack the viability of the essential stakeholder relationships on which any corporation depends ... Every successful campaign begins with extensive research designed to identify every stakeholder relationship on which the target company depends.
>
> Included would be relationships with such groups as its customers, bankers and creditors, shareholders and financial analysts, principal regulators, employees, advocacy groups and even civic and religious leaders. In

each instance, the antagonists seek out potential vulnerabilities they might exploit ...

Such a description understates the David and Goliath nature of social movements' campaigns against large transnational corporations, but it does encapsulate the basic elements of strategy that make such campaigns powerful. Despite being written from an anti-activist perspective, Manheim's description, and even the title, *The Death of a Thousand Cuts*, accurately depicts the thoroughness and perseverance that are needed to engage in successful anti-corporate campaigning. I often use the figure of speech 'death of a thousand cuts' to remind activists of how long a journey it can be to achieve success in a public interest campaign. It is ironic that activists can probably find more encouragement from Manheim's descriptions of the crippling effect of such campaigns on corporations than they usually can from the more sombre and often pessimistic assessments offered by people from within the social movements that are conducting such campaigns.

4.1.1 Generic anti-corporate awareness campaigns

The advent of the World Wide Web and the networking opportunities it has created have facilitated the growth and effectiveness of social movements using publicity campaigns to influence corporate activity. These campaign  groups range from single-issue groups targeting specific businesses through to more generic anti-corporate groups that address widespread problems with corporatization, including the weakening of public governance structures and democracy, misleading advertising, human rights abuses, poor labour conditions and poor environmental standards. Some prominent and useful examples of wide-issue corporate campaign groups include:

- Program on corporations law and democracy (www.poclad.org/)
- Adbusters (www.adbusters.org/)
- Wikileaks
- Indymedia (www.indymedia.org/en/index.shtml)
- Countercorp (www.countercorp.org/home)

Generic anti-corporate organizations and websites can be a useful source of links or useful as allies for new or smaller groups establishing new campaigns that target private bureaucracy.

In addition to the generic anti-corporate sites such as the examples given above, there are also numerous social movements and established non-government organizations that conduct publicity campaigns that target corporate wrongdoing around specific public interest concerns such as environmentalism, animal rights and human rights. A recent example of a successful campaign utilizing social media in such a campaign was the campaign by Greenpeace against the use of products in chocolate that destroy rainforest and specifically orang-utan habitat. Greenpeace released a disturbing short video on YouTube that depicted an office worker opening a KitKat chocolate bar and finding a bleeding orang-utan finger inside. As a result of this video and campaign, Nestlé has announced that it will stop using oils from suppliers identified as destroying rainforest to produce palm oil (www.greenpeace.org/international/campaigns/climate-change/kitkat/).

4.1.2 Corporate campaigning for local groups While the bulk of anti-corporate campaigning is conducted by larger, more established social movements and advocacy organizations, local campaigns can gain significant traction quickly by synchronizing some of their campaign activities with those of larger campaigns or by launching localized and fresh campaigns where required.

Some actions that are relatively cheap and easy to organize at the local level include:

- Retail actions: raising awareness locally about unethical products available in stores with shopfront actions. In most cases it would be wise to first ask retailers not to stock these items before launching an action against them, especially if they are small businesses.
- Producing brochures that describe the unethical products, and suggesting alternatives for customers.
- Producing small stickers to place on items and on shelves ('This product costs the earth'; 'Warning: rainforests were destroyed to produce this product', etc.).
- Encouraging local councils to change purchasing policies to reflect ethical choices.
- Holding demonstrations or street theatre actions at the main sites of offending companies, such as factory gates, head and regional offices and trade fairs and expos.
- Attending company meetings and leafleting shareholders with information.
- Purchasing shares and attending AGMs and asking difficult questions.

A useful web-based publication on local anti-corporate campaigns is produced by Friends of the Earth (UK) (www.foe.co.uk/resource/how_tos/cyw_26_corporate_campaign.pdf).

4.2 Consumer boycotts

Consumer boycotts often arise as a secondary tactic in an anti-corporate publicity campaign. Consumer boycotts are probably one of the most commonly recognized and widely used forms of direct action used for targeting corporations over social or environmental practices (Crane and Matten 2007: 421).

Consumer boycotts involve two aspects; one being the publicity generated by the boycott itself and the other being the intended economic impact on the companies' sales. In many cases the negative impact on branding may be a more powerful aspect than the raw economic effect of the boycott, but the real effectiveness of boycotts remains very difficult to measure. This is partly because companies are careful not to reveal information that would reveal this (Seidman 2007: 30).

Recent research in the UK suggests that the ethical consumer market is significant and growing steadily. The Cooperative Bank's Ethical Consumerism Report (2008, p. 3) estimated that food and drink boycotts alone accounted for over £1 billion of expenditure in the UK in 2007.

Consumer boycotts are most frequently instigated by existing campaign groups in response to corporate activities that offend those groups' values. So boycotts may be organized in response to environmental, human rights or animal rights concerns, concerns over labour conditions, or on the basis of other widely held values, such as in anti-corruption campaigns.

There are also a number of organizations that coordinate or at least list and publicize ethical boycott campaigns, such as Ethical Consumer. New groups and social movements wanting to launch boycott campaigns can get assistance through larger organizations or by utilizing services such as the Ethical Consumer site (www.ethicalconsumer.org/Boycotts/aboutboycotts. aspx).

4.3 Ethical consumerism

Ethical consumerism is a more recent proactive development that seeks to turn around the reactivity of boycott campaigns and promote ethical consumerism as a general practice for ethically oriented people. The strengths of this approach are many.

First, the campaign is proactive and aims to guide participants' consumption choices towards more ethically sound products and services. This is more instructive for the general population in that it provides options for what to do rather than simply suggestions for what not to buy or consume. It also means that a broad range of widely held social values can be coalesced into a generic category of 'ethical consumerism', and so the various individual campaigns can be brought together in a more integrated approach. Furthermore, in simplifying and identifying a range of values that together constitute ethical consumerism, corporations and businesses can be on notice as to what values are important in the marketplace and respond proactively themselves. The popularity of free-range eggs and the advent of 'ethically' oriented businesses such as the Body Shop are examples of the way in which ethical market choices can be effective.

Recent research in the UK suggests that the ethical consumer market is significant and growing steadily. The Cooperative Bank's Ethical Consumerism Report (2008, p. 3) estimated that overall ethical consumer spending in the UK in 2008 amounted to £35.5 billion, an increase of 15 per cent since the previous year.

4.4 Ethical investing

An important further arm of ethical consumerism is ethical investing, which seeks to encourage share market investors in particular to choose only companies that comply with published criteria for ethical investment, which can include human rights, workers' rights and environmental measures. There are now numerous ethical investment funds that provide stockbroking services for ethical investors, and the field is growing steadily in size and impact.

In 2010 the leading UK-based ethical investment research organization, Eiris, estimated that retail investment in ethical funds had grown to £9.5 billion. According to Eiris this represented approximately three-quarters of a million investors in ethical funds, up from around 200,000 investors in 1999, when around £2.4 billion was invested ethically in the UK (www. eiris.org/media.html#marketstats2010).

Ethical investment is probably even more powerful than ethical consumerism in that it targets a different set of stakeholders, namely investors, and so can directly affect share prices. Furthermore, it means that ethical funds eventually become large institutional investors in companies that can also have an influential effect on decision-making. Ethical investment funds also serve as important targets for collaboration for social movements. Social movements can use the results of their research into these funds as a way of helping to boost the information base upon which funds recommend or choose not to recommend certain companies for investment.

Taken together, ethical consumerism and ethical investment processes provide important leverage to social movements and activists in attempting to influence corporate decision-making. As we will see in the next section, such activities also work hand in glove with more sophisticated strategies for working from inside corporations.

5.0 Promoting shareholder activism

The use of shareholders' rights inside corporate meetings to undertake litigation or simply to raise awareness among shareholders about unsound corporate practices has become more widespread in recent years, partly accelerated by the growing market share held by institutional investors such as superannuation and pension funds and other fund managers.

The strategy aims to utilize the internal rights that shareholders possess to bring pressure to bear on directors. In order to be effective in influencing corporate decision-makers, advocates need a sound understanding of the nature of corporate decision-making, and of the legal framework in which it operates.

By obtaining even a very small portion of shares in a targeted company, or by activating existing shareholders with ethical leanings, activists can greatly expand their capacity to utilize internal means to influence corporate decision-making. Despite the fact that such small shareholdings may never command anything like a majority, corporations law can open the way to a number of powerful mechanisms for enforcing managerial accountability.

5.1 Shareholders' legal rights and remedies

Corporations law is very complex and differs significantly from jurisdiction to jurisdiction, but there are some general principles that remain more or less common throughout common-law countries. These general principles are designed to protect the interests of individual shareholders and shield them from oppressive conduct by boards of directors and in some cases even by majority shareholders. The underlying purpose of such provisions is certainly not a public interest one – rather, it is protecting the investments of individual shareholders – but there are ways in which activists can at times make strategic use of these general principles and the rights they create to pursue public interest agendas.

Shareholders' rights are detailed in both corporate constitutions (articles of association) and in applicable corporations laws in each jurisdiction. It's not possible to set these out in detail in this book, nor is it desirable, as such provisions can change quickly, but the purpose of this discussion is to alert activists to where to look and what to look for.

The relevant general principles include:

- Directors have a duty to act in good faith.
- Directors have a duty to act in the best interests of the company and its shareholders (often referred to as the directors' fiduciary duty).
- Directors have a duty to act competently and lawfully (sometimes called a duty of due diligence).
- All shareholders have the power to enforce the above duties.
- Minority shareholder groups have the right to be protected from 'oppression' by the majority.
- All shareholders are entitled to attend general meetings and can ask questions on notice.
- Relatively small groups of shareholders (sometimes 100) may be able to use embedded rights to requisition extraordinary meetings to discuss ethical issues in a target company.

5.2 Overcoming the question of standing

The first major advantage of obtaining a small holding is that it can overcome questions of standing to sue. Normally public interest advocates would not have standing to sue a corporation over its business practices (standing to sue is discussed in Chapters 1 and 10). Being a shareholder usually means having standing to sue the company and/or the directors for breaches of statutory and common-law duties.

Obtaining potential standing to sue is only one of the hurdles, however; the plaintiff shareholder also needs to be able to show a viable cause of action.

There are two main situations in which bringing an enforcement suit may be useful for a public interest advocate shareholder; these are:

- To enforce compliance with existing law (for example: environmental or human rights, anti-discrimination or other legislation) using shareholder rights and remedies.
- To promote public interest agendas (that may not be otherwise legally enforceable) through strategic use of shareholder rights.

5.3 Shareholder remedies to enforce compliance with existing law

Corporations are required to exist and operate lawfully within society. Like persons, corporations are subject to the law and are expected to obey it. Labour laws, consumer protection laws and environmental protection and anti-discrimination legislation all apply to companies. These laws provide a framework through which social movements and activists can target the business practices of corporations. In many situations government regulators may be unwilling to prosecute companies for relevant breaches, and a private citizen may lack legal standing to enforce these laws, but a shareholder has an ability to enforce such compliance indirectly as an element of enforcing the directors' duties to act in good faith.

The strength of the obligation to act in good faith is made explicit in the following cases. In *Anderson* v. *Corporation of the City of Enfield* (1983) 34 SASR 472, it was accepted that a manufacturer who failed to comply with regulations was negligent. And in the United States, in *Hutensky* v. *Federal Deposit Insurance Corporation* (1996) 82 F.3d 1234, the violation of loan regulations was held to warrant the removal of a bank director.

Conduct in breach of existing laws may also amount to a breach of a director's fiduciary duty to act in the best interests of the company.

The first proposition in this argument is that all citizens are bound to comply with the law. Obviously, persons may choose to ignore the law on moral grounds (conscientious objection) and accept the punishment of the state for disobeying the law if caught. Persons are considered in law and liberal philosophy (see John Stuart Mill and John Locke for discussions of liberty from the liberal perspective) to have an existence prior to the state which is the basis of their general entitlement to 'liberty'.

Corporations, on the other hand, are created by law and bestowed only with such capacity and legal powers as the law chooses to grant. For this deep underlying reason corporations and their managers must be considered to be absolutely bound to comply with the law. This situation is clearly spelt out, for example, in Australian law. Under s124 (1) of the Corporations Act a corporation is granted the general legal capacity and powers of an individual, subject to subsection (3), which provides:

> For the avoidance of doubt, this section does not:
> a) Authorise a company to do an act that is prohibited by a law of a State or Territory; or
> b) Give a company a right that a law of a State or Territory denies to the company.

It follows that the directors do not have:

- legal authority on behalf of the corporation to chose to ignore the law; or
- the moral privilege possessed by natural persons as a conscientious objector to make a personal choice to disobey a particular law (and accept the consequences).

Shareholders have significant rights to sue the company and its directors where the directors have failed to act in good faith, or where they have failed to act in the company's best interests. Intentional law-breaking by directors or by companies under their control is both a failure to act in good faith and a failure to act in the company's interests. Ethical shareholders are entitled to sue the directors to strictly require compliance with all of the company's legal obligations.

5.4 Shareholder remedies to enforce higher duties than legally mandated

We have already discussed the ability of shareholder activists to utilize shareholder rights to oblige company directors to comply with legal obligations. This strategy will be effective where the activist or social movement can identify specific breaches of environmental, human rights, consumer or labour law.

A more complex situation arises where a company's activities are breaching widely held social values but do not amount to any identifiable breach of existing law. This can often be the case, for example, in relation to animal cruelty and environmental destruction, where the company's activities can be technically lawful yet highly questionable morally.

There is a potential for activists to argue that directors who expose companies to sustained criticism for morally unacceptable (but technically lawful) business practices are not acting in the company's best interests (Beilefield et al. 2005).

The potential for successful suits against directors by activist shareholders in this situation is less certain and depends to an extent on the precise way the duties are expressed in different jurisdictions. Courts, particularly in the United States, are reluctant to interfere with the running of companies by directors unless the breaches of duty can be shown to cause identifiable harm to the company. The so-called 'business judgement rule' is designed by the courts to give directors some leeway to make risky decisions without being subjected to claims that they are not acting in the company's best interests. Such a rule is designed to protect directors from the risks associated with unstable market conditions. It may be less useful where complainants can point to almost certain damage to the company's reputation if certain questionable business practices are not discontinued.

At minimum it can be said that directors have a duty to take into consideration a long-term view of shareholder welfare. The long-term viability of a corporation may be threatened when a corporation engages in actions which, although not technically unlawful, involve serious environmental or social impacts which will continue to attract criticism of the company into the future.

Parkinson contends, for example, that 'a reputation for inflicting environmental damage will be harmful to profits ...' (Parkinson 2002).

The likely success of such an argument in court would depend very much upon the precise legislation defining directors' duties in a particular jurisdiction. In the USA, for example, directors would find some protection under the 'business judgement rule'. In Australia and Canada, directors' duties are defined in fairly neutral terms in s181 of the Corporations Act 2001 (Aust) and s122 of the Business Corporations Act 1985 (Can), simply reaffirming directors' duties to act in good faith in the best interests of the corporation.

5.5 Recent reforms in the United Kingdom

In the United Kingdom, however, recent legislative changes (Companies Act 2006, s172 (1)) has greatly strengthened the hand of public interest advocates in relation to directors' duties by specifically linking the duty to long-term effects and environmental and community impacts. Such a provision is a significant step forward in improving the potential for activists to promote corporate social responsibility.

> 172 Duty to promote the success of the company
>
> (1) A director of a company must act in the way he considers, in good faith, would be most likely to promote the success of the company for the benefit of its members as a whole, and in doing so have regard (amongst other matters) to—
>
> a) the likely consequences of any decision in the long term,
>
> b) the interests of the company's employees,
>
> c) the need to foster the company's business relationships with suppliers, customers and others,
>
> d) the impact of the company's operations on the community and the environment,
>
> e) the desirability of the company maintaining a reputation for high standards of business conduct, and
>
> f) the need to act fairly as between members of the company.

Using shareholder rights to enforce directors' duties to act responsibly is a powerful remedy. In jurisdictions other than the UK the success of such actions is less predictable because the legislation is less helpful, but even so such tactics are well worth pursuing. The publicity attendant upon public interest campaigns in the wider community can work hand in hand with this use of internal remedies by ethical shareholders to attempt to force companies to respond to public pressures for social accountability. There is a positive feedback loop that can be established by a well-orchestrated campaign, whereby the public criticism that the social movement is likely to subject the company to for its unethical behaviour becomes the very market condition that directors should be aiming to avoid. A failure to take account of the likely response of social movements could amount to a failure to act in the company's interests. The more sustained and publicly supported a particular campaign becomes, the more likely it is that directors could be seen to be in breach of their duties if they continue to subject the company to reputational damage. In turn, any actions by activist shareholders to challenge the directors over such issues serve to further advance the public awareness campaign. To critics this may appear to be a self-serving loop, but to public interest advocates it is simply a well-functioning strategy.

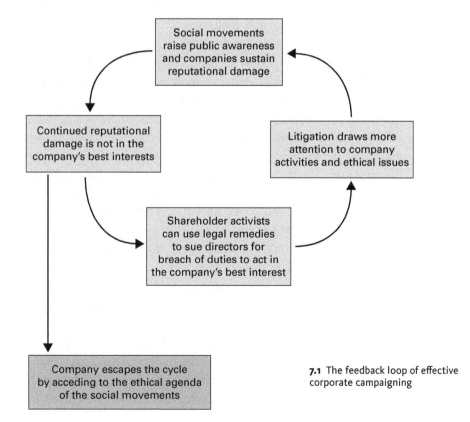

7.1 The feedback loop of effective corporate campaigning

Litigation is, of course, an expensive option, and it is best used only as part of a wider publicity strategy. There remain a number of important ways in which shareholder rights can also be used to pressure companies by using company meetings as a forum for alerting other investors to the questionable activities of the company. These techniques are cheaper and less risky than litigation. The following case study examines a successful use of this technique in relation to a uranium mine in Australia.

5.6 Non-litigious remedies: case study – Jabiluka and North shareholder campaign

In the late 1990s, as part of the national campaign to stop the proposed uranium mine at Jabiluka, in world-heritage-listed Kakadu National Park, by the company Energy Resources Australia (ERA), members of the Wilderness Society utilized the opportunity afforded by Australia's Corporations Act 2001, which permitted 100 shareholders, with as little as one share each, to requisition an extraordinary general meeting and put forward resolutions. The Wilderness Society targeted ERA's parent company North Ltd (North) and purchased a small parcel of shares. They also contacted other shareholders on the company's share register and built support inside the company to take some internal action (Beilefield et al. 2005).

As a result the 'North Ethical Shareholders Group' (NES) was formed, and the group used its shareholder rights to force an extraordinary general meeting to discuss their environmental concerns.

On 29 October 1999, around six hundred shareholders attended a specially convened EGM, and even though support for the special resolutions against uranium mining ran at an average of just under 6 per cent, the campaign made a significant impact upon North's parent company (ABC Radio, 'North Shareholder campaign – shareholder nation', *Triple J Morning Show*, www.abc.net.au/triplej/morning/shareholdernation/activism/default.htm).

North Ltd was subsequently bought out by Rio Tinto, and the campaign to stop Jabiluka continued throughout shareholder meetings in London and Sydney. Rio Tinto announced in 2001 that it would cease development of the mine on environmental, social and economic grounds, at least in the medium term. It has been observed that the shareholder campaign was instrumental in this decision (Rose 2001).

In more recent years activists have begun to focus on customers and members of large institutional investment funds. Large industry-based superannuation funds provide a great opportunity to target the thousands of rank-and-file investors. At times these campaigns can be supported by industry-based trade unions as well, which gives activists even greater access to the small investors in super funds. In the United Kingdom, the campaign to use pension funds to pressure for socially responsible corporate behaviour is well organized. A good source for information related to this avenue for corporate activism can be found at www.fairpensions.org.uk.

The following account is sourced from the fair pensions website:

> Early in 2010 FairPensions co-ordinated two shareholder resolutions, asking BP and Shell to publish details of the environmental, social and financial risks associated with their tar sands project ... [T]he Shell AGM saw 1 in 10 shareholders refusing to heed the company's recommendation to vote against the resolution, just weeks after 1 in 7 investors in BP (controlling nearly £10 billion in the company's stock) refused to back management on tar sands ... [S]ecuring this level of support (10% or above) is exceptional. In response to this unprecedented action, both BP and Shell rushed to meet with investors, and made important disclosures as a result. (www.fairpensions.org.uk/successes)

Far from being an abuse of process, shareholder actions in pursuit of environmental accountability by companies and their directors have the potential to reinvigorate shareholder democracy. As evidenced in the examples above, it is not necessary for activist shareholders to actually win majority support for a resolution to have a substantial impact upon corporate agendas.

The Corporate Responsibility Coalition (CORE) UK offers a very useful online guide to corporate activism at corporate-responsibility.org/act-now-a-campaigners-guide-to-the-companies-act/.

Shareholder activism is just one tool for the environmental activist embarking on corporate engagement, and it can be used in concert with consumer boycotts, direct lobbying of corporate executives, blockades, street marches, rallies, broader public education and political lobbying, and, as we have seen, litigation. At its most humble, securing a few shares in a target corporation can give a shareholder access to important company information and entitle them to attend general meetings. The intelligent use of shareholder rights and public awareness campaigns in tandem represents a very powerful medium for successful corporate campaigning.

Conclusion

In the final analysis it remains clear that the most significant aspect of all of the various tactics for influencing corporate decision-making revolves around the raising of awareness about the questionable activities of the company. Initially this is a process of alerting the public at large, which is a fundamental aspect of all campaigns. But when activists and social movements are engaged in the corporate sphere what is required is a deeper understanding of the way in which corporate lobbying differs from public sector lobbying and a strategic approach to applying pressure where it will be most effective. In general this means that activists need to conduct a lot of research into the business relationships of a target corporation and develop strategies for accessing and activating the range of stakeholders. These stakeholders can include:

- the general public;
- consumers;
- retail investors (mums and dads);
- ethical investment funds;
- institutional investors (superannuation funds, banks and investment houses);
- parent companies;
- major shareholding companies;
- major business customers;
- business competitors.

Corporate activism is a relatively new field and is certainly a less well-trodden path for activists and social movements than activism in the public sphere. Nonetheless, it represents an increasingly important and emerging focus of social change activism.

EIGHT | Direct action, protest and your rights

Introduction

The most exciting and highly visible aspect of activism and social change advocacy occurs when people take part in public political events. From radical events such as blockades, building occupations and direct action protests through to more sedate events such as public meetings, marches and rallies, such events are powerful, exciting and at times risky. This chapter takes a very practical approach to the staging of such events and carefully examines the usefulness, legality and pitfalls of particular types of action. We will also look at ways of ensuring that such actions remain effective and safe for the participants, through the use of effective police liaison and other techniques. Our analysis includes both lawful protest and civil disobedience, where activists may choose to place themselves in arrestable situations.

1.0 The right to protest

The first observation to make is that public demonstrations of every kind are an integral part of the practice of participatory democracy. Despite this, rights of protest are not well protected in modern legal systems such as those of the USA, the UK, Australia, New Zealand and Canada. The traditional common-law position is not to recognize any particular political rights except to allow that citizens have the right to do anything that has not been prohibited by law. The problem is that power-holders are often keen to outlaw the most effective forms of protest.

While a number of the jurisdictions under consideration have bills of rights (the USA, Canada and the UK), which are supposed to guarantee important civil and political rights, these are not usually expressed robustly enough to preserve rights of protest from significant legislative curtailment.

- Human Rights Act 1998 (UK): www.bailii.org/uk/legis/num_act/1998/ ukpga_19980042_en_1.html#pb1-l1g1
- Bill of Rights (USA): topics.law.cornell.edu/constitution/ billofrights#amendmentx
- Canadian Charter of Rights and Freedoms: lois.justice.gc.ca/eng/charter/ Charter_index.html

Where bills of rights are constitutionally entrenched, as they are in the USA and Canada, they do have the power to override legislation that is inconsistent with protected political rights. In practice the Supreme Court is ultimately called upon to decide the precise boundaries of protected rights, such as the First Amendment right in the US Constitution, which aims to enshrine the right to peaceful assembly. The judicial position tends to be that such rights can never for practical purposes be absolute, and so legislators aim to work around the various limiting or permissive principles set down by the courts. The USA Patriot Act (H.R. 3162) is a good example of the way in which legislators are able to work around bills of rights protections by the use of careful drafting, particularly where they are responding to moral panics such as terrorism.

The Human Rights Act in the United Kingdom is not constitutionally entrenched and as a consequence is limited in its effectiveness by the doctrine of parliamentary sovereignty, which enables Parliament to make and unmake any law. Despite these limitations the Act does provide some limited protection that would otherwise not be available at all.

The Human Rights Act 1998 UK allows judicial review of legislation and empowers the court to make a 'declaration of incompatibility' where legislation breaches the protected rights. Such a declaration does not have the effect of invalidating the legislation (which can happen in a judicial review challenge in the USA or Canada) but it is still a finding of important legal and political significance. Perhaps even more useful in practical situations is that the Human Rights Act can affect the way that courts interpret legislation that aims to control protests. The Human Rights Act provides in S3 (1): 'So far as it is possible to do so, primary legislation and subordinate legislation must be read and given effect in a way which is compatible with the Convention rights.'

Despite the limitations, bills of rights are important because they help to define the content of the recognized political rights of citizens in a country and help to foster a cultural attitude of respect for such rights.

The political culture of a country is an important factor in determining just how robust protest rights are likely to remain. Australia remains particularly vulnerable because of a lack of any recognized positive rights of protest or assembly.

1.1 The lawfulness of protests

Politicians and media commentators are fond of retreating to the line that protests are fine as long as protesters do not break the law, but this ends up as a circular argument where there are laws against protest itself. Certainly it makes sense to expect that protesters will not assault others or intentionally damage property, but such activities are traditional serious crimes that are adequately dealt with under existing laws. Non-violence is a core value of social movements described in this book, so this discussion relates to non-violent protest action, whether it is lawful or technically unlawful. Despite a commitment to non-violence, it is possible that any large group situation may nonetheless have the potential for sporadic eruptions of violence, and this is particularly problematic where police use violent means to prevent a political protest (horses, batons, shields, tear gas, capsicum spray, confrontational arrests). Experience has taught generations of protesters and probably police that any violent interactions between police and protesters will ultimately be presented in mainstream media as protester violence.

Outbreaks of violence invariably damage the credibility of the cause being pursued, so it is important that advocates are well informed about the law, police powers and effective methods of organization to minimize negative occurrences.

There is a myriad of laws in every jurisdiction which limit the public's rights to make political statements by way of public demonstration.

In the United Kingdom these include:

- Public Order Act 1986 (UK)
- Criminal Justice and Public Order Act 1994 (UK)
- Criminal Justice and Police Act 2001 (UK)
- Criminal Justice Act 2003 (UK)
- Terrorism Act 2000 (UK), and
- Anti-terrorism, Crime and Security Act 2001 (UK).

It is more difficult to provide a guide to the relevant laws regarding protest in Canada, the USA and Australia because those jurisdictions are federations and laws apply at both national and state or provincial levels and also vary significantly from state to state.

In Australia the national laws relevant to protests include:

- Security Legislation Amendment Act 2002 Cth
- Crimes Act 1914 Cth
- Criminal Code Act 1995 (Cth).

In Canada the most significant piece of national legislation that affects rights of protest is the Criminal Code Act 1985 (Can). In the United States the USA Patriot Act is an important piece of federal legislation that affects political rights, but in general most of the laws in the federations regulating public space are enacted at the state level.

New, more restrictive laws have in recent years developed as a result of fears about terrorism and as a result of the advent of special legislation for large events such as WTO, CHOGM, APEC and G20 meetings and other international events. Frequently these laws establish a power for police or police ministers to declare restricted areas (during times of international meetings) and to impose extreme levels of police control over public activities in those areas during those times. This is a new and worrying trend in that it continues to expand the situations in which legislators create a state of exception to 'normal' civil rights.

1.2 Intentional law-breaking and the conscientious objector

The common-law courts have long recognized the democratic right to be a conscientious objector. There is a difference between a real criminal who acts out of selfish motives, is often dishonest and may attempt to conceal an offence, and the genuine conscientious objector who honestly and publicly defies a law in order to make a bona fide political statement. While the courts recognize that citizens may validly see disobedience of the law as their moral duty (a variant of the fourth Nuremberg principle), the court will usually still convict the conscientious objector. Courts may be prepared to take the bona fides of a person's motivation into account in sentencing. In discussing intentional law-breaking by activists, we are discussing a subject which of itself is not a direct challenge to the rule of law, but an aspect of it. Conscientious objectors accept that they have the right to break the law, but that the state has the right to process them according to the law as a consequence.

2.0 Types of political event

This section explores a range of public protest activities, ranging in general from the most passive to the more confrontational. It is by no means exhaustive, but it will provide the opportunity to discuss the issues which arise. Generically all of these types of activity can be referred to as 'actions' or 'events'.

The section will discuss actions and events that fall into the following categories:

* public meetings;
* rallies;

- marches;
- protests/direct action;
- sit-ins and occupations;
- blockades.

Each different type of political action or event attracts a different level of legal response or restriction.

A very useful guide to public order laws in relation to each type of action for readers in the United Kingdom is provided by Liberty in their publication *Your Rights: The Liberty Guide to Human Rights* (www.yourrights. org.uk/yourrights/the-right-of-peaceful-protest/index.html).

In a multi-jurisdictional publication such as this it is not possible to exhaustively discuss the likely legal implications of each type of action. This is made particularly difficult in the nations with a federal system (the USA, Australia and Canada) as the main legislative authority in relation to public order offences is normally located at the sub-national level (state/province).

In order to provide some general guidance, however, the likely legal consequences of particular actions will be discussed using examples drawn from the United Kingdom (which is simpler because there is only one legislature), Australia, Canada and the United States. Activists should always consult their local laws in detail when planning actions or events.

2.1 Public meetings

Public meetings are frequently used as the first stage of an emerging campaign and are usually aimed at gauging (and perhaps demonstrating) support for an issue, networking with other concerned people, and developing a group focus on how to proceed farther. Usually they will attract no police interference, and can normally be organized to take place in public parks or in halls, offices or clubs by arrangement with the owners, or in private homes. Public meetings are an obvious starting point in the process of participatory democracy; this is where new campaigns are born and the initial networking that leads to the formation of a new group occurs. Chapter 4 provides some more detailed guidance on how to approach your first public meeting in order to make the most productive use of the event.

2.1.1 Generating media Local media can sometimes assist in publicizing the proposal to hold the meeting. This is because the fact of local people gathering to discuss an issue of concern is generally considered by journalists to be a news event in itself. The ability to publicize the meeting often allows a new group two free splashes in the media if they handle their publicity well. First, you can usually get some coverage of the fact that the meeting is going to be held, and this will help attract more people, and secondly, you may be able to get the local media to report on some outcomes of the meeting. If an outcome of the meeting is the formation of a new group some time down the track, this can also often be used to generate another media story later.

2.1.2 Collecting contact information The most important priority activists should have in these early meetings is to collect names and contact details of as many participants as possible. There is nothing more tragic than having an effective meeting of one hundred or more people, then realizing at the end that you have no means to contact those people again. The other important issues to be aware of in organizing such meetings are to be inclusive of all attendees (opportunities to be heard), to have prepared information available to distribute if possible, to seek commitments from people about how they can help, and if possible to achieve group agreement to meet again to undertake a further step in the campaign.

One of the potential difficulties you may face is that the group of people who attend will not necessarily agree with your particular response to the issue. You can partly forestall this by being careful how you describe the purpose of the meeting in your initial publicity for the event. You may need, for example, to make it clear that your meeting is for people who are concerned about the negative impacts of the proposed lead refinery. If you have done this you may still need to accommodate a range of views from those who are outright opposed and those who seek modification of the proposal so as to build a community consensus and keep your group open and inclusive. But you need to be able to draw a boundary in relation to people who may attend whose approach is diametrically different to yours. You can be polite but firm, explaining that you respect their opinion but that this meeting has been called by and for people who oppose the current proposal in some form. Unless you are dealing with professional provocateurs, which is unlikely at a first meeting, then you should be able to politely work around these people.

2.1.3 Setting direction Once you have some broad agreement on the range of outcomes that the people in attendance may want to achieve you can begin the process of identifying an immediate goal (as discussed in Chapter 4). It may not be possible or even desirable to try to achieve too much in a first meeting; it is probably better to use your public meeting for some basic logistical outcomes rather than risk alienating people by getting into the details too quickly. So, for example, a good set of outcomes of a first meeting would include:

- Gathering a reasonable number of concerned people around your issue.
- Identifying a broad approach that is consistent with your purpose but broad enough to be inclusive of a range of approaches.
- Collecting names and contact details and if possible gauging individuals' levels of skill and enthusiasm.
- Establishing a core organizing committee to progress the issue and planning for a follow-up meeting.
- Generating some positive media for your campaign.

2.1.4 Follow-up meetings At follow-up meetings you should be able to proceed with better defining the group's aims. This can be a good time to engage in the campaign mapping and planning processes discussed in Chapter 4.

Public meetings are a low-risk way to start a new campaign and to gauge or gather support for a campaign at a local level. This discussion has mostly linked public meetings with new campaigns, and this is predominantly the case. There are times when established campaigns or social movements also use public meetings, but usually this is in the context of a new issue developing within the framework of the existing campaign. There are few risks of negative police response to public meetings, provided they do not obstruct traffic or cause other forms of public disturbance.

2.2 Rallies

Rallies are like public meetings but on a grander scale. Rallies are useful for demonstrating levels of public support, for bringing an issue to the public's attention and for providing an important opportunity to network with supporters. Rallies are usually called by existing campaign groups or social movements which have already moved beyond the initial stage of gauging support and are often timed to coincide with important trigger events.

2.2.1 Demonstrating support Rallies can be most useful for allowing popular social movements to demonstrate high levels of support. A good example was the massive worldwide rallies that took place at the start of the second Iraq War in 2003. Globally the peace movement is one of the oldest, most complex and largest of all social movements. The rallies against the Iraq War in March 2003 were estimated to involve between six and ten million people worldwide (BBC News, 17 March 2003, news.bbc.co.uk/2/hi/europe/2765215. stm) and possibly represent the largest-ever mobilization of the public for a political cause.

Rallies are a powerful way to demonstrate widespread support but campaigners should be careful not to overestimate the likely response to calling an action. To illustrate, a public meeting attended by thirty people in a local area can be a success, but a rally attended by only thirty people is not. Rallies need to be well publicized beforehand and well organized, and should usually relate to an issue for which there is already demonstrable community support, e.g. peace, the environment, refugees, climate change. This tends to suggest that rallies are better organized by well-established campaign groups or social movements, but they can be useful for fairly new groups provided they relate to a burning local issue that is arousing passion in the community. It is impossible to put a number on what constitutes a successful rally; this needs to be judged in context according to what would be seen by ordinary people as a strong show of support. Obviously a rally of 100 people in a small rural community may be significant, whereas in London or New York this would tend to demonstrate low levels of support.

2.2.2 Networking and belonging Demonstrating support is, of course, not the only value of a rally; rallies are important face-to-face networking events that are very useful for fostering a sense of belonging among supporters, are inclusive of new people and allow for the ongoing collection of contacts and dissemination of information.

Successful rallies should have some form of adequate public address equipment available, credible speakers, information to distribute, and if possible some relevant forms of entertainment and refreshment. All of these help to hold the crowd and encourage new supporters to take part or remain active. It is a grave mistake to let your crowd disperse without involving them, informing them and collecting their contact information.

2.2.3 Legal issues related to rallies Traditionally, provided a rally takes place in a public place, and does not cause obstructions to traffic, there should be no adverse response from police. This was certainly the traditional common-law position, but this basic right of peaceful public assembly has come under threat from legislative interventions in a number of jurisdictions.

In the United Kingdom, for example, s14 of the Public Order Act 1986

(UK) provides police with powers to impose conditions on public assemblies that may impose limits on matters such as location, duration and numbers of people attending. The section creates offences for persons who fail to comply with such conditions. This section clearly imposes a serious restriction on the underlying right to public assembly.

Similarly in the Australian states there is legislation that creates procedures requiring organizers of public political events to notify police, and which empowers the police to approve or object to the proposal. S23 of the Summary Offences Act 1988 (NSW) provides such a procedure and stipulates that persons who take part in an 'authorised public assembly (or procession)' will not be liable for a range of offences related to assemblies and obstruction of vehicles provided the terms of the approval are complied with.

Interestingly, neither of the provisions outlined above necessarily require prior notification or approval of a gathering that will take place on public land (such as a park) and which will not cause any obstruction to vehicles or the general public. So rallies, as distinct from marches or processions, occupy an ambiguous position in this regard. Organizers should make a strategic decision based on local laws and conditions as to whether approval should be sought.

Under the Canadian Criminal Code 1985 (Can) (s63) public assemblies are prima facie lawful unless they appear to be leading to a breach of the peace, in which case various sections for the suppression of riots become effective. This flexible process makes it difficult for participants to determine the lawfulness of assemblies ahead of the event, and has allowed authorities to utilize extensive 'riot' powers in relation to protests over events such as G8 meetings and APEC meetings.

2.2.4 'Free speech zones' and designated exclusion areas In the United States, despite the First Amendment protecting the rights to peaceful assembly, a practice has emerged in which legislators restrict the freedom to assemble by limiting the time, manner and place in which these assemblies can occur. The rather misleading term 'free speech zones' has come to describe the places (often away from political or media action) where authorities are prepared to tolerate political assemblies. Obviously the idea that a specified area is a 'free speech zone' implies that free speech rights are being abrogated elsewhere.

The selective sealing off of public areas during specific events and the creation of contained areas away from the action where protesters can gather is an alarming but growing trend in many jurisdictions. This technique is especially prevalent in relation to the security preparations surrounding major global meetings and summits, such as those of the World Trade Organization (WTO), Asia Pacific Economic Cooperation (APEC), G20, G8, etc.

Free Speech Zone

In Australia, for example, special legislation, the APEC Meeting (Police Powers) Act 2007 (NSW), was created to provide increased security for the APEC meeting held in Sydney. Parts 4 and 5 of the Act gave police extensive powers to close public areas and remove all unauthorized persons from such areas.

Powers to create 'designated areas' in which special laws prohibiting entry and assembly can be enforced are also contained in sections 128 and 132 of the Serious Organized Crime and Police Act 2005 (UK).

Provincial legislation in Canada is also used to supplement the Criminal Code and achieve the equivalent of the notorious free speech zones (De Lint 2004: 43) seen in the USA and Australia.

2.3 Marches

Marches are more problematic than rallies from a legal perspective. This is because, unlike static rallies, they are likely to involve some obstruction to roadways as they usually involve a crowd of people walking along a thoroughfare, and this is where your action can run into difficulties with the law. Before examining the legalities of marches, we should first consider their usefulness.

2.3.1 Usefulness of marches Marches usually need to begin with some kind of rally as a mustering point and end with some kind of rally as a destination point. So for this reason all of the considerations that apply to rallies apply to marches, but there are further complexities that also arise. Like rallies, marches are not suited to actions involving small numbers of people. A group of thirty or so walking down the street, chanting or holding banners, is likely to appear very marginalized, and to attract anger from inconvenienced shoppers and drivers, and potentially enforcement actions from police. Marches also have the tendency to disperse the crowd you started with (at your rally) unless you have a clear destination and a clear programme of events at the destination. It is important to remember that many people attending a political action may not be nearly as committed as the organizers and could be easily alienated by confusion, lack of organization or lack of a clear and empowering focus or object.

Given the challenges in organizing successful marches, what, then, is their value? Ideally a march attracts more attention than a static rally, and gives people more of a sense of spectacle and celebration. At their very best marches have the capacity to draw in members of the public spontaneously as they see the march moving past and decide to join in. This is most likely to occur where the march relates to a widely held social value that is being breached by a current trigger event. Many of the marches against the Iraq War, for example, gained in size dramatically as onlookers spontaneously joined in. Organizers need to be realistic about whether their march is likely to encourage such spontaneous recruitment, or whether it may conversely have the effect of angering onlookers who are being inconvenienced in proceeding with their normal activities. Of course, there will always be some people who are angry at being inconvenienced, but that is in part the price we pay for living in a democracy.

2.3.2 Legal implications of marches Street marches are not prima facie lawful without prior authorization from the police; they expose marchers to the prospect of charges for the obstruction of the roadway. In the UK it is obstruction of the highway which constitutes the offence – s137 of the Highways Act 1980 (UK) – regardless of whether a vehicle has actually been obstructed.

Conversely, under the Australian provision found in s6 of the Summary Offences Act 1988 (NSW) it is the obstruction of a person or vehicle which constitutes the offence, whether or not they are travelling on a public road. Under this formulation of the offence, all that is required is that free passage of a person or vehicle is prevented without reasonable excuse. This has allowed a novel defence on some occasions: if the vehicle or person being obstructed was not involved in a lawful pursuit, then the obstruction would arguably be for a lawful purpose. This technicality has allowed some protesters blockading logging operations that were later found to be unlawful to be acquitted of obstruction charges, because the logging equipment they obstructed was not part of a lawful pursuit.

Such a defence may not apply to the offence as it is constructed in the UK legislation. These minor local differences in the nature of the offences can have important consequences, and organizers should always investigate the precise nature of local laws. A particular risk for activists in Canada is that under s423 of the Canadian Criminal Code, actions that cause obstruction of a highway can fall under the definition of the more serious crime of 'intimidation', which is discussed in more detail in the next section.

The prospect of being charged with obstruction offences together with the unpredictable consequences (violent enforcement) that may occur if police choose to move against an unauthorized march mean that marching is an action which needs to be carefully considered before a decision to proceed is taken.

Most jurisdictions have legislation that provides a procedure for obtaining police approval for a march or procession, and in most situations following this is advisable.

2.3.3 Prior notification of marches S11 of the Public Order Act 1986 (UK) requires that police receive advance notice of all processions and creates an offence for organizers where notification requirements are not met. Sections 12 and 13 of the Act provide powers for police to impose conditions upon and in some cases prohibit processions altogether. It is not clear in those sections whether acting in accordance with the imposed conditions can provide any positive defence to charges under other legislation – for example, for obstruction.

A similar procedure exists in Australia under s23 of the Summary Offences Act 1988 (NSW) to obtain police authorization for a march. Under s24 this authorization specifically has the effect of protecting participants from finding themselves in breach of laws relating to obstruction.

Similar provisions on obstructions and notification requirements for processions and marches can be found in state legislation in the United States and provincial legislation in Canada, but they vary in their precise legal formulations. For this reason organizers need to remain mindful of the legal risks and alert to the exceptions and procedures that apply at the local level.

Marches are a potentially powerful way to engage the public's attention, but clearly there are also a number of pitfalls that need to be avoided.

2.4 Public political events held on private land

So far we have been discussing rallies and marches that occur on public land, but at times the public protest event may involve private land – for example, where there are protests on mine sites, at building demolitions and against logging or other environmentally destructive commercial activities. The legal context of any political action will depend upon whether it takes place in a public place or on private land/premises. In short, in a public space a range of public order laws will apply, whereas on private premises the issue of trespass becomes most significant.

2.4.1 The traditional law regarding trespass

Trespass is a traditional cause of action in private law (a tort) under the English common law and still exists in most common-law jurisdictions, including Australia, the United States, Canada and New Zealand. A person trespasses when they enter the property of another person without their consent or remain there after consent has been withdrawn. There are many complexities regarding the concept of implied consent which protect individuals who innocently encroach on another's land unaware that the owner may have some objection.

Implied consent operates in a broad cultural setting; unless owners display signs prohibiting entry, or specifically request a person to leave, then use of private premises in ways that are usual for the public will be tolerated. For example, it is usual for members of the public to be allowed to enter retail and other commercial premises, or to knock on the front doors of residential properties or move across large rural properties without needing specific consent. These implications protect usual usages of private land at least until an owner expressly prohibits entry. They will also protect individuals

involved in protest actions to some extent, depending on the nature of the action and whether there has been any withdrawal of consent communicated.

Trespass as a civil action can be used against protesters who conduct their activities on private property, although as the process of a private lawsuit is lengthy and costly, this is not a very common outcome. More relevant to protesters is the fact that in most jurisdictions a parallel statutory offence of trespass has been created which empowers law enforcement officers to remove trespassers and charge them with a minor offence, usually follow-ing a complaint by a property owner. Statutory offences of trespass are frequently used against demonstrators, blockaders, picketers and squatters. Statutory trespass offences exist in the states of Australia and the USA and the provinces of Canada, and in New Zealand and the UK, but the precise coverage of such offences varies considerably.

The issue of whether a protest is occurring on public or private land is a significant issue in the UK, where public order laws tend to diverge according to whether the events in question are taking place on highways, in public places or on private property. Where public political events are taking place on public lands they are more likely to be dealt with under Part 2 of the Public Order Act 1986 (UK). In relation to private lands the Criminal Justice and Public Order Act 1994 (UK) contains detailed provisions in Part 5 that pertain to trespass. Part 5 is intended mostly as a means of controlling travellers and rave parties but also contains provisions for preventing 'trespassory assemblies', which would include political protests intended to take place on private lands.

In Australia a slightly different approach has been taken, whereby private premises can temporarily be deemed public when they are being used by the public for the time being.

For example, in the Summary Offences Act 1988 (NSW), s3(b), public place means: 'a part of premises, that is open to the public, or is used by the public whether or not on payment of money or other consideration, whether or not the place or part is ordinarily so open or used and whether or not the public to whom it is open consists only of a limited class of persons ...'

This allows a range of public order laws that would otherwise not apply to be applied during a protest, even where it occurs on private land. In *The appeal of Camp* [1975] 1 NSWLR 452, the court observed, 'the definition does not distinguish between public property and private property, a public place is a place where the public go, no matter whether they have a right to go or not'.

This actually has the effect that a private place becomes a public place for the purpose of charging people under public order laws such as the Summary Offences Act merely by the fact that the public go there to hold a political demonstration.

In a South Australian case (*Semple* v. *Howes* 91985 38 SASR 34) dem-onstrators entered land, as trespassers, where uranium mining was taking place; they were held to be in a public place for the purposes of the South Australian Summary Offences Act 1953.

This approach has the effect of creating an increased jeopardy for protesters entering private lands. Where a protest event takes place on private premises, activists may be subjected to trespass laws as well as more general public order laws. Trespass laws should not discourage activists from taking actions that may involve private premises; they are merely another part of the legal fabric that needs to be taken into account in strategic planning.

2.5 Protests/direct action

Protest is a very wide term that can refer to a variety of actions, with the unifying factor that they are usually a protest against something, even though they are usually also in support of an alternative. This negative connotation of the word 'protest' is a feature which requires some examination. Frequently advocates have no choice but to protest against the status quo, and even when they attempt to present their argument in a positive form, they are still portrayed by media and other commentators as protesters. For example, environmentalists seeking to preserve old-growth forests are routinely described in the media as anti-logging protesters rather than as being in favour of preserving old-growth forests. This being so, it is always important for advocates to clearly express what it is that they advocate in any protest situation. Unlike marches and rallies, protests do not always have to be supported by large numbers of people. There are numerous examples of effective one-person protests, or small-group protests. Protests can occur in public or on private premises (e.g. corporate offices, shareholder meetings), and the observations made above about the legal implications of protest on private land are equally applicable.

One issue that activists should consider is whether they should simply protest about something or whether their protest should take the form of a more direct and positive act. This latter form of active protest is known as direct action.

2.5.1 Direct action Direct actions occur when a group of people (often a small group) take an action which is intended to reveal an existing problem, highlight an alternative, or demonstrate a possible solution. These types of action have become very popular with social movements in the last thirty years. Actions such as burning draft cards, releasing factory-farm animals, disrupting duck hunts, delivering rubbish back to the steps of fast-food outlets and disrupting whale hunts are all examples of direct actions that are colourful, bold and informative and which graphically highlight an aspect of the issue being promoted.

2.5.2 The theatre of protest Novel, informative and provocative forms of direct action are more politically effective than many of the conventional models of protesting, such as simply gathering at a location and displaying banners and placards, or public speaking. Successful direct action protests contain an element of theatre. The key advantage of theatrical styles of direct action is that the actions speak for themselves and don't rely on onlookers to read placards and banners to deliver an effective message. If you looked at the action from the perspective of an onlooker, the question 'Why are these people waving placards?' can be transformed into 'Look at all those dead waterbirds collected at the duck hunt' or 'Look at that bleeding baby whale being dragged on to that boat'.

Direct action protests particularly suit the format of TV news in that a quick visual grab can be very effective. This is especially important in the context of shallow media portrayal of political events; an event that speaks for itself conveys a message beyond the way it is described by newsreaders.

The power of theatre in direct action has been the subject of a separate article by the author:

> This understanding of theatre is ... intended to encapsulate a whole range
> of psychological devices associated with protest that can be intricately
> woven into the fabric of the experience. Devices such as imagination, ritual,
> ceremony, romance and symbolism, when combined with bold physical
> acts of protest, disobedience and defiance, produce a powerful medium for
> asserting dissent. (Ricketts 2006: 77)

2.5.3 Empowerment of participants Direct action has other advantages; in particular, it is empowering for those involved because it allows them to directly do something (however symbolic) about a problem, rather than simply beseeching power-holders to respond to the problem. This is what is *direct* about direct action; activists actually take it upon themselves to stop a hunt, return rubbish or stop a logging operation.

As observed by Rogers (1998: 148): 'The power of direct action should not be underestimated. Direct action provokes rebellion, creates cohesion and often changes the values and philosophy of the participants.'

It is also empowering because it gives protesters the ability to portray a new vision of society and even to attempt to enforce this vision rather than adopting the inherently passive position of simply protesting against the status quo. In this sense direct action can challenge the status quo in a very immediate way.

2.5.4 Decentring of opponents When protesters assert control of a space, as they do in blockades, sit-ins and other forms of theatrical direct action, they often also assert some authority. Although these assertions may be short lived they still have an unsettling effect on the people who are the targets of the action because this event may be the first time that person has had their authority, or the authority of their employer or even of the state itself, challenged in such a bold way.

> Theatre in this sense involves not only defying the physical power of the state to prohibit, control, arrest and to punish, but also more importantly defying the power of the dominant paradigm to define the events or even the outcomes for the participants. Through asserting themselves in new and more empowered roles, activists contradict the assumptions and worldview of their opponents ... by the skilful use of theatre, the public appearance of the event is gradually transformed and begins to more and more closely reinforce the interpretations being asserted by the activists. (Ricketts 2006: 80)

2.5.5 Direct action does not need to rely on mass support A key advantage of direct action protest is that it can have a major public impact, yet it can be achieved by a very small group of activists. This is a major advantage for new or cutting-edge campaign groups which do not always have the luxury of being able to mobilize large numbers of people for protests, nor the time to build a campaign to the point where this is possible. Groups of between eight and twenty people can quite successfully accomplish effective direct actions (ibid.: 78).

2.5.6 Lawful direct action protests Although many kinds of direct action are unlawful to some extent, it is possible to conduct direct action protests that are lawful; a good example would be Michael Moore taking a group of people with throat cancer to sing Christmas carols at the offices of a major tobacco company (www.youtube.com/watch?v=eB286VdOkCM).

Sometimes relatively ordinary kinds of political action can be enhanced by the use of theatre without adding to their unlawfulness. A good example of how a lawful procession can be embellished by direct action is a protest against Australian terrorism laws in 2003, in which a campaign group obtained police permission for a procession from a politician's office to a police station. The procession consisted of thirty 'accused' persons chained together and wearing signs around their neck accusing them of quite innocent and formerly lawful acts of political expression that could constitute potential terror offences under the new laws. As part of their supervision of the event, police walked at the front and back of the procession. The presence of the police became part of the theatre of the event, making the procession more visually convincing. Unwittingly the police escort became part of the theatre of protest.

2.5.7 Direct action involving intentional law-breaking Direct action protest does not have to be unlawful, but in practice the most bold and effective actions often are.

It isn't lawful to dump the carcasses of birds killed in a duck hunt on the stairs of the legislature, for example, although in the confusion of a novel action the best that local police may be able to do in such a situation is issue littering fines. If you are lucky, the action will be so novel that there is no law against it yet – for example, riding a surfboard in the bow-wave of a nuclear naval ship (Cohen 1997).

Nonetheless, in many cases activists may have to accept the possibility of criminal charges as the consequence of an otherwise highly successful action. For example, the activist who famously painted 'No War' on the Sydney Opera House on the day the Iraq War started was charged with a graffiti offence and required to pay a substantial clean-up bill as well (*Sydney Morning Herald*, 17 April 2003, www.smh.com.au/articles/2003/04/16/1050172650756. html).

Fortunately, because direct action protests often are novel and surprising, the police may apply inappropriate charges which can be successfully defended later in court, so arrestees should be careful not to admit to charges prematurely.

Arrest and charges are a risk to be weighed up, but the courts are sometimes lenient in sentencing where a peaceful political action has breached the law if it has not involved harm to persons or significant harm to property. This leniency cannot be relied upon, however, and there is an increasing trend towards courts ordering criminal compensation payments from protesters who damage property or delay commercial activity.

As detailed later in the section on intentional law-breaking, the strategic principles behind conscientious acts of disobedience usually suggest that the calculus of the effectiveness of placing an activist or oneself in a knowingly arrestable situation is the effectiveness of the action compared to the gravity of the legal consequences. The more political clout you achieve for each arrest, the more worthwhile it has been.

2.6 Sit-ins and occupations

Sit-ins and occupations are a particular kind of action which usually take place in buildings, but can take place in other areas such as mine sites, woodchip piles, etc. Sit-ins are more commonly associated with large groups, particularly students occupying university or government offices, and occupations involving smaller-scale direct actions by environmental activists. Generally there is an issue of trespass involved, as these kinds of action usually take place in buildings controlled by government agencies, departments or private corporations.

The difference between a sit-in and an occupation mostly relates to style, method and intention, and exemplifies well the role of theatre in framing the way the action appears to onlookers. A sit-in is a basic form of protest usually involving a significant number of persons entering a building and refusing to leave, coupled with the display of banners, placards and information explaining the reason for taking the action. Sit-ins are meant to remain non-violent but, because they are based upon mass disobedience, there is always a risk of unintended action by some participants in the passion of the moment. This is particularly a risk when police attend and begin to remove and arrest protesters, usually using statutory trespass powers (discussed above).

An occupation is a similar action but more pointedly designed as a form of robust direct action. In an occupation the intention of the protesters can be to actually take over the premises, and consequently, and in contrast to a sit-in, they may utilize various technologies to effectively seal the building or premises. Occupations may not need to involve large numbers as more passive sit-ins do, they can be achieved by a small but dedicated group of activists, but the legal consequences are usually more serious than simple trespass charges.

2.6.1 Building occupation: a case study A particularly daring example of a building occupation took place in Sydney, Australia, when the North East Forest Alliance occupied the offices of the state's Forestry Commission in 1992. NEFA already had a long track record of successful forest blockades but aimed to demonstrate its ability to also target the central offices of the Commission.

In that action the entire multi-storey building, including the executive offices and the personal suite of the Forestry Commissioner, was seized by a small group (about twenty) of highly skilled activists. The activists intentionally used a theatrical approach to style the action as more than a sit-in or occupation, and conceived of it as a symbolic coup. NEFA called itself the 'People's Commission for Forests' and issued its own new 'Forestry Charter' and media releases and a list of demands to the state government.

The highly controversial action was executed with precision. Activists had already staked out the building in the days leading up to the action and  had obtained detailed floor plans and fabricated metal devices for holding doors closed from the inside. They had also calculated the precise time that the building's security systems were deactivated in the morning to start allowing workers to arrive. The aim was to take the building unoccupied, and the moment the security gates in the underground car park opened, two carloads of people were delivered into the area and immediately took both lifts and stairwells to predetermined target sites. Within minutes the protesters had secured (closed) all access from the ground floor and basement, occupied the executive floor and commissioner's office (sixth floor), disabled the lifts (by placing pot plants between the doors) and gained access to the roof, where abseilers were able to hang a giant banner proclaiming 'Under New Management'. The group entered with prepared media statements and their new 'Forestry Charter' and proceeded to use the commissioner's official fax machine to send the new charter out to all regional offices throughout the state as an 'urgent directive'. Outside support for media and police liaison had also been arranged beforehand. Detailed description and analysis of the action are available in an article by the author (Ricketts 2006).

This action was highly controversial, attracted a great deal of media and political comment and led to charges not only of trespass but also of intimidation, which is a more serious criminal offence. The action shocked the government, the media and many less radical members of the environment movement. Debate continues about whether such a confrontational action is advisable politically, particularly in the more recent context of heightened sensitivities aroused by fears of terrorism.

The action was a non-violent action and certainly not a terrorist operation in any way – no one was armed (or harmed), no one's identity was concealed, all interactions with staff in the building were respectful, care was taken to minimize property damage as far as possible, arrests were all conducted peacefully and no one resisted arrest when the police finally gained access to the building. Nonetheless, even in the pre-9/11 atmosphere of 1992, allegations of terrorism were made by opponents of the group on the day, and anyone conducting a similar action today would be advised to carefully check existing anti-terror laws because the definitions of terrorism offences have been drawn so widely and vaguely that a great number of quite peaceful political actions could these days be caught in the anti-terror net.

What was powerful about the action was the way in which it was presented as a coup, as a people-power action to remove a corrupt government agency and institute new measures. One of the coordinators of the group later observed that all eleven demands of the people's charter were subsequently achieved several years later (Corkill, personal communication, 4 April 2011).

2.6.2 Legal implications of sit-ins and occupations Sit-ins and occupations obviously lead to trespass charges, but more serious charges are possible. In Australia, at both the federal and state level (and in other relevant jurisdictions), there is a serious criminal charge of 'intimidation' (sometimes also called 'watch and beset'). It was originally developed to criminalize various activities associated with trade union pickets in which direct action would be taken by unionists to prevent work from taking place, such as pickets, lock-outs and lock-downs of tools and equipment. These charges have also been used frequently against protesters involved in other forms of direct action. The Australian offence is found in Section 545 (b) of the Crimes Act 1900 (NSW), and an almost identical provision can be found in the Canadian Criminal Code at s423. This offence includes but is not limited to the use of violence or intimidation to prevent a person doing that which he has a lawful right to do. Despite the fact that the offence is often referred to as intimidation, there need be no element of intimidation involved. The section is very wide and makes it an offence simply to hinder any person in the use of tools. Clearly this is wide enough to be a risk for activists who take direct action to try to stop environmentally destructive activities, or conduct sit-ins or blockades. In the Australian case of *Keenan* (1994 76 A Crim R 374) the appellant was convicted of an offence under s545 (b) after having chained himself to logging equipment to prevent logging in forests in the south-east.

In the United Kingdom harassment laws in various pieces of legislation, including the Protection from Harassment Act 1997 (UK) and the Serious

Organized Crime and Police Act 2005 (s125), cover similar circumstances to those coming under 'intimidation' laws elsewhere, specifically being triggered where conduct is designed to discourage people from engaging in a lawful activity.

It is also important to ensure that the original entry to the premises is conducted lawfully; entering a closed or locked building outside of usual hours of business could lead to charges for housebreaking-type offences.

The above discussion is meant to alert activists to some of the more common legal consequences, such as charges of statutory trespass (discussed earlier in this chapter) and more serious charges such as intimidation or harassment. Obviously the precise laws will differ from one jurisdiction to another and laws are continually changing. Activists and organizers should always consult local laws at the time. The discussion also presupposes that participants are engaged in entirely non-violent activities, and consequently regular criminal charges in relation to assault, resisting arrest or assaulting police, or in relation to property damage, have not been discussed.

2.7 Blockades

Blockades have been a regular feature of environmental protests, particularly in relation to threatened old-growth forests in the United States, Canada and Australia since the 1970s. They are also common in relation to campaigns to protect heritage buildings from demolition, which is a more common context for blockades in the UK. Blockades as a tactic reflect the urgency felt by activists when irreplaceable aspects of the natural or built environment are being destroyed.

2.7.1 Usefulness of blockades Blockades by themselves rarely prevent the destruction for long, because the overwhelming force of the state is usually brought to bear against blockaders, but used in conjunction with other tools of advocacy blockades are a powerful political tool. The sheer physical nature of blockades can be indispensable in protecting areas from immediate destruction while other, slower strategies are pursued, such as seeking injunctions through the courts, or seeking longer-term political change. Blockades also generate large amounts of media interest and publicity and elevate conflicts over icon areas into major political issues.

Interference by Greenpeace and Sea Shepherd activists with Japanese whale hunting in the southern oceans is a prominent example of blockade-type tactics being used to resist physical destruction while also generating compelling visual images to support a wider political campaign.

2.7.2 Blockades, non-violence and personal risk Blockades require high levels of organization, skill and courage, and usually involve key participants being charged with minor offences. To be effective in stopping heavy earth-moving equipment activists are required to place their own bodies on the line, usually in ingenious blockade installations, and rely on their opponents to stop short of causing them serious physical injury or death. Obviously this tactic works only where there is a clear cultural restraint against causing death and injury and routinely enforced legal consequences for any acts that intentionally or negligently cause harm to others. Blockades in developed countries are conducted within the cultural context of non-violence and respect for human life, but they have also been used by some indigenous peoples, such as the Penan in Malaysia, to resist rainforest logging (intercontinentalcry.org/malaysia-penan-blockade-demolished-let-the-deforestation-begin/).

2.7.3 Blockade devices Blockaders, particularly in the forests of Australia and North America and in heritage building and anti-motorway demonstrations in the UK, have utilized a range of devices, such as:

- tripods (where a protester sits at the apex of a 5–6-metre-high tripod to block a road, risking injury if tipped off);
- burying of people in roads, sometimes inside concrete drainage pipes;
- the use of steel locks (often called 'dragons') on devices to lock arms around machinery or into road surfaces;
- occupation of and locking on to machinery such as bulldozers and tower cranes;
- other devices to slow down the movement of earth-moving equipment.

The use of blockade devices is intended to make it time-consuming to safely remove the protester who is obstructing continued disputed work. Despite the apparent dangers, it is usually far safer to attempt to conduct blockades using a small number of people with well-constructed and robust blockade devices than to attempt to resist by use of large groups of people simply staring down developers, contractors or police.

Large group actions are volatile and usually result in 'rugby scrums' between protesters and protestees which lead to mass arrests and often to unnecessary charges such as assault and/or hindering police.

By contrast, where blockaders are well entrenched with robust devices which require expert removal by police rescue squads, the atmosphere is likely to remain calm and largely professional, and there is little likelihood of renegade actions by opponents. What is vital in blockades is concern for the safety of those attached to devices; simply keeping watch is a lawful activity which all the other supporters can engage in while one or a few brave souls are cut free or otherwise extracted from blockade devices.

The underlying strategic approach to the use of blockade devices is not only to achieve maximum physical effect, but also to reduce the potential for violent flare-ups, minimize arrests and ensure that the maximum time delay is achieved for each arrestable situation.

Blockade devices come in many forms. An excellent guide to how to construct and use an array of blockade devices called the 'Intercontinental Deluxe Guide to Blockading' is available at the NEFA website (nefa.org. au/ or nefa.org.au/icdgb/files/icdgb.htm).

2.7.4 Legal implications of blockades Blockaders are usually subject to a range of charges previously discussed, including:

* statutory trespass;
* obstruction;
* intimidation or harassment.

In addition to the above offences there can also be site-specific offences where specific legislation creates special offences or powers of exclusion in relation to state-controlled forest areas, military establishments or mine or industrial sites. These need to be investigated at the local level.

In Australia, for example, the prevalence of forest blockades has led to the creation of special legislation that empowers forest officers to issue orders to individuals to leave an area and creates an offence for failure to leave. See, for example, the regulations in the Forestry Act 1916 in NSW.

These very arbitrary powers created to prevent forestry blockades were used as a template in designing regulations to apply to the site of the Sydney Olympics, and almost identical provisions now appear in the regulations of the Homebush Bay Operations Act 1999 (NSW).

This pattern of establishing special zones within which conventional civil liberties are further restricted in areas where protest is likely is a growing trend in the United States, Canada, Australia and the United Kingdom, and is discussed earlier in this chapter under its US descriptor of 'free speech zones'.

3.0 Avoiding unnecessary arrest

The forms of political action described above are all non-violent, and with the exception of rallies and marches can all be achieved effectively with quite small numbers of activists, minimum arrests and maximum impact.

There are a number of important considerations to remember when undertaking political action that may involve 'arrestable situations', including:

- Make sure you have a clear understanding of what the arrestable situations are.
- Keep these to a minimum and provide opportunities for the rest of the group to participate in non-arrestable roles.
- Sometimes the delineation between arrestable and non-arrestable situations may require some negotiation and clarification with senior police in attendance, but police are usually happy to be consulted on this topic.
- Generally avoid mass arrest scenarios as a tactic.

Strategically, large mass arrest actions are seldom effective unless you have a very large group, willing to be arrested, or sometimes where it is the last line of defence, or where you are confident that for various reasons the police will not logistically be able to cope with mass disobedience (insufficient police in attendance, insufficient transport for arrestees, etc.).

Usually, successful direct action depends on ensuring that arrests are kept to a minimum and that every arrest is justified strategically by reference to what is achieved by the person in the arrestable situation. For example, one activist arrested for dropping a huge banner from a building or bridge, or one arrested after several hours locked on to a bulldozer, is usually worthwhile. Mass sit-down arrestees, on the other hand, are quickly removed, achieve little in the way of a lasting strategic outcome and tie your group down in bail procedures and conditions and court appearances and fines for months to come. Where you have minimum arrests, your group also has the advantage of being able to concentrate on the legal defence against the charges as they come to court.

3.1 Avoiding unnecessary charges

As discussed earlier, conscientious objectors have a moral claim of entitlement to break the law, provided they are non-violent, do not destroy property and do so openly and for the purpose of making a bona fide political statement. It is vital that in choosing to do so they do not commit other collateral offences unrelated to making that political statement. The most common charges that fall into this category are those related to resisting arrest. There are various different names for such offences in different jurisdictions, but in all relevant jurisdictions there are common criminal offences in relation to hindering police, resisting arrest and assaulting police.

3.1.1 Do not resist arrest An activist in an arrestable situation should, once apprehended and removed from any obstacle to which they may be attached, cooperate with the police. Attempts to evade capture amount to hindrance, and worse still any act of striking or pushing a police officer will lead to further charges of assaulting police. These charges are to be avoided. They are unrelated to making the political statement, they look bad when reported in the media, they damage the fragile relationship between protesters and police, and they will stick even if the initial charges for which the person was being arrested are later dropped or defeated.

Frequently activists oppose operations that themselves are of dubious legality. In these situations it is common for charges to be dropped on the basis that the protester had a lawful excuse for their actions in that they were preventing a greater offence (e.g. illegal destruction of forest). In these circumstances, any charges of resisting, hindrance or assault will still stand because they are a separate offence to the initial charge of obstruction, trespass or intimidation.

3.1.2 Avoid offensive behaviour or language Another area in which unnecessary charges can be applied is in relation to offensive behaviour or language. Offensive language charges can be laid where protesters become impassioned and use profane words that are not acceptable in public settings. Offensive behaviour charges can also be laid where protesters use offensive gestures or display banners or placards that can be viewed as offensive. Again, such arrests have little or no relationship to the political statements being made and usually generate negative publicity for the campaign.

3.1.3 Graffiti offences Another source of collateral arrests is charges in relation to defacing property and graffiti. These were once minor offences, but in most jurisdictions the penalties for such offences have risen dramatically over the last twenty years as authorities become more concerned about the prevalence of graffiti.

Of course, it is important to point out that graffiti charges may not always be a form of collateral arrest. If the main form of civil disobedience that is being practised in a direct action is daubing graffiti, then obviously this is an intentional arrestable offence rather than provoking a collateral arrest. A good example of such an action would be the famous painting of 'No War' on the Sydney Opera House in 2003. In such a case the graffiti offence is the direct action, and the collateral charge to avoid would be resisting arrest.

3.1.4 Avoid unnecessary property damage Property damage that is not absolutely necessary for successful execution of a direct action should be avoided carefully as it is another way of provoking unnecessary collateral arrest. There are times when minor property damage may be unavoidable – where, for example, protesters are digging lock-on devices into roads, breaking locks to gain access to protest sites and so on – but these should be kept to an absolute minimum.

The spirit of non-violence that informs responsible social movements requires that property damage be kept to an absolute minimum. While whether this is a necessary caveat for non-violence is contested by some more radical commentators, it is more generally accepted that techniques that involve widespread property damage are harmful to the public image of campaigns and are likely to provoke violent responses from the owners of damaged property and from authorities. For this reason the small groups of black-clad youths that seem to turn up at many major global protests and engage in property damage are a major embarrassment to the responsible social movements involved, and a counterproductive force.

The issue of minimum necessary property damage is discussed in more detail in Chapter 2.

3.1.5 Keeping intentional law-breaking in perspective Protests that involve arrestable situations invoke the traditional common-law recognition of the role of the conscientious objector. There is some extant degree of sympathy in the general community and among liberal judges for such conscientious law-breakers, but this sympathy cannot be expected to extend to collateral actions that constitute unnecessary and separate criminal offences. It must be remembered that the most important work of a social movement is to foster change in community values around a particular issue, and this means soliciting and building public support. Excessive use of confrontational tactics tends to erode public support and can consequently be counterproductive.

4.0 Ways to make political actions safer and more effective

There are a number of good practices that will help to keep political actions safer and more effective. This is important both at the time of the event and as a longer-term strategic consideration, because it is important that people are encouraged to attend political events and many people will be discouraged if they become violent or disorganized, or if misbehaviour is not responded to appropriately.

4.1 Police liaison

In any political action in which police attendance is likely it is important to have a specific person appointed to act as police liaison. The role requires someone who can be both confident and courteous. The police liaison person is responsible for maintaining contact and communication between the body of protesters and the police in attendance.

It is helpful for this person to introduce themselves at the earliest possible opportunity to the most senior police officer in attendance. Police dislike mob scenes where they need to try to talk to many people at once, and will usually appreciate a clear and courteous liaison person.

4.1.1 The police liaison person is not in control It is usually necessary to point out to the police that as the liaison person you are not an organizer, you have no power to control the group, and that they are all individuals acting voluntarily. Your role is only to assist the police to communicate with the assembled group and sometimes to help negotiate some 'understandings'. It is absolutely essential that the police liaison person does not present themselves as a protest leader or organizer or describe themselves as having any authority over the group or any other individual.

Maintaining a clear line that you are able only to assist with communication but have no control means that police cannot give you any directions beyond your own capacity as an individual citizen. They cannot order you to give instructions to the crowd or to prevent any other person's behaviour, nor can you be held responsible for the acts of any person or group. There are a number of offences under various pieces of legislation that pertain to 'organizers'. It may even be wise to carry a card with an explanatory note that defines the nature of your role and hand this to the police. In the event that you were charged with offences as an 'organizer' this would constitute important evidence in your favour in subsequent court hearings.

4.1.2 Clarify arrestable and non-arrestable situations Most importantly, the police liaison person should explain to the police that the majority of the people in attendance do not intend to break the law or be arrested and they should ask the most senior police officer where these people can remain if they do not wish to be arrested. It is at this point that the liaison person may need to be a little firm if the police officer gives instructions that exceed their powers.

In most situations a senior officer will let you know that 'provided the rest of the people stand over there they will not be arrested', and you should communicate that to your group.

Your role may involve some negotiation with police about what actions are going to be seen as acceptable; in negotiating in this way make sure you act only as the messenger between the group and the police – do not make the mistake of appearing to be in control of the crowd.

4.1.3 The right to be arrested and processed according to law If there are to be arrestable situations, the liaison person must explain to the police that some members may choose to place themselves in an arrestable situation and accept arrest as a consequence, and that no attempt will be made to hinder or to assault police.

In some cases police take offence at the fact that some people are knowingly going to break the law. It is a good idea to explain that they are making a political statement, which they have a right to do, and if they break the law 'they have a right to be arrested and processed according to the law'. This rather odd-sounding 'right to be arrested' is an amazingly simple way of clarifying the difference between a riot and an orderly demonstration of civil disobedience. From personal experience, this explanation usually calms the police officer down and defuses confrontation.

It is surprising how good relations can sometimes be between police and protesters where a few simple ground rules are observed. It needs to be remembered that police often deal with aggressive people or criminals who are dishonest and trying to conceal their actions. It can be very refreshing for police to deal with polite, honest and respectful law-breakers.

4.2 Legal observers

Legal observers perform a different role to that of police liaison. They are responsible for observing an action to ensure that police and other personnel (the other side) comply with the law. They are responsible for the collection of evidence, statements and statutory declarations, evidence of police malpractice such as assaults against protesters, and following up on the treatment of arrestees, bail and so on. This function has a role in assisting in all legal follow-up that may be necessary after the event, including court appearances and complaints about police behaviour. It may be useful to identify legal observers with badges or T-shirts so that your opponents or the police can see that you have this kind of back-up available. Law students are often a good source of candidates for this role.

4.3 Cameras, videos

Cameras are great peacekeepers. Video cameras are even better. They can be used to gather evidence that can later be used in court. Even when they are not working they are still excellent to give police or opponents (of whatever kind) the impression that your group will record and follow up any unacceptable behaviour towards non-violent protesters.

4.4 Media liaison, generating your own media

As important as good police liaison is good media liaison. Publicity is usually a core motivation behind direct action, and writing good media releases, inviting media to attend well beforehand and even providing them with broadcast-quality digital video snippets can be very rewarding. Journalists will not usually warn police or your opposition of an intended action when you have offered them a scoop. If they do, no scoops again ever! If it is absolutely essential that your action has an element of surprise, then it may be useful to prearrange media releases and have a set time at which they are sent, just as the action begins but too late for any leaks to be a problem.

4.5 Two-way radio, mobile phones

Good communication is an essential. Especially in large group situations or remote terrain, it assists with safety, with strategy and with providing good information to the media. Chapter 9 on digital activism discusses the various uses of mobile phones in modern protests.

4.6 Follow-up support for arrestees (bail, legal defence, fines)

This is essential. Arrestees are your martyrs and should be treated with great respect, especially in the boring, inconvenient days and weeks of court processes that follow. If police liaison and legal observers have been doing their job your group should be able to offer valuable support to arrestees. There are publicly funded lawyers in most jurisdictions who can offer basic assistance to arrestees in court, but you will often be able to find private lawyers who sympathize with your cause who will offer some pro bono assistance for your arrestees as well.

4.7 Complaints

Protest actions usually generate a myriad of individual complaints about police heavy-handedness. Usually it is impossible to usefully process these because of a lack of reliable evidence. In addition to collecting evidence by having active legal observers at protests, complainants should be encouraged to make statutory declarations immediately after such events, and these should be collected to be taken up either with senior police or appropriate complaint-handling bodies such as the Office of the Ombudsman. Such complaints cost protesters nothing, but are a major headache to police. Police will be better behaved at protests if they think your group has the skills and determination to bring them to account for every significant procedural breach.

5.0 Terrorism and anti-terrorist laws

It is essential in a democracy to preserve the right to non-violent direct action and political protest. Unfortunately many governments around the world have seized upon the spectre of terrorism as an excuse for imposing draconian and anti-democratic regimes of suppression of dissent. Terrorism laws should not be an issue for non-violent protesters, but unfortunately the unnecessarily wide reach of such laws in many cases means they need to be considered.

As one of the few countries that lacks any comprehensive bill of rights instrument, Australia has some of the widest, most ambiguous and most draconian anti-terror laws of all the countries being considered in this book. The bills of rights in Canada, the United Kingdom and the United States have provided some boundaries to legislative inventiveness in drafting anti-terror laws, although even in those countries these laws are also very far-reaching.

5.1.1 Wide definitions of a 'terrorist act' The definition of terrorism in Australia is extremely wide, and it is vital that activists remain zealously faithful to a code of non-violence and the avoidance of serious property damage if they are to avoid being demonized under this label. Even so, some extremist politicians will probably still attempt this. An act of terrorism as defined in the legislation can include any politically or ideologically motivated action which leads to serious property damage or personal harm. A similar basic definition of a terrorist act is used in Australian, UK and Canadian anti-terror laws.

5.1.2 Secondary offences Anti-terror laws around the world constitute a substantial threat to existing rights of political association and free expression. This unnecessarily wide reach of anti-terror laws occurs because such legislation typically creates a new range of serious criminal offences based upon a broadly constructed definition of 'an act of terrorism', together with secondary offences for providing training or other assistance to 'terrorist organizations', and increased powers of surveillance, detention and interrogation of those suspected or accused of terrorism-related offences, or of having information about any suspects.

The offences established under such legislation are often wide enough to seriously restrict the rights of persons to take part in international political campaigns, even by way of sending donations, medicines training or providing support generally for independence or even pro-democracy movements of their choice in other countries. Had these laws been in force during the apartheid struggles in South Africa or East Timor's struggle for independence from Indonesia, then any support offered by citizens of developed countries to support resistance movements in those countries could have constituted a terrorism offence. This is remarkable given that Nelson Mandela and leaders of the East Timorese resistance have since been awarded Nobel peace prizes. It goes to show that one person's freedom fighter is another person's terrorist.

More worrying still is the fact that these laws provide increased powers to security personnel that could be used not just against genuine terrorist sympathizers, but against any politically active citizens who are accused of such offences (Ricketts 2002). Anti-terror legislation affecting the UK, the USA, Australia and Canada includes the following:

Canada
- Anti-terrorism Act 2001, c. 41 (Can)
- Criminal Code 1985 (Can) Part 11.1

United States
- The USA Patriot Act (H.R. 3162) (USA)

United Kingdom
- Terrorism Act 2000 (UK)
- Anti-terrorism, Crime and Security Act 2001 (UK)
- Terrorism Act 2006

Australia
- Anti-terrorism Act 2004
- Anti-terrorism Act (No. 2) 2005
- Security Legislation Amendment (Terrorism) Act 2002
- Criminal Code Act 1995 (Cth) Part 5.3

Conclusion

Public political events and actions are an important part of most campaigns and an essential part of the practice of participatory democracy. It is important from a strategic perspective for activists to be aware of the advantages and disadvantages of particular forms of public event, and to be able to effectively plan for any legal implications that may be applicable. It is not possible in an international publication to provide precise advice about the laws in place in particular places at particular times, but this chapter has examined the main forms of legal regulation that apply to protests in the jurisdictions under consideration. Whether organizers aim for strict compliance with all laws or accept that some limited form of civil disobedience is required, it is important to be aware of the ground rules for safe and effective public political events.

NINE | **Digital activism**

Introduction

Digital technology has dramatically expanded the range of tools available to the modern activist. In this chapter we examine the way new technologies 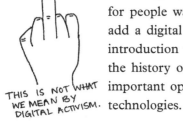 are being used by activists and provide practical advice for people wanting to launch a new digital campaign or add a digital component to an existing campaign. As an introduction to the bigger picture we also briefly explore the history of digital activism, and consider some of the important opportunities and challenges of using the new technologies.

1.0 What is digital activism?

Modern communications technology is transforming the way social change work is undertaken. It is important to ask ourselves what digital activism is, and to what extent it is actually different to or separate from the kind of activism that came before it. The term digital activism (Joyce 2010) is used for this chapter because it is wide enough to include the use of a range of online tools as well as the growing use of mobile-phone-based technologies. Terms like net activism, cyber activism and online activism may not be wide enough to include mobile and SMS technologies.

Digital activism describes all of the ways in which activists harness the power of digital networks. The term is used with the intention of distinguishing digital activism from the more conventional non-digital forms (snail mailing, street theatre, face-to-face networking and graffiti campaigns, etc.) for the purposes of discussion. In practice, however, there is no definite divide between digital and non-digital activism because most successful campaigns combine elements of both.

It is also difficult to exhaustively list the precise forms of media that are encompassed by the term digital activism, simply because the field continues to expand rapidly. However, a current if non-exhaustive list would include:

- the Internet;
- e-mail;

- social media (Web 2.0);
- currently popular and influential social networking tools such as Facebook, Twitter, YouTube;
- mobile phones; and
- dedicated websites for digital activism such as Move On, GetUp and Avaaz.

This list could be endlessly expanded to include a wide range of specialized and non-specialized software applications that can facilitate campaigning and activist activities and numerous websites that offer training in relation to digital activism.

Digital activism has enormous potential to expand the capacities of activists and social movements, but it is important to remember that it is not separate from more 'traditional' or even novel non-digital forms at all. The strategic background, core values and basic purpose of activism and social change work have not changed, but the tools and the tactics may have. Ultimately it's the activism which is the important part rather than the chosen tools, technologies and infrastructures. It's also important to appreciate the interlocking and mutually reinforcing nature of digital and non-digital forms of activism. While it can be very satisfying to generate a lot of activity in the digital world, the important test of effectiveness is how well such activity translates to change in the real world.

1.1 Digital activism: a very brief history

The use of digital technologies for activism is in a state of rapid growth and constant change and refinement. Digital and electronic forms of communication have expanded rapidly since the US defence research network known as ARPANET first appeared in the 1970s. During the 1990s the Internet was progressively opened up to public use as it developed into the World Wide Web. Since that time development has been rapid, in terms of both commercial and perhaps more surprisingly non-commercial usages, as evidenced by the open source movement and the ever-growing availability of free online applications, software and a variety of other tools (Scholtz 2010: 17–32), as well as an explosion in digitally based political activism.

One of the most widely known and prominent examples of the early use of digital activism tools took place in the context of the protests against the 1999 World Trade Organization meeting, often referred to as the 'Battle of Seattle'. During that event digital activism contributed to the effectiveness of the protests in several key ways, including the establishment and usage of the independent media centre IndyMedia (ibid.: 23), the use of smart mobbing tactics whereby activists used SMS communications to coordinate actions and evade police (Cullum 2010: 58), and distributed denial-of-service attacks (DDoS) designed to jam the e-mail and Internet systems being used by the WTO (Radcliff 2000; www.networkworld.com/research/2000/0529feat2.html).

Today the Internet is awash with activist sites, campaigns and lively use of social media to promote political causes. It has become essential for major campaigns to maintain an active digital campaign presence and important for new groups and new campaigns to put energy into developing the digital side of their campaign plans.

1.2 The basic toolkit

This section takes a very brief look at the main tools that are important for modern activists and social movements to engage with. A more detailed examination of each tool and tips on how to make best use of them is provided later in this chapter.

1.2.1 Web 2.0 social media More recent innovations, including social media tools such as Facebook, YouTube and Twitter, have greatly enlarged the range of digital tools available to activists. While these tools are largely designed to provide access for recreational and commercial purposes, their popularity and in particular their capacity to allow messages and information to 'go viral' have meant that they have become important sites for digital activism. These tools have provided easily accessible platforms through which individuals and groups can download, upload and share information, photos and digital video, without needing to have unusual levels of technical expertise.

1.2.2 Mobile technologies The ever-increasing ubiquity of mobile phones and of mobile Internet connectivity has also greatly expanded the scope for digital activism using these technologies. As a result of massive growth in mobile phone usage, particularly in developing countries, it has recently been estimated that there are around five billion users of mobile phone technology worldwide (UN News Centre 2010).

Mobile technology is particularly well suited to facilitating largely spontaneous public demonstrations and has proved particularly effective in a number of repressive regimes where other forms of communication are being censored or blocked. Mobile phones were used to facilitate street demonstrations during the 2004 Orange Revolution in Ukraine (Cullum 2010: 50).

In 2007, SMS messaging was used to help organize the gathering of an estimated one million people in Xiamen, China, to protest against the building of a proposed toxic chemical plant (ibid.: 50). In popular uprisings in the Middle East in 2011, mobile phones were used both to organize protests and to spread photos and other images of violence by security forces (www.mobiledia.com/news/82525.html).

1.2.3 The emergence of 'host' organizations Host organizations represent a very real way in which digital technology has actively encouraged the evolution of relatively new forms of activist organization. Host organizations aim to establish themselves as a service available to any number of issue-based campaigns to further their campaign aims. They are easy to join and invite members to suggest and become involved in new campaigns. Campaign methodology is mostly by means of e-mail and online fund-raising and petitions.

Host organizations differ from more traditional groups because they deliberately lack a central issue around which the organization is built, although obviously they do have unifying ethical and political focal points. At times the host itself becomes the campaigner, but even in this setting the campaign is only one of a number of completely separate campaigns being run simultaneously. MoveOn.org in the USA, GetUp.org in Australia and Avaaz.org internationally are good examples of this relatively new style of activist 'host' organization.

Both GetUp and Move On centre their activities around parliamentary or representative politics by providing a means for members to contribute to campaigns aimed at pressuring politicians to respond to particular concerns.

GetUp in Australia has more recently broadened its range of campaigning activities. In addition to targeting government and politicians, GetUp now raises funds to run advertisements on chosen topics, including campaigning against corporate targets (www.getup.org.au/campaigns/save-our-forests/no-harvey-no/the-ad-they-dont-want-us-to-see).

GetUp has also been successful in running test cases through the courts. In the lead-up to the 2010 general election in Australia, GetUp was instrumental in running a constitutional challenge in the High Court of Australia that overturned previously existing legislation that limited the ability of new voters to enrol to vote after an election had been called (*Rowe & Anor* v. *Electoral Commissioner & Anor*, 6 August 2010). Within weeks of that successful case, GetUp also succeeded in establishing the legality of enrolments submitted online (*GetUp Limited & Ors* v. *Electoral Commissioner*). It is quite possible that these actions by GetUp could have helped affect the balance of votes in a national election that was one of the closest on record.

At the international level Avaaz.org performs a similar role, boasting on its own website: 'In 3 years, Avaaz has grown to 5.5 million members from every country on earth, becoming the largest global web movement in history' (www.avaaz.org/en/about.php).

The membership base and outreach of these groups are impressive, and where they combine purely digital activism with more traditional forms of activism they become even more potent as change agents.

Both Move On and GetUp have begun to move beyond purely digital campaigning and are actively re-engaging with face-to-face meetings as a means of more effectively grounding the campaigns in local communities. In most instances this involves mobilizing people to attend specific rallies and actions or to work at polling stations. Move On also has a network of locally based Move On councils, which provide an opportunity for face-to-face networking in local communities. Similarly, GetUp has begun to establish local community get-togethers to organize for events such as elections (www.getup.org.au/community/gettogethers/series.php?id=28).

This combination of digital campaigning and more intimate face-to-face meetings is likely to strengthen the networks and to enhance the effectiveness of their digital campaigns.

2.0 Digital tools and their impact on modern activism

The dual evolution of the Internet as both a site of commercialization and an active and surprisingly open community of information has triggered much debate about its emancipatory capacity. What is clear is that the tools made available by emerging digital technologies continue to be taken up by social movements and activists all over the planet as part of the ongoing evolution of the art and practice of activism.

Activist use of digital technology includes the use of both dedicated activism websites and even dedicated activist tools together with the co-option of mass popular platforms for communication such as mobile phones and networking media such as YouTube, Facebook and Twitter, as well as the use of blog sites and wikis. Activist use is facilitated not just by the technologies themselves, but also by new forms of organization that have begun to grow around them. What has occurred in recent years is that more traditional social movement campaign organizations (political parties, NGOs, small campaign groups) have taken up digital activism and incorporated it into the larger picture of their campaign activities.

Loose networked social movements existed long before digital activism tools became available, but there is a productive interplay between the potentials of the new tools and the networked nature of non-formal campaign organizations which has allowed non-formal networked groups to propagate and expand more rapidly than they could previously. Loosely networked digital activist groups, including host organizations, in many ways resemble the community-based environment centres of the 1980s that acted as a host to a multitude of local campaign groups; however, the scale and professionalism of these newer digital organizations are greater by an order of magnitude.

2.1 Current debates about digital activism: is it merely placebo activism?

It is easy to become enthusiastic about the potential of new technologies to revolutionize the work of activists and social media, but it is also important to consider the possible risks or downsides and to make sure that older and more established methods for achieving social change are not discarded prematurely. There is currently much debate about the effectiveness of digital activism, but for current purposes it is sufficient to quickly summarize this and move on to more practical issues. At its simplest, at one end of the scale are those who probably overestimate the emancipatory capacity of the new technologies, and at the other those who criticize them as little more than a distraction.

Wilhelm (2000) characterized three distinct positions in such debate as represented by the following descriptions:

- *dystopians*, whom he described as being wary of the potential of emerging technologies to disrupt social and political life, particularly face-to-face political interactions, which are seen as more authentic;
- *neofuturists*, whom he described as having an uncritical faith in progress and an acceptance of novel emerging technologies as juggernauts; and
- *technorealists*, who occupy the middle ground and seek to critically assess the role that tools and interfaces actually play in everyday life (ibid.: 15).

Few people would openly identify themselves as being other than realists these days, but what is important is to ascertain the real effectiveness of digital campaigning and whether large online or SMS-based networks really facilitate effective political action on the ground.

A good example of a critique of digital activism appeared in a recent article in the *Guardian* newspaper. In a strongly worded critique of digital

activism and the tactics employed by host organizations such as MoveOn.
org, Micah White argues that

> This model of activism uncritically embraces the ideology of marketing. It
> accepts that the tactics of advertising and market research used to sell toilet
> paper can also build social movements ... Political engagement becomes
> a matter of clicking a few links. In promoting the illusion that surfing the
> web can change the world, clicktivism is to activism as McDonalds is to a
> slow-cooked meal. It may look like food, but the life-giving nutrients are
> long gone ... they unfairly compete with legitimate local organisations who
> represent an authentic voice of their communities ... Digital activism is a
> danger to the left. Its ineffectual marketing campaigns spread political cyni-
> cism and draw attention away from genuinely radical movements. Political
> passivity is the end result of replacing salient political critique with the logic
> of advertising. (Micah White, *Guardian*, 12 August 2010)

White's critique is polemic, but it does alert us to the risks of having
uncritical faith in the seemingly large demographic reach of digital activist
technologies. The digital age has made surfing through vast quantities of
information possible, entertaining and even potentially addictive for many.
But there is a danger that a significant proportion of the online activity that
appears in the quantitative analysis of activism sites does not really translate
into effective political action that achieves results. Facebook 'causes' are a
good example. Some well-run campaigns use Facebook groups and causes
to good effect (see, for example, Australian Youth Climate Coalition, www.
facebook.com/AYCC.org.au?v=info#!/AYCC.org.au?v=wall), but the overwhelming majority of even the serious causes (excluding the ever-growing
multitude of joke causes and groups) are little more than placebo groups
where the only real contribution supporters make is to join or to click a
'like' button. The real impact of many of these causes upon power-holders
is likely to be very small unless they also effectively harness the support
and translate it into real outcomes that are felt by power-holders. The risk
of 'placebo activism' can be that individuals feel a sense of having been
heard or having made a difference when they haven't.

What this critique of 'clicktivism' or placebo activism leads us to is the
realization that amid all the masses of statistics that we can collect, we need
to develop some measures of campaign success.

2.1.1 Measuring success How should we measure the success of a campaign?
It might seem logical to measure the success of a campaign by its political

impact, but this can be very difficult during the currency of the campaign. Most campaigns require the raising of public awareness over time, the building of political pressure and quite often far-reaching changes in widely held social values. For this reason we often cannot really measure political effectiveness until after the campaign has ended.

Quantitative measurement is also problematic. In traditional campaigning quantitative measurement may have included numbers of people attending protests, numbers of names on petitions and so on. These numbers had meaning only because of the previous experience of campaigners and the knowledge they had about what level of support was needed to achieve political impact. Digital activism technologies lend themselves to extensive and detailed quantitative analysis, where visitors to sites, hits, names, posts, online petitions and other activities are easily measured. Unfortunately there have not been enough studies done, nor experience gained, to really establish what levels of support are likely to translate into significant political shifts.

The practical answer is that there is no harm in collecting data, and certainly no harm in using technologies that enable massive outreach and which make different levels of participation easy for people, but that measurement of success needs to be tempered with some realism. A practical approach to measuring success in an ongoing campaign is to set staged campaign goals from the outset so that there is some ability to monitor progress towards these stages as the campaign progresses. Some ways of measuring campaign success were discussed in Chapter 3. It will never be an exact science, but the value of statistics is in the knowledge base we use to interpret them, so measuring participation statistics and correlating these with campaign sub-goals is an important way to institute some internal mechanisms for assessing progress.

2.1.2 Digital technologies: emancipatory tools or surveillance technology?

An even more worrying critique of the emancipatory capacity of digital activism is provided by those who argue that it also carries a high risk of facilitating surveillance by state-based agencies. While there have been some impressive instances of digital activism unleashing significant displays of popular resistance in eastern Europe, China and the Middle East, for example, there is an ever-present risk that oppressive governments can also use the new technologies to enhance their own surveillance and suppression activities.

Social networking, then, has inadvertently made it easier to gather intelligence about activist networks. Even a tiny security flaw in the settings of one Facebook profile can compromise the security of many others ... Despite what digital enthusiasts tell you, the emergence of new digital spaces for dissent also lead to new ways of tracking it. Analogue activism was pretty safe: if one node in a protest network got busted, the rest of the group was probably OK. But getting access to an activist's inbox puts all their interlocutors in the frame, too. (Morozov Evigeny, 'How dictators watch us on the web', *Prospect*, 165, 18 November 2009, www.prospect magazine.co.uk/2009/11/how-dictators-watch-us-on-the-web/)

Debates about the real value of digital activism are worth heeding, not only to gain a more realistic view of the risks and opportunities presented

by the digital age, but more importantly to encourage us to develop more strategic ways of using the technologies. The position advocated here is that activism is activism and tools are tools. Tools are only as good as what they are being used for and the skill and experience of the persons using them. The effectiveness of all the tools and techniques will still depend upon the strategic focus and planning of the campaigners using them. It is this practical view of digital activism which informs this chapter, and in the pages that follow our focus will be on examining the tools with a view to uncovering the best ways to use them to achieve campaign success.

Once we are aware of the range of tools available, it becomes important to consider how they can be integrated into a particular campaign in a beneficial way. If they don't actually lead to a substantial benefit then they may not be worth the investment of time and possibly money.

3.0 Choosing and using digital tools

The first trap to be avoided in choosing whether to use digital tools for campaigns is to assume that adding such tools will automatically make the campaign more effective. Instead, like any campaign decision, it is a strategic decision which needs to be made in the context of the campaign as a whole.

There are often a lot of inflated expectations that accompany the introduction of new technologies, and some technologies meet or surpass these expectations and become embedded in social practice, and others don't. To add to the complexity, it may not always be the technically best tool which becomes the dominant tool in the marketplace; it may be the cheapest or the most user friendly.

MySpace, for example, could be argued to be a superior tool for the promotion of social movements, owing to the greater control exercised by site users and the more public nature of the tool, but the popular ascendancy of Facebook means that to achieve maximum outreach via social media, activist groups have little option other than to include a Facebook presence in their activities.

Predicting which tools and technologies will achieve dominance or maintain dominance is also very difficult. So activist groups have to constantly review the appropriateness of the choices they make (Shultz and Jungherr 2010: 40).

3.1 What do you want to do with it?

In choosing which tools to employ in a given campaign, the first strategic consideration is to be clear about what it is you are aiming to achieve by using digital campaign technologies. The two main reasons for adopting such technologies are:

- internal communication, networking and organizing; and
- outreach into the wider community.

Your group may be primarily concerned with either or both of these, and the extent to which these are separate considerations may also depend on the nature of the campaign group itself. For example, some new groups may be aiming specifically to establish themselves primarily or solely as digital campaigners, whereas other groups may be intending to have a more local face-to-face focus but require some additional tools for networking and outreach. Established groups can include loose networked social movements or more formal organizations, but again their needs are usually going to be a mixture of the communication and outreach functions.

Internal communication is a simpler proposition, as it does not contain as many unknowns as the outreach function. To add to the complexity, the same tools can often be used for both functions.

The principal tools for internal communication include:

- e-mail;
- dedicated websites;
- dedicated activist networking tools (e.g. crabgrass);
- social media such as Facebook groups, Skype; and
- the use of simple SMS networks.

Outreach functions will involve all of these tools with the addition of many more, such as:

- IndyMedia;
- YouTube;
- MySpace;
- Google+;
- Twitter; and
- sophisticated SMS processing systems.

Listed below are some of the basic rules of good practice for engaging with the more common and available tools – e-mail, social networking sites and SMS.

3.2 E-mail for activists: rules and tips for optimum use of e-mail

E-mail needs little introduction, but as you move from personal use to group and campaign use of the tool it becomes important to think about proper e-mail etiquette. Basic rules of etiquette and practice can make communication a lot more effective and avoid some serious pitfalls.

3.2.1 Subject lines and signatures A simple but often overlooked practice is to encourage members to use a coherent subject line on all e-mails, and to change the subject line if the conversation moves on to a new track. This is an important piece of advice for keeping conversations traceable, coherent and much easier to archive and retrieve. Additionally, all members should be encouraged to have a practical e-mail signature that provides information about who they are and how else they may be contacted.

3.2.2 Carbon copies and blind carbon copies Rules need to be established about the use of CC (carbon copy) and BCC (blind carbon copy) fields to protect the privacy of members and the security of the network. Large CC fields are never advisable, and large group postings should always be done by way of BCC. This prevents the individual details of all the addressees going out to every single other addressee and greatly reduces the risks of spamming, hoaxes and advertising penetration. It can also have important security implications if the membership of the group needs to be kept confidential. It is also just bad manners and likely to repel supporters if your group can't be trusted with their information.

3.2.3 Don't press send ... Another very important rule of etiquette is to try to avoid 'flaming' or the sending of provocative or emotionally charged e-mails. Flaming can be a problem because people often feel more emboldened to be rude or offensive to others from a distance. Everyone also has to bear in mind that insult sometimes also occurs because e-mail provides a fairly limited means of human-to-human communication. Without the added subtleties of body language, tone of voice and syntax, communications can be easily misconstrued. Just think of all the different ways we can say 'I'm sorry' or 'fine' to each other in spoken conversation (where the meaning can even be reversed in context) and you will get an idea of how easily such terms could be misconstrued in an e-mail.

A good rule of thumb is to never send an e-mail when you are angry. This could be called the 'don't press send' rule. Sometimes it can be very therapeutic to pour out exactly what you want to say in a long e-mail, but it's best to then save to draft, go for lunch and then come back and reconsider it before you press send. You will be surprised how many times you will be glad you didn't send it. E-mails are a form of written communication, but unlike letters they are posted instantly, so the 'cooling off' period that traditionally existed between writing a letter and posting it is not available.

On group e-mail lists it is all the more important to avoid flaming because people are likely to feel much more aggrieved when you have attacked them in what is effectively a public forum than if it was a single person-to-person e-mail. Group e-mail sites can become dangerous places and can fuel disintegration of the group if proper etiquette and respect are not maintained.

3.2.4 Maintaining contact lists A very important aspect of using e-mail well within a social movement is building and maintaining a useful list of contacts.

Some excellent tips on using e-mail for advocacy are available online from the NetAction collective at www.netaction.org/training/index.html.

NetAction advises activists and groups to be ever vigilant in collecting names and contact details from all of the people with whom they have contact; this includes members, supporters and volunteers, the media, your contacts in legislative offices, your funders and anyone else you communicate with regularly (www.netaction.org/training/index.html, accessed 25 August 2010).

3.2.5 E-mail action alerts One of the most significant uses of e-mail for outreach purposes is e-mail action alerts. E-mail action alerts are designed to alert as many people as possible to some upcoming event or action or to request people to take part in some useful process connected with the

From info@getup.org.au
Subject In your neighbourhood
Date 14 July 2010 7:43:22 PM — Clear date and time
To activist@gmail.com
Reply-to info+1205_551347@getup.org.au — Return address

Dear friend, A GetUp community is being established in each neighbourhood, leading the charge on issues like climate change, asylum seekers and mental health. Next week we've got the opportunity to build this community by coming together in homes and cafes across the country, including in your neighbourhood. On Thursday July 22 from 7pm - 8.30pm, GetUp members like you will be getting together.

Click on the link below to find an 'Election Action GetTogether' already organised in your neighbourhood - or host your own.

www.getup.org.au/community/gettogethers/series.
php?id=28

Here's how it works: — Clear explanation of event and what the reader needs to do

– Click below and enter your postcode to find a GetTogether in your area.

– Come along on Thursday week to meet the lovely GetUp members of your neighbourhood. Everyone brings some snacks or a plate of food.

– Together you go through GetUp's easy step-by-step guide and pick one or two local actions to take this election.

If every group holds one enrolment drive, or one local event, or covers one polling booth on election day, together we can create an election effort to rival the big money of political parties.

Can you help make it happen?

This election, GetUp isn't about the parties, the pollies or the pundits. We're about the issues: turning around rising carbon pollution; fixing our broken mental health system; and demanding a more compassionate approach to asylum seekers.

www.getup.org.au/community/gettogethers/series.php?id=28

We'll see you there, — Embedded website for further information

The GetUp team

GetUp is an independent, not-for-profit community campaigning group. We use new technology to empower Australians to have their say on important national issues. We receive no political party or government funding, and every campaign we run is entirely supported by voluntary donations. If you'd like to contribute to help fund GetUp's work, please donate now! If you have trouble with any links in this email, please go directly to www.getup.org.au. To unsubscribe from GetUp, please click here.

Information promoting the group and a pitch for donations

campaign, such as letter-writing, or coordinated actions in different locations at the same time. E-mail alerts may also be coordinated with SMS alert systems and similar rules should be applied.

There are some important rules of effective practice to be observed in using e-mail action alerts, and again one of the best detailed sources for these rules is NetAction's virtual activist trainer (www.netaction.org/training/index.html).

While it is recommended that activists and groups should consult Net Action's more detailed resource, it is important to observe at least the following rules:

Make sure addressees know:

- who sent the action alert;
- how to contact the organizers and where to get more information;
- what the alert is actually about (include a clear subject line);
- exactly when and where the action is meant to take place;
- why the action is important;
- how to provide support in other ways (e.g. donations).

Groups that issue a lot of e-mail action alerts may find it useful to adopt a scaling code to indicate the level of emergency preparedness involved. The North East Forest Alliance, for example, had a colour code as follows:

- Green alert (notification of likely future action);
- Yellow alert (definite future action, but exact time unknown);
- Orange alert (action is imminent; be prepared);
- Red alert (urgent!).

These scales enable the organization to maintain a complex conversation with supporters and keep them alerted without running the risk of overwhelming them with everything being urgent. This system is particularly useful in uncertain situations such as physical protest actions, where the exact time and place of the action may remain fluid until the last moment.

3.3 Facebook for activists

Facebook is becoming increasingly popular as an activist tool, but users need to be aware of some of the limitations of this social networking site. Foremost among them is that it was not designed as an activist tool specifically; rather it is a social networking tool. Data privacy, and even copyright issues, can be problematic for Facebook users, and you should investigate the terms of use thoroughly before you get started. That having been said,

Facebook has grown into a huge network so it is a useful way to build online activism communities.

One of the big challenges with using Facebook for activism is making sure that you are promoting real and effective action rather than placebo activism. In general this means you should not measure your success by the number of people who join or 'like' the site, but by your capacity to convert that passive engagement into real political action.

There are vast numbers of causes and groups on Facebook and most seem to have very little engagement outside of the Facebook environment; some even become polluted by other groups and various kinds of advertisements. To see a fairly dysfunctional example that appears to be a good cause, visit 'Make 2010 the year of peace' at www.facebook.com/reqs.php#!/group.php ?gid=194516228089&v=app_2344061033.

Apart from the fact that the group has remained in place since 2010, its sole aim appears to have been to become a very large Facebook group with no real programme for converting any ambient support into real political action. There's nothing wrong in principle with establishing a feel-good Facebook group, but from an activist perspective such sites have little practical use.

As with all other aspects of campaigning, it is essential to first have a clear strategic plan for your campaign before you start to go public. The campaign mapping exercises in Chapter 4 of this book should always be completed prior to going public with social media like Facebook.

DigiActive have provided a very useful publication online which offers sound advice on Facebook activism and gives some great examples. See www.digiactive.org/2008/06/28/guide-a-digiactive-introduction-to-facebook-activism/.

The basic steps that DigiActive recommend for setting up a Facebook activist group are similar to those needed to establish more traditional campaign groups which we discussed in Chapter 4.

The basic rules of good practice for setting up and maintaining a good Facebook site include:

- Clearly identify your overall objectives and goals.
- Engage in active networking to expand your support base. Facebook itself helps to support this process.
- Stage events both online and offline that can help bring people together to share resources, links and contacts as well as foster a sense of belonging and effectiveness.
- Link your Facebook site back to your own group website. Your group will

have much greater control of the website and can use it permanently for information, news and other forms of communication.

- Network with existing organizations and share links.
- Generate external publicity via mainstream or alternative media, other social media and the Internet.
- Periodically review your campaign goals and successes and evaluate the effectiveness of your digital campaigning.

For an example of an effective site that is linked to a real campaign organization visit Australian Youth Climate Coalition: www.facebook.com/AYCC.org.au?v=info#!/AYCC.org.au?v=wall.

You will see that this Facebook group ticks most of the boxes in the list above. It is linked to a real-life activist group, provides a link to its own external website, is networked with other groups and organizes real-time political events.

Combining the campaign planning advice and exercises provided in Chapter 4 with the recommended steps above should ensure that your Facebook group is well focused and effective. In particular you should note how closely the list above corresponds to the strategy maps, power-holders maps and friends and foes maps introduced in Chapter 4. This correlation in itself reinforces the general point that digital activism is really just a new way of going about traditional activism.

Facebook is significant because of its sheer popularity at present, but there are significant concerns about the privacy of information on Facebook. Google has recently launched Google+ as a competitor to Facebook and is promising better control over privacy settings. It is worth keeping an eye on emerging sites like Google+ to ascertain their suitability for activism applications in future. One would expect that if rival social networks become well established in the future then some form of cross-compatibility will ultimately need to be introduced to allow users of different networks to communicate with each other. Where activist groups are seeking to use social networking sites for internal networking, services that provide higher information security are likely to be favoured by such groups.

3.4 YouTube and MySpace

Similar strategic considerations apply to utilizing YouTube and MySpace for campaign outreach activities to those set out above in relation to Facebook. First, you need to have completed the important planning and mapping stages of your campaign before you start to go public with content. You should also ensure that all your outputs are designed to:

- work within your campaign plans and mapping;
- build your organization or campaign profile;
- build your support base;
- link to external websites for further information;
- link to existing compatible networks;
- promote some real-life impact;
- generate wider media coverage;
- continue to feed into the ongoing campaign.

It would be a great missed opportunity, for example, to produce a groundbreaking video that went absolutely viral worldwide, but fail to closely identify it with your organization and generate support and contacts, and thus not be able to fully harness its popularity for promoting your campaign aims.

Probably one of the most important disciplines is to always remember that your video, Facebook group or MySpace page is never an end in itself; it is simply a tactical use of a social networking tool for a campaign purpose.

If your organization lacks the profile to launch its own YouTube hits, there are some sites that are designed to promote activism content, such as CitizenTube, which provides a non-stop feed of alternative news on YouTube (www.citizentube.com/).

For an example of a more focused offshoot of CitizenTube that concentrates on issues of homelessness in the USA, go to the Invisible People project at www.citizentube.com/2009/07/invisiblepeopletv-giving-voice-to.html.

For an example of a more specific YouTube project focusing on human rights issues, see www.youtube.com/witness.

There is also a MySpace activism group that aims to provide a convenient source of general alternative news and information, promote like-minded groups and events, and help connect activists to one another. Go to www.myspace.com/1205522.

3.5 SMS activism

As observed earlier, mobile phones have become the most ubiquitous digital communication device on the planet, recently estimated as having reached 5 billion users by the end of 2010 (UN News Centre 2010).

For activists this massive global network (even massive domestic networks) provides great potential for outreach and communication. Mobile phones and SMS-based communications allow for both organized and non-organized dissemination of information, which can assist in the organizing of public protest events, as well as real-time communication of events as they unfold.

One of the most exciting possibilities opened up by mobile phone technologies is what is known as 'smart mobbing'. This is when large groups are assembled and even moved from place to place at very short notice using SMS technology (Rheingold 2002).

> A smart mob is a self-organizing group of people who operate like a swarm of bees or a flock of pigeons ... [F]orming into a group that is controlled by no single person, yet which moves as if it has a mind of its own. Since mobile text-messages can be instantly forwarded ... the mobs frequently involve masses of people who have never even met. (Ramey 2007)

One of the most widely reported early examples of effective smart mobbing was the series of protests surrounding the 1999 World Trade Organization meetings in Seattle. Phones were used to coordinate demonstrations and evade police, and groups were able to be moved from location to location with great efficiency (www.npaction.org/article/articleprint/607/-1/%7B category_id%7D/).

Mobile phones have become an integral part of the mass organizing of protests and demonstrations in many countries around the world. They have provided a means of communication between organizers and supporters, and between friends, and have also facilitated the dissemination of news and images at times when governments have shut down other major forms of communication.

Mobile phones and other digital technologies played a major role during coverage of recent mass protests in the Middle East in 2011. The increasing effectiveness of these digital tools also led to many governments shutting down access to parts of the digital networks during the unrest (www.technology-digital.com/sectors/online/middle-east-protests-and-social-media-savior).

Attempts by governments to suppress digital activism by shutting down networks can have a temporary effect, but at great social and economic cost, and they cannot be sustained indefinitely. The use of viral peer-to-peer (not centrally organized) text messaging has been particularly useful in countries that otherwise attempt to suppress organized political activity, such as Iran and China; this is far more difficult to selectively block or monitor because of its disorganized nature.

3.5.1 Dispersed or centralized networks? Most activist groups with large or rapidly expanding campaigns will eventually reach a crossroads where decisions need to be made about investing in a more centralized SMS network. Leaving aside the issues of networking in repressive regimes, there are a number of generic logistical issues that can influence the choice between centralized and peer-to-peer networking options. Generally smaller activist groups may prefer to use a dispersed network, but larger, more established organizations, incorporated NGOs and groups relying on large mass support are more likely to opt to use a centralized SMS gateway.

3.5.2 Phone pyramids For small groups still reliant upon basic decentralized SMS capabilities, the efficacy of SMS in campaigns can be greatly enhanced by the use of phone trees or phone pyramids within the organization. For

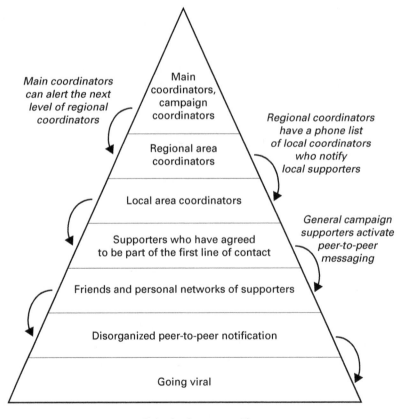

9.2 A simple phone pyramid

example, if a networked group has a list a of principal or nodal coordinators, each of whom has a local list of potential activists on their phones, a pyramid-like SMS structure that has the capacity to fan out and include a large number of people very quickly can be activated quickly and effectively. At the final and most populous stage of the pyramids it can be suggested that all recipients then forward the message to as many recipients as they can. This last step will increase the coverage substantially, but at the risk of cross-postings.

Phone pyramids represent a way in which smaller groups can get started with text campaigns without the need for any specialized services or tools. As the campaign grows in magnitude, or if the campaign is intended to be mostly SMS-based, it will be necessary to use service providers to establish a more centralized and flexible mobile network. There are two basic options for establishing a more centralized system. These are:

- web-based service providers;
- use of a mobile vendor (gateway service).

3.5.3 Web-based service providers Web-based service providers are a good way to get started for small organizations because they can be readily accessed, set up online and the group can begin to experiment with the functionality provided. The disadvantages are that they tend to end up becoming costly and they do require some expertise to derive the maximum benefit (mobileactive.org/research/generation-2-0-practical-guide-using-new-media-recruit-organize-and-mobilize-young-people).

3.5.4 Mobile service provider Larger and more established organizations are more likely to opt for the use of a commercial mobile service provider, which will streamline the logistics of operating the system by making it easier for members of the public to join and by having safeguards against cross-posting.

There are a number of advantages to signing up with a mobile service provider. They will be able to provide technical assistance and advice to enable your organization to make the most of the available functionality. The use of such providers opens up a whole range of new options for advocacy campaigns, in addition to providing a more functional platform for activities like rapid communication and smart mobbing.

A primary advantage of working with a provider is that it becomes very easy to promote your network and for people to 'opt in' (recruitment). Typically, an organization that subscribes to a vendor will be given one or more short codes (a five- or six-digit phone number) that enables individual users to opt in to receiving messages from the organization or even to provide other data or donations. So during a large public event your organization may be able to recruit large numbers of people quickly by asking supporters to text the word 'support' or 'join' or 'activ8' to the short code number. This will cause all incoming messages to be recorded into the database of the service and replies can then be sent automatically. At any later stage it becomes very simple to text the entire membership list simultaneously (text blasting). Follow-up texts can also be used to elicit further information from supporters, such as e-mail addresses, location and age.

The use of large mobile phone networks also holds great promise for fund-raising for organizations, because supporters can each be asked by text to agree to have a small donation added to their phone bill. This kind of donation strategy can be very productive for large networks. The costs associated with this process at present would probably discourage its use by smaller groups.

3.5.5 Data collection A key advantage of using mobile technology for advocacy is the enormous amount of quantitative data that is generated. It becomes easy for organizations over time to determine which messages or tactics are most effective (Generation 2.0A n.d.: 10) or to gauge which kinds of alerts in which locations generated the greatest response from users.

In non-repressive societies there are not a lot of disadvantages to using SMS vendor service providers, but in oppressive societies they are not recommended owing to the increased risk of shutdown or government authorities seizing the information and harassing individual activists (Ramey 2007).

The best advice for small, newly forming activist groups is to start by using phone pyramid structures and viral messaging tactics until they reach a stage where the demands of their organization suggest that moving to a service provider is required. Obviously factors such as traffic volume and the cost of establishing a relationship with a service provider will influence individual decisions.

There are some existing web-based organizations that offer advice, discussions and training guides for organizations considering engaging with SMS campaigning.

3.5.6 User guides
- MobileActive.org (mobileactive.org/about) is one of the more useful sites, providing practical training guides as well as the downloadable

publication *Using Mobile Phones in Advocacy Campaigns* (mobileactive.org/howtos/using-mobile-phones-advocacy).

• Generation 2.0A offers a practical guide for using new media to recruit, organize and mobilize young people (mobileactive.org/research/generation-2-0-practical-guide-using-new-media-recruit-organize-and-mobilize-young-people).

4.0 Working digital activism into your existing campaign

Probably the single most important principle to bear in mind is ensuring that all new tools and tactics are worked into the totality of your campaign plan. The campaign planning processes outlined in Chapter 4 are of utmost importance in orchestrating a successful campaign and determining where new tools and technologies will be necessary or more effective.

One of the key reasons why constructing and maintaining a comprehensive campaign plan or strategy map is so important is that it allows all component aspects of the campaign to be kept within the context of the whole campaign. Unless your whole group understands the hierarchy of objectives, goals, strategies, tactics and now, in the case of digital activism, tools as well, there is a very great risk of being sidetracked, of confusing a lower-order function with a higher one or generating unnecessary internal conflict.

Conflict in organizations often occurs because participants obsess about a particular tactic or tool and mistake it for the campaign itself. If an organization chooses to utilize a particular digital tool, some members engaged with the process may become very passionate about its importance for the overall campaign. There is a risk that they could become myopic and start to believe that the digital part of the campaign *is* the campaign or is the 'single most important' aspect of the campaign. When this kind of confusion of the hierarchy of strategy, tactic and tool sets in, it can not only unbalance the campaign, it can also lead to conflict as members lose respect for the work being done by others in other component strategy areas such as public awareness raising or media work.

It's important to have passionate digital activists in your organization but they must not become digital fundamentalists. Endless arguments of detail can erupt within your group if individuals become obsessed with their particular contribution to the campaign, and the very best insurance against this is to have and to constantly revise a whole-of-campaign planning map. This enables every activist to see their part in the whole, or at least be reminded of it if need be.

Digital activism is a tool, not an end in itself; you could have one of the

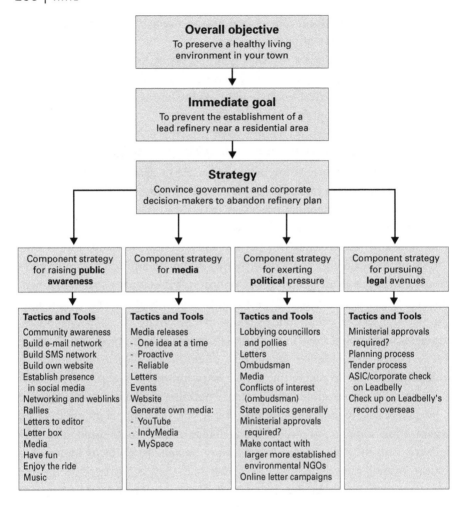

9.3 Example of campaign plan with digital media tools/tactics included

best digital campaigns on the block and still fail to be successful if there are major shortcomings in how this campaign is delivered on the ground. So the essential discipline is to make sure your digital campaign is worked into your overall plan.

4.1 Longevity of digital campaigns

Achieving longevity for digital campaigns involves similar principles to traditional campaigning:

Well-thought-out objectives, goals, strategies and tactics This has already been covered above; you must have a whole-of-campaign plan so that the digital component fits within a coherent process.

Inclusiveness Your campaign should be accessible and welcoming to a broad range of people. This includes having positive and welcoming messages, but also providing simple ways for people to become involved.

Appropriate form of organizational structure Digital activism tools have actually made it easier to build and maintain loose and largely horizontal networks rather than having to rely upon top-down organizational forms, although in reality such looser forms of collective, alliance and affinity groupings have been a feature of activism groups and social movements since long before the digital tools came along. Choose a structure that works well with the aims of your group and the underlying ethics.

Remain current Maintaining a good website or Facebook group can require a lot of work and constant maintenance. Sites that obviously contain out-of-date information are an instant turn-off for the average punter. There's nothing worse than seeing an 'urgent' action alert for three months ago on the main page. So if you are going to establish a digital presence, make sure your group can sustain it and keep it current.

Integrate the online and offline worlds It's important not to become lost in the digital world and lose contact with the real world on the streets. Successful and durable digital campaigns are those that balance well-coordinated digital networking with real physical and face-to-face interaction and political action.

Avoid personal and organizational burnout Burnout is the biggest single enemy of sustainable activism both at the personal and the organizational level. Pay close attention to the advice provided in Chapter 12 to avoid burnout and build empowerment and renewal practices into everything you do. The world needs you to remain healthy and productive.

Conclusion

Digital activism is an exciting and constantly evolving field of practice. The purpose of this chapter has been to introduce the basic concepts, debates and tools and to provide practical tips on how to work these new tools into your campaign. An underlying message is the need for activists to treat digital activism as simply another tool for activism generally and to incorporate it into existing campaigns in a coherent and holistic way. There is a huge number of resources available on the web to give guidance on every aspect of using the tools, and some of the best sites are listed below, but ultimately political success will always depend on campaign planning, strategy and execution, and the tools can never do this for you.

Networking resources and help

Activism host organizations
www.moveon.org/; www.avaaz.org; www.getup.org.au

Social media host sites
www.citizentube.com/; www.youtube.com/witness;
www.myspace.com/1205522

Organizations offering digital activism training packages
www.digiactive.org; www.tacticaltech.org/; mobileactive.org;
www.netaction.org/training/; meta-activism.org/;
advocacy.globalvoicesonline.org/; crabgrass.riseup.net/

TEN | **Strategic litigation**

Introduction

Bringing a lawsuit against a government or a major corporation can be a powerful way to promote change and generate publicity for your cause. This chapter looks at practical issues involved in dealing with lawyers and going to court, and also discusses the important strategic, organizational, financial and political issues involved in the use of litigation as a campaign tactic.

1.0 Have a realistic idea of what is involved before you get started

Legal action is not always fun. It is hard work and often takes place under very stressful circumstances. If you want the court action to be successful you must put in the time and effort necessary to achieve your goal. Wins in court don't come easily, and losses can certainly occur because of rushed or poorly prepared or poorly organized cases.

Don't make the mistake of thinking that you can simply hand your case over to lawyers and let them do the work; this is not how it works. Your lawyers will guide you in relation to the applicable law and procedure, but the all-important work of proving your argument is going to depend on a huge amount of work by you and your team. Your lawyers will require you to do the groundwork to produce high-quality evidence, and this is the most time-consuming part of the litigation. Legal professionals will require you to perform to their standards and timetables. If you want their help, in their specialist area, you will need to play by their rules.

1.1 Law as strategy; litigation as tactic

Before we start to think about using the law in our campaign, we need

to be clear about what the strategic advantage of litigation is likely to be. Activism is, after all, about building support and consensus for social change in our communities. Winning a legal challenge may be a strategic way of propelling an issue to public attention, it can be a powerful way of exposing the wrongdoing of power-holders or of revealing injustice or stopping some destructive activity, but usually it is not the end purpose of your campaign; rather it is part of the process of building public support for your campaign.

A good way of understanding how litigation might fit into your campaign is to go back to your overall strategy map and see where it slots in. You will notice for a start that in the template strategy map in Chapter 4 litigation is listed as a 'tactic', not as a strategy in its own right. Successful litigation can be a very powerful tactic, but we need to be clear that court cases on their own rarely bring about the kind of broad social change that is really needed in the long term.

1.2 Some common pitfalls to avoid

Remaining clear about where litigation fits into your overall campaign helps to avoid some of the very common pitfalls. Once you or your group become involved in litigation it can become very all-encompassing. Unless you keep reminding yourself that it is not the whole campaign but merely a significant contributory tactic it is easy to fall into the trap of exaggerating the importance of the litigation. This has a number of negative consequences:

- It can lead to the neglect of other important aspects of the campaign (such as public-awareness-raising, political lobbying, media work and other forms of campaigning).
- This loss of holistic focus in the campaign can generate conflict within your group, as the members running the litigation tactic may start to show disrespect for the work of others.
- It may generate resentment in other campaign workers over the amount of time, money or campaign focus that is being sucked up by the litigation tactic.

A sure warning sign is when you start to hear yourself or others saying things like 'all that's important now is that we win this case; if we don't the whole campaign is pointless'. Once people start to place such a singular emphasis on a single tactic, the campaign as a whole is likely to suffer.

There is a further reason why centring your campaign around a court case can be dangerous, and that is because court cases are inherently unpredictable. If both sides knew beforehand what the court would decide there would not be a dispute. If you allow the whole of your campaign focus to shift to a court action and it fails, your campaign will be in a sorry state.

Before we leave this part of the discussion it's important to identify another risk. Court cases can be useful in attracting a lot of public or media attention to an issue, but the case may deal only with a small aspect of your overall campaign. Again, you need to be careful in all of your public statements to keep reminding people of the bigger issue. You also need to explain what your group will do if it loses the case. In most cases the answer is 'just keep campaigning'. You need to be careful that you don't hand all of the power to the court. The court can decide the case at hand, but that does not decide the wider moral, social, political or other issues involved in the campaign as whole. You have to be wary of painting yourself into a corner where you feel obliged to accept the court's decision as the 'umpire's' decision on your whole issue.

2.0 Strategic litigation

Having started with the warnings about the pitfalls, let's now go on to discuss the many ways in which litigation can fulfil a very useful strategic function in your campaign.

Public interest litigation is almost always also 'strategic litigation'. This means it is used in conjunction with other social change strategies, and it also means that at times winning the case is not the only way to achieve a successful outcome. For example:

- You may be simply trying to expose an injustice.
- You may be trying to demonstrate the inadequacy of existing law.
- You may be trying to buy time and delay your opponent.
- You may simply be using the litigation as a platform for publicizing an issue.

To understand strategic litigation we can contrast it with more conventional forms of litigation. Most people engage in litigation only to advance their own personal interests and, as such, winning their case is usually a vitally important or even uniquely important aim. For the average individual litigant, there is not usually a wider social issue that envelops their case (although at times they may be propelled by a sense of justice as well as a desire to gain some advantage).

Public interest litigants are different, in that the litigation is rarely about achieving any personal outcome for them, and it's usually part of a wider campaign. In this context, there can be times when a case is brought knowing it has no real chance of success, simply because of the strategic advantage of the attention or delay associated with the litigation.

It's probably rare even for campaigners to bring a case they know they can't win, but it does happen. In a famous indigenous land rights case in Australia (*Coe* v. *Commonwealth*, 53 ALJR 403; [1979] 24 ALR 118) the plaintiff, Coe, brought a test case challenging the legal basis of the establishment of British law in Australia. The case could not succeed because there was no way the Australian courts would undermine their own jurisdiction by making a finding adverse to the entire Australian legal system, but nonetheless the plaintiff was successful in his application in raising serious questions about the process of colonization in Australia and in forcing the courts to adopt a defensive stance. Such a case is a clear example of strategic litigation that aims merely to raise an issue with no real prospect of success. The case helped publicize the land rights cause, and helped to lay some of the political and legal groundwork for the more successful land rights cases of the early 1990s.

More commonly, a campaigner brings a case in which winning is only one of a number of useful outcomes they are aiming to achieve. This represents a very intelligent and strategic use of litigation as a tactic, and shows that the campaigner has a broader strategic framework within which they are working. You should aim to identify these collateral aims when choosing litigation as a tactic, because this will help you frame your publicity properly.

2.1 Strategic litigation against public participation (SLAPP suits)

It is important to be aware that it's not only social change activists who may use litigation to achieve a collateral aim outside of the courtroom. Corporations and other target groups often use defamation-style actions as a strategic form of litigation designed to intimidate community activists out of speaking their mind. These kinds of action are also known as SLAPP

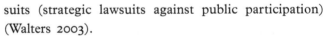

suits (strategic lawsuits against public participation) (Walters 2003).

These are usually undertaken by corporations or governments to intimidate public interest advocates. There are numerous examples available, but one of the most famous worldwide is the 'Mclibel case': *McDonald's Corporation, McDonald's Restaurants Limited* v. *Helen Marie Steel and David Morris* [1997] EWHC QB 366.

The Mclibel case is an interesting story because of just how much the litigation backfired on McDonald's, even though they were technically successful in court. As such it is a good example of the power of court cases to bring information into the public eye, and of the fact that the winner politically in such actions is not always the same as the winner in court.

Even though the plaintiff (McDonald's) was technically successful in their defamation action against the activists, the amount of negative publicity generated by the case was probably more damaging than the original campaign leaflet. The award of damages was relatively small, and in the process of delivering judgment the court made a number of findings that confirmed some of the criticisms originally levelled by activists. In particular, the court found:

- some evidence of health risks associated with regular consumption of the food (para. 127);
- evidence of the use of advertising specifically targeted at children (140–1);
- evidence of animal cruelty attributable to the activities of the corporation (151–60); and
- that the company does pay its workers low wages, thereby helping to depress wages for workers in the catering trade in Britain (187).

In the years since the case public criticism has continued, including the production of a popular feature-length movie and a permanent anti-McDonald's website (www.mcspotlight.org/case/index.html).

Of course, not all cases are as high profile or as positive as the Mclibel case in terms of turning the tables on the power-holders who are using the tactic. There is no doubt that the fear of defamation actions, and even the fear generated by threats of defamation actions made against public interest activists, can have a detrimental and chilling effect on free speech.

There has been another high-profile case in Australia in recent years, known as the Gunn's 20 case, in which a timber company instituted legal action against twenty high-profile environmentalists (*Gunn's Limited* v. *Marr* [2005] VSC 251).

> On December 14, 2004, Gunn's – one of Australia's largest forestry companies – lodged a 216-page writ against 20 Tasmanian environmentalists and groups seeking A\$6.3 million for actions it claims has damaged their business and reputation. The case never went to full trial and by 2009 all of the claims were either dropped or settled out of court. And the company ended up paying large amounts of costs to the environmentalists. (www.sourcewatch.org/index.php?title=Gunns_20)

The case made an impact internationally, as well as with a group of influential lawyers in the UK who wrote a letter to the *Guardian* newspaper condemning SLAPP suits and the Gunn's claim (www.guardian.co.uk/world/2006/apr/03/australia.mainsection).

While the case failed badly for the company, there is still no doubt that these kinds of tactic have a negative effect on public freedom of communication, that they tend to intimidate people from speaking their minds, and at the very least can massively distract activists from pursuing their campaigns. Experience shows that the majority of SLAPP suits do not succeed in court, but we should not underestimate the effect they have upon activists and ordinary citizens. Because of the fear they inspire, SLAPP suits remain popular with controversial industry groups and remain a threat to public interest advocates worldwide.

In order to remain empowered and to avoid being unnecessarily intimidated, activists need to understand local defamation or libel laws well enough to know what they can and can't reasonably say, and be prepared to tough it out if threats are made. Owing to the prevalence of SLAPP suits in Australia and New Zealand in recent years there is a lot of information available on the web for activists to consult. A good site is the Sourcewatch website discussion of SLAPP suits (www.sourcewatch.org/index.php?title=SLAPP's_in_Australia).

One of the more entertaining and useful sites is 'The bush lawyers' guide to using legal threats as wallpaper' (users.senet.com.au/~gregogle/wallpaper.htm).

2.2 Impediments to public interest litigation

Before we go on to consider the various kinds of legal action that activists may choose to pursue, it is worth also discussing the various impediments that are often faced.

The first thing public interest advocates need to be aware of is that the common law (the judicial systems in the UK, the USA, Australia, New Zealand and Canada) is primarily concerned with enforcing the vested interests of individuals, in particular private property interests. This is an important threshold concept that needs to be grasped in order to go on to understand the general body of common law as it applies to public interest campaigns (see Chapter 1).

To put it bluntly, the common law is not naturally well suited to being used to pursue public interest agendas; it exists predominantly to protect and enforce private rights. From this knowledge flows the important realization that public interest activists will nearly always need to use the common law in a careful and strategic way in order to bend it towards a more public purpose than it was really designed for. This is not just a critique of common law; it is very important in helping your strategic understanding of the nature of common-law rights, and causes of action, their enforcement and the possible remedies.

2.3 The law of standing

One of the best examples of the way in which the common law tradition-ally resists allowing public interest advocates into court is provided by the traditional common-law rules of standing. Australia probably has the most outdated and restrictive standing rules among the major common-law legal systems owing to a very conservative High Court judgment delivered in 1980 in the case of *Australian Conservation Foundation* v. *The Commonwealth* [1980] 146 CLR 493 (discussed in Chapter 1).

The Australian Conservation Foundation (ACF) was seeking to obtain an injunction to prevent the construction of a resort on sensitive coastal land. The court ultimately decreed that the ACF were prevented from even bringing the action because the Foundation did not have a 'sufficient inter-est' in the subject matter of the proceedings. In effect, because the ACF's involvement was of a public interest nature and did not affect their private rights, the court held that they could not bring the litigation.

Fortunately subsequent cases in Australia show that the courts are becom-ing more willing to allow public interest cases to proceed, but the underlying restriction remains in place for now. In the United Kingdom, by contrast, there has been a significant positive shift in the courts' preparedness to allow public interest advocates access. The older, more conservative position was evident in the case of *R* v. *Environment Secretary, Ex parte Rose Theatre Trust Co* [1990] 1 All ER 754. In that case, the remains of an important theatre from Elizabethan times were discovered during commercial excava-tion work in London. A company was then formed to preserve the remains. The Secretary of State decided not to include the site in a list of protected archaeological areas, and the company sought judicial review of this decision. The High Court held that the company did not have 'sufficient interest' to apply for leave to bring proceedings for judicial review.

However, the English courts have demonstrated a significant shift in approach, as seen in the subsequent case of *R* v. *Inspectorate of Pollution, Ex parte Greenpeace* [1994] 1 WLR 570, [1994] 4 All ER 329. In that case, officials in a pollution control agency licensed a company to reprocess nuclear fuel. The court held that an association formed to protect the environment had standing to apply for judicial review of this decision. In this case, the court expressly declined to follow *R* v. *Environment Secretary, Ex parte Rose Theatre Trust Co* (above).

The Supreme Court in Canada has adopted a different and more flexible approach that recognizes a general judicial discretion to recognize public inter-est standing. See *Finlay* v. *Canada (Minister of Finance)* [1986] 2 S.C.R. 607.

In the United States, standing to sue continues to be a difficult legal issue for public interest advocates, although the rules in the USA differ significantly from the other common-law countries discussed. See *Allen* v. *Wright* 468 US 737 (1984).

Standing is a technical legal issue which activists in all jurisdictions need to discuss with competent legal representatives.

2.4 Statutory standing rights

The above discussion relates to standing rights at common law, but it is important to also note that individual pieces of legislation may grant rights of standing to enforce aspects of the legislation to much wider classes of persons than are traditionally available at common law. Where the standing provision allows 'any person' to bring an action it is known as an 'open standing' provision.

See, for example:

Section 123, Environmental Planning and Assessment Act 1979 (NSW)

(1) Any person may bring proceedings in the Court for an order to remedy or restrain a breach of this Act, whether or not any right of that person has been or may be infringed by or as a consequence of that breach.

But not all statutory grants of standing are so wide. Standing may be granted to a specified class of persons such as neighbouring property-holders (in the case of local government legislation) or to people who previously objected to a certain process. Sometimes the legislation uses terminologies similar to some of the common-law tests to describe standing rights, such terms as 'person aggrieved' or persons with a 'sufficient interest', and such terms are usually seen as an attempt to invoke some of the limitations that existed traditionally under common law. These statutory formulations need to be interpreted by domestic courts before we can be certain of just how wide the grant of standing is.

Once again it is impossible to go into all the different formulations that may be encountered in the different jurisdictions. This discussion is meant to alert campaigners to the need to ascertain statutory standing rights and to seek accurate legal advice before proceeding.

3.0 Effective use of public interest litigation

Despite the limitations, litigation can still be a useful part of an overall strategy. It can be used to:

- bring a simmering issue into the public spotlight;
- embarrass or expose particular power-holders;
- cause delay or extra cost to one's opponents;
- bring about a timely change in the law itself;
- actually stop a particular destructive, unjust or discriminatory practice;
- be a catalyst for a long-term political solution.

The key to using it well is to always locate litigation as a tactic within your overall campaign plan and strategies. Used wisely in this way, it can be a powerful tactic in propelling an issue or provoking change.

3.1 Particular types of legal action

There are a number of common types of action that characterize public interest litigation, and these include the following:

- Test cases: these may be actions by private individuals that develop the law in a particular area.
- Class actions: collective actions by a class of people affected by some activity.
- Third party appeals: where organizations or individuals bring cases to enforce law or public policy (e.g. environmental litigation).
- Amicus curiae: where an advocacy organization intervenes in a private case to put a public interest perspective to the court.
- Judicial review: where the lawfulness of a governmental decision is reviewed by the courts.

3.1.1 Test cases Test cases in pure legal terms resemble any other private action except that they involve a new and uncertain issue and a deeper public interest aspect. Sometimes a test case involves an area of law that has been in flux for some time, and some party feels the time is right to take it to the courts for a new ruling; in other instances it is simply a previously untested idea.

The famous Australian indigenous land rights case of *Mabo* v. *Commonwealth* (www.austlii.edu.au/au/cases/cth/HCA/1992/23.html) is an example of a test case. In that case the plaintiffs felt the time was right to ask the High Court in Australia to overturn more than a century of legal decisions that had denied the existence of prior native title rights in Australia. It is a classic example of a successful test case because the court actually swept away hundreds of years of prior decisions and established a new legal paradigm for Australia.

When considering bringing a test case, it is vital to make sure that the applicant and the set of facts that will be relied upon are best suited to represent the particular legal issue that will be in question. A poorly prepared test case runs the risk of setting a negative precedent and can be a setback for the campaign for years to come. The case on *locus standi* mentioned previously, *ACF* v. *Commonwealth*, was an example of a test case that ended up setting a negative precedent that is to this day still holding back developments to the law of standing in Australia.

3.1.2 Class actions Class actions occur where a large class of people are affected by the same harm. By all joining together as parties they are able to share the legal costs of an action, and they also usually have the advantage of attracting a lot more media and political attention because of the large numbers of affected parties. Often the cause of action is one that relates to widespread harm, such as 'public nuisance', for example, but it does not need to be. Class actions can be brought in relation to negligence, for example. The biggest challenge with class actions is making sure that the facts and issues are identical for all the plaintiffs, otherwise the action can become chaotic.

Class actions are very useful in circumstances where it would be too costly for one individual to bring the action alone. The parties all benefit from sharing the costs and also share in any damages or compensation awarded.

Class actions are common in cases of industrial disease, or contamination of neighbourhoods. They have also been a common feature of litigation concerning the health effects of tobacco smoking. One of the earliest and most famous class actions saw 170,000 women compensated by the company Dow Corning over faulty breast implants (Parker 2010). In Canada's largest environmental class action based on pollution, mining giant Vale was ordered to pay $36 million compensation to approximately seven thousand local residents because certain pollutants escaped from the refinery and devalued their properties (Briggs et al. 2010).

In Australia there have been a number of test cases and class actions brought in relation to the health effects of asbestos in workplaces; see *Banton* v. *Amaca Pty Ltd* [2007] NSWDDT 29 and *Moss* v. *Amaca Pty Ltd* (Formerly James Hardie & Co Pty Ltd) [2006] WASC 311.

3.1.3 Third party appeals Third party appeal is a generic term used to describe situations where a third party (such as an environment or human rights advocacy group) brings an action to overturn a government decision. Usually this will be by way of judicial review (discussed below), but on some occasions the third party appeal rights may be statutory rights to bring a specific appeal against a decision on its merits. Merits appeals are a statutory creation and are sometimes provided for in specific legislation, such as local government, environmental or pollution control legislation. Activists and advocates need to become familiar with the legislation under which decisions are made by power-holders and explore whatever opportunities are provided for review of those decisions. The difference between merits appeals and judicial review is also discussed in Chapter 6.

3.1.4 Amicus curiae Amicus curiae (friend of the court) is a process whereby the court allows a public interest intervener (a third party) to present evidence or information to the court.

Sometimes the court may request such information from an independent and authoritative source, and sometimes the amicus curiae will of their own accord seek the court's leave to intervene and present evidence.

The decision on whether to admit the information is at the discretion of the court. When there is an application to present evidence as an amicus curiae, the process is known as presenting a brief of amicus curiae to the court. This is a process that is more common in North America, but there are examples from the UK and Australia. In the UK the nature of amicus curiae is discussed in the case of *Allen* v. *Sir Alfred McAlpine & Sons Ltd* [1968] 2 QB 229. An Australian example of the use of amicus curiae is found in the case of *Levy* v. *Victoria* (www.austlii.edu.au/au/cases/cth/HCA/1997/31.html).

Levy is a case involving the scope of the freedom of political communication, in which the court allowed an association of media proprietors to intervene by way of amicus curiae.

In the USA, the rules for bringing amicus curiae applications are set out in the Federal Rules of Appellate Procedure (FRAP) rule 29 (www.law.cornell.edu/rules/frap/rules.html#Rule29).

An important limitation with amicus curiae is that the intervener is only there to help provide information to the court and does not become a party as such and cannot recover damages or other remedies in their own right. For this reason the process tends to be attractive only to professional public interest organizations such as human rights, civil liberties and environmental organizations.

3.1.5 Judicial review Judicial review is another very significant way in which public interest cases come before the courts, and probably one of the most common procedures for this purpose.

The superior courts in all jurisdictions (the UK, Canada, the US, New Zealand, Australia) have an inherent jurisdiction to enforce all of the laws of the nation. This means they automatically have a power to judicially review governmental and public decision-making bodies to ensure they have acted within the law, and a power to quash any decision that contravenes the law. This power is usually referred to as the power of judicial review. In addition, the courts have over many years built up a body of principles that define the way in which such bodies should go about making decisions, and these are often called the principles of due process or of natural justice and fairness. Judicial review of administrative decisions is a complex area of the law. An excellent publication describing English administrative law in detail entitled *The Judge over Your Shoulder* is available online and provides a very good background to administrative law (www.tsol.gov.uk/Publications/services.htm).

In some jurisdictions the older, more complex common-law rules have been replaced by more modern legislation that generically deals with the review of governmental decisions. See, for example:

- Australia: Administrative Decisions Judicial Review Act 1977 (www.austlii.edu.au/au/legis/cth/consol_act/adra1977396/);
- Canada: Judicial Review Procedure Act 1990 (www.canlii.org/en/on/laws/stat/rso-1990-c-j1/latest/rso-1990-c-j1.html);
- United States: Administrative Procedure Act of 1946 (www.law.cornell.edu/uscode/5/usc_sup_01_5_10_I_30_5.html).

Because judicial review is only about reviewing the way in which the decision was made and not the merits of the decision itself, it has the disadvantage that the quashed decision may later be made again by the original decision-maker, provided they follow the correct procedures. Judicial review is, however, a powerful remedy because it applies across the board to all governmental and public decision-making bodies whether there is specific legislation to provide for review or not, and the courts are very reluctant to allow exemptions from this general supervisory jurisdiction that they possess.

This discussion serves only as a guide to the various common ways in which public interest litigation is presented in the courts. In practical situations there is no substitute for reading the legislation, and the policy documents of the decision-maker, and making sure you lodge any requests for review within the time limits specified and in the form specified. If you are considering bringing an action in the courts you will need to have the assistance of lawyers.

3.2 The practical side of public interest litigation

The legal niceties of your particular case are something you will work out with your advisers and your legal team, but before you get to that point you and your organization have to make sure you are ready.

The next sections give some practical advice on:

- getting legal advice;
- dealing with lawyers;
- financial issues.

3.2.1 Getting legal advice You should obtain as much general legal advice as possible before you think about engaging lawyers professionally. Many lawyers will offer a first free consultation to discuss your case, but if you decide to go any farther you need to consider the costs.

You can often obtain useful preliminary advice from experienced activists, law students, university lecturers and community legal centres, or from professional public interest advocacy organizations such as those listed below:

- The Public Interest Advocacy Centre NSW Australia: www.piac.asn.au/about/
- Public Interest Advocacy Centre (Canada): www.ic.gc.ca/eic/site/oca-bc.nsf/eng/ca01928.html
- Public Interest Advocacy Centre British Columbia: bcpiac.com/
- Public Interest Lawyers (UK): www.publicinterestlawyers.co.uk/

These kinds of organization often also have very informative websites with fact sheets about litigation.

Non-governmental organizations such as the public interest advocacy centres will have limited resources, so they will choose whether to take on your case based on its merits and importance to their overall aims and objectives. Even if they can't take on your case, they are usually a good source of information about what your other options may be.

3.2.2 Dealing with lawyers Before you choose a lawyer, ask around to find out who is an expert in that particular field. Good lawyers are specialists, and it's best if you choose a lawyer who is trying to build up a reputation in that particular field. This will mean that they have a vested interest in going the extra mile to win your case.

Before you hire lawyers, be sure you know exactly what you want them to do and be ready to ask specific questions. Be aware that they cannot offer you a magic bullet to win your case, and be sure to heed their advice, even if it is not what you want to hear, particularly about your chances of success.

3.2.3 Financial issues For most campaign groups financing litigation is the most problematic aspect. There are various ways in which public interest advocates may be able to reduce the cost burden. In some jurisdictions legal aid schemes operate, although they are not always geared to supporting public-interest-type cases. A popular approach is to seek 'no win no pay' deals with lawyers, but this will not protect you from paying the other side's costs if you lose.

When you are seeking lawyers for public interest litigation you may be able to find firms who offer pro bono (free of charge) public interest work.

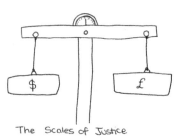

The Scales of Justice

Despite the bad reputation lawyers enjoy in the community, it is surprising how much of their time they often donate to community groups and social movements (some lawyers, that is). In most jurisdictions there are schemes operating in which lawyers and law firms take part in pro bono public interest litigation that is coordinated by some representative body. The public interest advocacy centres and similar organizations often coordinate this.

You need to be aware, however, that even where your lawyer agrees not to charge fees, or to work on a 'no win no pay' basis, this will not protect you from a lot of other expenses, such as filing fees, payments for expert evidence, or costs orders against you if you lose. On rare occasions the courts are prepared to vary the usual rule (that costs follow the order, i.e. the loser pays) in favour of public interest applicants, but this cannot be relied upon. See *Oshlack* v. *Richmond River Council* [1998] 193 CLR 72 (www.austlii.edu.au/au/cases/cth/HCA/1998/11.html).

The advantage of the rules related to costs, of course, is that if you win your costs will be paid by your opponent, but you should expect settling the bill to take months – up to a year or even more!

Another way in which some public interest advocates try to deal with the risk of adverse costs orders being made against them is to make sure that the actual person or organization that puts its name down as the applicant has no assets (the man of straw). This will mean that if you win your opponent will have to pay the costs to you, but if you lose the other side may just give up on pursuing the costs, or else an individual will simply file for bankruptcy or an organization will fold and have to be replaced later by a new group. This is a remarkably effective strategy, although sometimes the defendants will be able to convince the court to require a surety as to costs before the litigation proceeds, which means you will be required to put up a sum of money to cover costs in the event of your case not succeeding.

As you can see, litigation is a complex and financially risky business.

3.3 The legal arguments and the evidence

Don't expect that you can simply place your case in the lawyers' hands and sit back; litigation involves a huge amount of work for the applicants and you will find that the lawyers demand a lot of information from you, some of which may never ultimately be used.

Most cases involve two distinct aspects: the legal arguments and the evidence, which is used to establish provable facts. The legal argument is usually the simpler process because although there may be uncertainty about the law or how it will be applied in this case, the lawyers are well equipped to deal with this aspect of your case. It is largely an on-paper theoretical exercise.

The evidence aspect is usually much more problematic. This is because you may know certain facts but courts are an evidence-based institution, so you need to be able to present persuasive and reliable evidence to support every aspect of your claim. This may require that you go to great expense and effort, even hiring expensive expert witnesses to prove a fact that to you was obvious all along.

The lawyers handle the law, but you will be responsible for gathering the evidence, and it is a difficult and time-consuming and often expensive task. Different cases have a different balance of law- and evidence-based arguments. If your case is based on proving some obvious procedural defect – for example, that a government authority failed to provide the required notice period when it made a decision or took an action – then the evidence aspect may be quite straightforward. If your case requires you to prove complex facts about other people's actions, beliefs or motivations, or if you are required to present medical, scientific or environmental data, then the evidentiary side of your case may be very challenging. Part of assessing the affordability of your case is knowing at the outset how much evidence you are going to need to produce.

One final but very important caution is that you should not assume your case will end once it has been decided in the primary court. If you win, you need to be ready for your opponent's appeal, and this could prove more expensive than the original case. Fortunately appeal courts often do not require a rehearing of the evidence; often the appeal focuses purely upon the legal arguments, which can be a bit simpler to manage. Usually, however, the legal costs grow substantially as you move into the higher courts.

3.4 The legal issue may not be the same as your campaign issue

A very important aspect of litigation that activists need to be aware of is that courts define issues within a very narrow and specific legal framework. You may have brought your case because to you there is a major issue of public, political, environmental or moral significance at stake, but usually the litigation will revolve around a very narrow question about the application of the law to a particular set of facts. The wider political or moral values are most often considered to be entirely or at least substantially irrelevant to the judges.

In many cases the narrowness of the legal question may completely exclude your real moral motivation for bringing the case in the first place. This can be frustrating for public interest applicants, but it is actually something that judges pride themselves on. They deliberately approach cases from the perspective of applying the law as they see it, largely independent of the wider social ramifications. This is generally but not universally the case; of course judges do keep an eye out for the public policy implications of developing the law in a particular way, but they are careful not to allow the court to be seen to be the umpire of wider social or political issues.

This deliberate disconnection between the legal issue and the wider social issue can be frustrating for activists who are relying on the court to deliver what they see as a just outcome in the case at hand. For an example of this, see the Tasmanian Dams case (www.austlii.edu.au/au/cases/cth/HCA/1983/21.html).

In that case, environmentalists in Australia had been campaigning in an internationally famous protest to prevent the construction of a dam in an important wilderness area in the state of Tasmania. Following its election to office, the national government took steps to stop the construction of the dam, and the state government challenged the national government's legislation as being unconstitutional. This led to a situation where there was an important case that would determine whether the dam was built or not. However, the court was not there to decide whether the dam was a good idea or not – that was largely irrelevant; the only question was a constitutional one of whether the national government had the power to override state legislation in that instance. Fortunately for the environmentalists, the court upheld the exercise of power by the national government, but the case demonstrates how the issue in court and the issue in the eyes of the public may be two completely different things.

The danger of this kind of litigation is that a loss in court may send a message to the public that the court has somehow legitimized your opponent's position on the larger issue. Public interest advocates usually choose litigation as a tactic in a wider social or political campaign, and they need to be very careful at all times to remember the bigger picture. In developing a campaign plan that involves litigation there is a need to ensure that your campaign is prepared for a loss as much as for a win in court. You need to be able to articulate your broader message before, during and after the case, and you may need to make it clear that you will not stop your campaign if you lose in court.

If you make the mistake of making too much of the litigation and you lose, you may be faced with a situation where you are expected to accept the court's decision as though it was an umpire's decision on your whole campaign. You should never allow yourself to end up in this position.

4.0 Other ways to use the law

This chapter has mainly examined the advantages and potential pitfalls of litigation as a tactic in public interest campaigns. There are other ways in which activists can use the law to further their campaign aims without actually becoming plaintiffs in formal legal actions. These other processes are usually established in various pieces of legislation that create rights to obtain information, participate in decision-making or lodge complaints or seek reviews of the decisions of government and public decision-making bodies.

These other statutory participation rights were discussed in Chapter 6 in relation to activism in the public sector. It is important for activists to obtain copies of the legislation relevant to their campaigns and look for opportunities that may be available to participate, complain or seek review or information. These processes are usually widely available and relatively low cost to initiate.

Conclusion

This chapter has aimed to provide practical advice for activists and advocates about using litigation as tactic in a campaign. The central message is that you need to start from the perspective of your overall campaign plan (see Chapter 4) and then see where litigation may or may not fit in as a useful and cost-effective strategy. There are many advantages but also a lot of potential pitfalls in going down the road to litigation, and this chapter aims to make campaigners aware of these considerations. Certainly it can be concluded that litigation is no silver bullet that will ensure campaign success, but used properly and strategically it can be a powerful tactic in a wider campaign.

ELEVEN | **Social change and conflict resolution**

Introduction

Although we have strongly promoted non-violence as a core value in public interest work, this does not mean that there is no place for conflict. On the contrary, conflict is often unavoidable, and sometimes there can even be a need to deliberately generate some conflict to bring an issue into public awareness. What is critical is our approach to conflict and how we manage it. Conflict and conflict resolution are important topics, both in the external environment in which social movements and activists operate, and within the internal structures of organizations. This chapter explores the context of conflict in social change work, then goes on to explore some practical tools for conflict resolution, including strategic questioning, negotiation and mediation.

1.0 Attitudes to conflict

Conflict is an opportunity. Although conflict usually conjures up a negative mental image, it is also what attracts a lot of attention in our society. Conflict can be an important precursor to beneficial change.

Justice Murphy in the Australian High Court eloquently described the value of agitators and the social conflict they can produce in his famous judgment concerning an indigenous rights activist who was jailed for a minor assault:

> That Mr. Neal was an 'agitator' or stirrer in the magistrate's view obviously contributed to the severe penalty. If he is an agitator, he is in good company. Many of the great religious and political figures of history have been agitators, and human progress owes much to the efforts of these and the many who are unknown ... Mr. Neal is entitled to be an agitator. (J. Murphy, *Neal* v. *R* [1982] 149 CLR 305 at p. 317)

1.1 Invisible conflict and voiceless victims

Sometimes conflict is the only effective way to bring people's attention to an issue. The reason for this is that the victims of violence in society are often invisible to the everyday person. Whether these victims are prisoners, disadvantaged groups such as homeless people or children, or non-humans such as animals or the environment itself, it is often very difficult to convey their suffering to the mass of the population until there is some event, often conflict, which brings people's attention to the issue.

The issue of logging of old-growth forest is a good example. These forests are usually very remote, which is why they have survived until now, so they are in places where the average person may never see them. The harm suffered by the forests and the species that are dependent upon them is unlikely to register with the great mass of people unless and until some event brings it to their attention. Protests and blockades are a powerful way in which environmentalists have been able to draw attention to the conflict that already exists between human economic activities on the one hand and environmental sustainability on the other. In a sense what a forest protest does is transport some of the inherent conflict out of the forest and into the human social world. Blockades cause nature's suffering to become a conflict between human and human, and then there is a greater chance that steps will be taken to resolve that conflict.

Similar principles apply to animal rights activists, for whom there is a need to first relocate the locus of the problem in the human community in order to provoke a response. Countless other issues rely to some extent upon conflict as a means of promoting change and resolution.

Conflict and violence are not synonymous; conflict can be as little as strident disagreement or taking a stand and being heard. Sometimes conflict exists merely because different people have incompatible ideas about how a resource should be used. At times a social movement needs to deliberately provoke a level of conflict in order to bring an issue to public attention. Obviously such a strategic use of conflict carries risks and the decision to pursue it is not one that should be taken lightly, but nor should we be afraid to admit to ourselves that the first step in our campaign may be to step up, make a stand and be prepared to generate an appropriate level of conflict.

How individuals and groups handle conflict is, of course, critical. Conflict can be an open invitation for us to succumb to our feelings of fear and aversion and react rather than respond to a situation. Shields (1991: 34–9) explores the way in which a person's past experiences, often childhood experiences, can cause them to have strong or even extreme reactions to certain situations. Where these kinds of reactions are present they are mostly unhelpful to a campaign. When people are proceeding from deeper personal issues that colour their perceptions of an external event there is a greater danger that they will act inappropriately and alienate onlookers, allies and opponents. While it may be important to generate some controlled conflict, it is also important to try to prevent people within the movement using this as a justification for aggression.

Shields (ibid.: 35) describes 'the rebel' as a common aspect of the personality of many social change activists. The rebel persona has a lot of positive motivating qualities for activists, but can also tend to be unreceptive, rigid and unwilling to listen. If people identify too closely with their inner rebel, there is a danger that they may end up investing more in maintaining the problem than in contributing to the solution. Useful as it may be at first, it is not desirable to maintain conflict as a permanent state; your campaign needs to be on a path towards resolution.

The value of conflict is the opportunity it creates for debate, discussions and exploring new approaches; it is rarely constructive on its own. To get to the constructive side of conflict it is important that all participants genuinely want resolution.

There are many techniques for dealing with conflict and we will examine some of them; however, techniques are not a substitute for a deep understanding of non-violence, which is at the heart of conflict resolution. Non-violence is much more than not being violent, and it is not the same as simply being passive. The best approach is to be hard on the problem in a collaborative way and soft on the person (Fisher et al. 1991: 55). Another way of saying this is that as activists we should be firm and assertive but not aggressive. Bringing a level of respect and concern to conflict situations is the best foundation for dispute resolution. This attitude can be very challenging personally because often there is a fear that it will make you soft on the person *and* the problem.

A distinction is often drawn between external and internal conflict in social movements. It should not be seen as a strict dichotomy; on the contrary, it is important to maintain a high degree of skill transference in social movements between outside and internal approaches to conflict resolution. Conflict resolution processes are essential in relations within the group, but it is exactly these skills which are also needed externally in developing allies and resolving conflict with intelligent opponents. For this reason the skills needed for internal or external conflict resolution have not been completely differentiated in this chapter.

2.0 Reducing internal conflict through inclusive structures

Today's social movements tend to have relatively flat structures with participatory decision-making, whereby all members are involved to some extent. Ideally there is also an awareness of sites of oppression such as sexism and racism. Such awareness is essential, although it can bring with it the danger that groups get paralysed in a mire of political correctness and lose sight of their goals. This is commonly referred to as 'analysis paralysis'.

2.1 Consensus decision-making

Participatory decision-making is often based on consensus. Issues are discussed until a decision is reached that all participants can 'live with'; this is called a 'working consensus'. Consensus that requires absolute agreement from all participants is absolute consensus and is usually reserved for the most important decisions.

Group processes are a fine balancing act for social movements. On the one hand processes need to be inclusive so that people have a voice in decision-making, have a chance to grow in the movement and the opportunity to make a contribution that is commensurate with their skills and ability. On the other hand the social movement is not there to provide a totally supportive environment for those involved; the movement exists to achieve particular aims encompassed within a vision of how the world could be.

As Katrina Shields (1991: 82) points out, it is very important to avoid the 'tyranny of structurelessness'. Usually this happens when a group is reacting against traditional conservative structures of decision-making. The result generally is that the individual or group with the greatest stamina and/or the loudest voice dominates the others. What this means is that it is necessary to find the right group processes. Choices about group structure need to be informed by the size of the group, its values and the nature of the decisions being taken.

Absolute consensus may not always be achievable; it can sometimes lead to oppressiveness of its own, whereby dissenting members are pressured to stop 'blocking consensus'. There has to be a place for legitimate dissent, whereby members of a group accept a decision which they may not agree with, but maintain (or even record) their dissent. This is preferable to the majority assuming that convincing these people to change their minds is essential. It may not be necessary at all.

For this reason, working consensus is a more realistic aim, offering general agreement on aims and methods, and sufficient agreement on the actions to be taken to allow a group to go ahead and make their plans.

2.2 Decision-making under pressure: affinity groups

Sometimes there is some urgency to a situation and a section of the group needs to make a decision quickly without the luxury of consulting more widely. This can often arise, for example, in intense conflict situations such as street protests and blockades. A more truncated method of decision-making can be achieved that is consistent with the group's overall values by adopting a systematic approach in which a series of threshold questions are applied, such as:

- Is the activity being contemplated in line with the current strategy of the group?
- Is it consistent with the group's overall values?
- Are there sufficient people who want to undertake the activity?
- Are participants prepared for the legal implications?

If the answer is 'yes' to all of the above then people may go ahead and organize the activity. A particularly useful process, if the above preconditions are met, is for those taking part in the action, and only those intending to take part, to form an 'affinity group' to plan the details. This avoids lengthy and often theoretical discussions with non-participants. This approach has several advantages: it is fast and flexible and it can also serve to confuse the opposition, because actions can happen almost spontaneously with little apparent leadership.

Group processes such as consensus decision-making and affinity groups are explored in more detail in the next chapter. What is important is to ensure that internal processes within groups are open enough to allow people to feel included in decision-making, inclusive enough to encourage the broadest range of people to take part, and flexible enough to permit the group to take action, sometimes quickly where required. Running a group's internal affairs in a way that minimizes conflict means that the group can focus more intently on the external issues and conflicts that are associated with its objectives.

3.0 Core conflict resolution skills

In this section we are going to look briefly at a few basic skills that are useful in conflict resolution; these include strategic questioning, negotiation and mediation. This is a specialist area, but this guide should provide some insights and signposts for people wishing to further develop these skills. Hopefully we will be able to reveal some of the core concepts that underlie good conflict resolution processes.

3.1 Strategic questioning

Strategic questioning is also a form of active listening and it is a powerful technique for resolving conflict and promoting change, both within groups and even more powerfully in interactions with other stakeholders, including intelligent opponents. It is a gentle but surprisingly effective means of inviting other stakeholders to define and possibly alter their positions. One of the most prominent writers associated with strategic questioning as a technique for social change work is Fran Peavey. Her book *By Life's Grace: Musing on the Essence of Social Change* is a good place to look for more information on this topic.

Strategic questioning requires the questioner to adopt a very open-minded, even curious, approach to the person they are talking to. The idea is to invite resolution of an issue by encouraging an exchange in which the other party is encouraged to explore their own values and needs and to explore other options for meeting those needs or addressing those values.

Strategic questioning demands active listening. Strategic questioning is not the same as the way a lawyer may cross-examine a witness in court. Cross-examination is conducted with a view to eliciting a predetermined response from a witness, or at least causing them to become confused or appear unreliable. Strategic questioning is not about outsmarting the other person, although hopefully it does proceed initially at least from a position where the questioner has a broader awareness of the issue than the other party. Strategic questioning requires the questioner to use their open-mindedness and inherent respect for the other person as a means to invite the other person to see things differently.

Peavey (1994: 89–93) identifies a number of key features of strategic questioning, paraphrased below.

The questions should be open ended enough to encourage motion and invite new ideas and solutions. So instead of asking, 'Why don't you just stop?' you could ask, 'Are there any other options available to you?' The questions may also aim to dig deeper by uncovering underlying values or motivations: 'What are the values that influence your choice?'

The questions usually avoid starting with 'Why', because this can appear aggressive and confrontational to the person being questioned; instead of inviting alternatives it can have the effect of causing the person to justify their position even more strongly, which tends to entrench their position rather than open it up. It is definitely advisable to avoid questions that require 'yes' or 'no' answers. This is because questions that present a binary choice leave the person being questioned in a passive role and are often subtly an attempt to manipulate the person being questioned.

Another key approach is to try to ensure that the questions can create a degree of empowerment. 'What different conditions would you need to see to help you make this decision?' Such a question allows the person to suggest and define possible solutions for him- or herself.

Finally, it may be necessary sometimes to be courageous and to ask the unaskable question: 'What would it take to encourage you to change your decision?' Such questions should obviously be used sparingly and only after a significant amount of opening up has already occurred, but they get to the crux of resolving what may otherwise be a dispute.

Strategic questioning is a powerful skill that is unlikely to be learned overnight. It runs counter to much of our cultural baggage in that it requires us to stand back and be curious and even respectful of our opponents. The attitude required is one of genuine curiosity, an eagerness to uncover the reasons why a person takes a different view to you. The great value of the technique is that often in the process we discover a lot of common ground between the parties to the conversation, the areas in dispute are minimized and there is more likelihood of the parties feeling a desire to reach further accommodation of each other's position.

It's perhaps useful to contrast the idea of strategic questioning with the way in which many will argue over ideas with people they disagree with. It's actually very unlikely that someone will succeed in arguing another person out of their chosen position; most arguments cause each party to validate and further reinforce their own existing position. Strategic questioning aims to give people the scope to explore their motivations and to find new ways of looking at an issue without feeling that they need to change their underlying values.

Obviously there will be situations where parties are so entrenched in their position that they will be resistant to any attempt to open up to new options, but you should not be the one to assume that. What is important is to ensure that you are open minded enough to leave some room for the possibility of change in your opponent's position. Assuming, for example, that a business person will 'only be interested in the money' may be a grave strategic error, when a little probing may uncover a broader range of values in the person which could have been activated as part of a conflict resolution process.

3.2 Negotiation

Negotiation is a key skill for conflict resolution. Superficially negotiation is an ordinary skill that all people need to use in their daily lives in dealing with partners, children, colleagues, neighbours and in business dealings. In many of these situations its role in resolving conflict goes partly unnoticed because it is often effective in preventing latent conflict from becoming manifest. While we all use negotiation in our daily lives it is a skill that we mostly rely on our intuition and past experiences to develop. Negotiation can also be a professional skill for lawyers, diplomats, business people and, of course, for activists and people engaged in social change work. These more formal settings often require a little more practice and training.

Negotiation has been defined as a process which 'Involves parties with perceived conflicting interests working towards an understanding or outcome as to how they can best resolve their differences' (Alexander and Howieson 2010: xxiv).

3.2.1 Principled negotiation
As the context for negotiation moves from the purely personal to a more formalized setting, personal intuition may not be sufficient as a guide to the negotiation process, so some guidelines become necessary. Four critical elements of principled negotiation that have been described by Fisher et al. in their seminal work *Getting to Yes* (1991) are:

1. *Separate the person from the problem* (ibid.: 17–19) In high-conflict situations this is more easily said than done. This element reinforces the necessity for people committed to social change not to be motivated by fear and aversion. It's hard to negotiate effectively with a party that you have demonized. Developing fixed negative ideas about the other parties is highly counterproductive. Apart from the disrespect it shows and the subconscious

tension it can bring into a situation, it also hampers effective negotiation. If you start from a position of believing negative stereotypes about the other party you actually limit your own ability to imagine or envision solutions, or to invite them to offer solutions.

It is also important to ensure that both parties' emotions are acknowledged and hopefully expressed early in the negotiation (ibid.: 30–3). Venting of emotion in a controlled way can be very significant in clearing the table for the substantive negotiation. This is especially important in very personal negotiations such as family law situations, but it is also surprisingly important in professional settings as well. The form that emotional venting will take will vary depending on the circumstances. In a professional setting it may be done away from the other party; in a less explosive setting, such as an internal conflict within an organization, it may be appropriate to allow it to take place (in a controlled way) between the parties as a preliminary step to negotiation.

2. *Work with the other parties' interests not their positions* (ibid.: 41–57) Interests are what underlie positions. Positions are a result of interests. Conflict begins because both sides adopt opposing positions. These positions reflect a person's own limited perception of what is possible or desirable. Both parties identifying their interests offers the opportunity for these interests to be served in a variety of new ways. There is never only one solution to a conflict. Working with interests also allows more opportunities for mutualizing or establishing common ground.

3. *Invent options for mutual gain* Once each party has revealed their interests and needs, it is critical to explore as many options for satisfying those needs as possible. One of the most difficult things in negotiation is to ensure that both parties' needs are adequately explored before options for solution are discussed. It is human nature to want to fix a problem; unfortunately, unless needs are explored, parties end up simply arguing about solutions with little basis for decision-making. Brainstorming, where all options are put forward without judgement, can produce surprising results (ibid.: 58–83).

4. *Use objective criteria* Objective criteria should be used to assess the options, e.g. a valuation or a scientific report (ibid.: 84–98). This can be very useful in public as well as private disputes.

Negotiation can be a key element in a campaign. It is especially likely to form a key strategic component of the later or final stages of a successful campaign (Moyer 2001: 73). Like most things in social change work there's no substitute for preparation.

3.2.2 A framework for your negotiation

In Chapter 4 we examined a number of conflict maps that were useful for framing and mapping a campaign. In a similar way it can be useful to develop a map of the parameters of an issue prior to commencing formal negotiation. Alexander and Howieson (2010: 106) suggest the use of a negotiation navigation map that explores the following aspects of the process:

- frame the negotiation: this means defining what you see as the parameters of the dispute or subject of negotiation;
- identify the stakeholders;
- identify the interests of stakeholders;
- identify potential options for negotiated outcomes;
- identify sources of independent criteria (valuations, precedents, benchmarks, etc.);
- develop alternatives;
- define the bottom line – both yours and the likely bottom line of others;
- identify more potential options.

Developing a map of this kind will help you clarify your own aims and help you be prepared to respond to suggestions, offers and negotiating tactics.

In trying to understand or predict what another party's interests may be, you should be careful not to underestimate them. It's easy to assume that their interests are very simple ('they just want money'), especially if you have demonized them in your own mind. Such an approach is unhelpful because, for example, your opponent may place a high value on saving face, or on a more certain business or personal environment, and for this reason may be prepared to compromise to achieve this.

In analysing your own interests and bottom line you should think carefully about what you could walk away without and still feel OK about the outcome. These negotiable items become part of what you have to offer the other side to achieve agreement.

3.2.3 The dynamics of negotiating for a group

When negotiating on behalf of a campaign group or social movement the situation is much more complex than when negotiating as an individual. These issues about your own interests and what's negotiable and non-negotiable become a group decision and it may be difficult to gain agreement beforehand. As a negotiator representing a group, you are in a difficult position because you will be held accountable for any strategic concessions that you may make. It's important to develop a clear understanding with the group before you begin negotiation about just how far your personal scope for making concessions extends. It may be that all you can do in negotiation is indicate to the other parties your personal openness to a position, but that you require time to go back and discuss this with the group.

Negotiating on behalf of an activist group can be fraught with risks. Negotiation usually takes place towards the end of the life cycle of a campaign or social movement, when the campaign is nearing success. You need to ensure that you know your campaign's strengths and weaknesses, whether it has the underlying tenacity to keep fighting if the negotiations fail, and whether you can achieve more through negotiation.

We have previously discussed the role of rebels in social movements. Rebels are useful allies in the early stages and trigger events (Moyer 2001: 24), but people who identify too closely with the rebel persona are uncomfortable with negotiation and even more uncomfortable with compromise. You run the risk of encountering severe internal opposition if your compromises are seen to be too extensive. This is where really knowing your organization is essential. There may well be a small group of extremists who will never support a negotiated outcome and you may just need to trade off their support for the greater good if you and the rest of the group are sure that the negotiated outcome is the best.

3.2.4 Your best alternative A useful tool for determining whether the negotiated outcome is better than what could be achieved without negotiation is what is called your 'BATNA', which stands for your 'best alternative to a negotiated agreement' (Fisher et al. 1991: 101). As Fisher et al. explain, your BATNA 'is the standard against which any proposed agreement should be measured. That is the only standard which can protect you both from accepting terms that are too unfavourable and from rejecting terms it would be in your interests to accept' (p. 104).

In negotiating on behalf of a campaign group or social movement it is very important to have first involved all participants within your organization in considering the likely outcome of not reaching a negotiated agreement. There may be idealists who will rail against any compromise, but if you can show that the compromise is streets ahead of the most likely outcome of persisting with conflict, then you should be able to at least persuade the vast majority of your group to support a negotiated outcome.

In negotiation it's good to have a small team that has different perspectives and skills, e.g. a person with good strategic knowledge of negotiation, a person with lots of information about the issue, and a person who can strongly put across your party's interests. Whether your negotiation will involve a team, of course, depends on how formal the process is and how large your group is.

3.3 Mediation

Mediation includes elements of negotiation but it is a more structured process whereby an impartial third party assists the parties in developing an agreement between them. Mediation is generally employed where negotiation is too difficult. Mediation has the advantage that there is a facilitator who can supervise the conduct of the parties to ensure that it remains respectful and constructive. Mediators may also be skilled at uncovering the needs of the parties and at helping to suggest possible solutions.

Beyond this brief description it is not easy to define mediation as a process. Mediation can be a purely private matter to which the parties commit voluntarily and a suitable private mediator is employed at the expense of one or both parties, or it can be a more institutionalized process, such as family-court-supervised mediation, which is required in many jurisdictions as part of the litigation process (Boulle 1996: 4).

Boulle (ibid.) cautiously describes the core features of mediation as follows:

- it is a decision-making process;
- in which the parties are assisted by a third person, the mediator;
- who attempts to improve the process of decision-making;
- to assist the parties in reaching an outcome to which each of them can assent.

Mediators do not make the decision, though; the mediator's role is, as the name suggests, simply one of assisting the parties themselves in reaching agreement. A process in which a third party has the power to impose a decision on the parties is usually called arbitration and we do not discuss arbitration in this book. Mediators are there to facilitate the process, but not to impose a solution on the parties.

The role of a professional mediator largely consists of encouraging the parties to engage in a productive negotiation process in which the key features of good negotiation that we identified earlier are promoted, including:

- assisting communication by encouraging parties to focus on the issues and not upon their personal conflict;

- seeking to uncover the needs and interests that lie behind the parties' adopted positions;
- seeking a broader range of possible outcomes.

Mediation in the context of social change work is likely to take place either in internal organizational disputes or as part of a formal process for resolving a public interest dispute. Where mediation is used as a means of resolving a public interest issue, the process will usually be a formalized one initiated by government power-holders. Some examples of situations in which activists and social change advocates may find themselves involved in formal mediation processes include:

- neighbourhood disputes;
- landlord and tenant disputes;
- disputes arising under anti-discrimination legislation;
- telecommunications complaints;
- complaints about police misconduct;
- indigenous and native land title claim disputes;
- industrial and trade union matters;
- environmental disputes;
- consumer disputes;
- complaints and appeals against the decisions of government agencies generally.

Social change activists taking part in mediation processes will usually be doing so on behalf of organizations that they represent or on behalf of the clients of support services that they provide (e.g. tenant support, trade union matters, anti-discrimination issues, etc.). In these situations the individual will be constrained by their professional or organizational role and may be further constrained by the internal politics of the organization that they represent. The discussion in the section above regarding negotiation and the risks of alienating parts of your organization that may be opposed to compromise apply equally to individuals who take part in mediation processes on behalf of a public interest group or organization.

4.0 Summary: conflict resolution processes

There are overlaps between all of the three processes – strategic questioning, negotiation and mediation – that we have discussed here. There are clearly some important underlying skills and values that remain common to all three. In a nutshell, you should always approach the other party with respect, open-mindedness and a willingness to find solutions that meet each other's needs. The main awareness you need to bring is that each party comes with a 'position' that represents their understanding of the outcome they want, but that what is important is to dig deeper and uncover the underlying needs or interests that they are seeking to satisfy by adopting that position. Once this is undertaken by both parties then it's possible to start to imagine ways of better accommodating both sets of interests.

4.1 Strategic considerations

Conflict resolution processes are designed to bring a conflict to a close by encouraging realistic compromise between the parties. There are times when this will not be the right approach for your campaign, or at least not the right approach at this time.

Most obviously you need to assess whether your campaign has progressed far enough through its own process of building support and momentum to allow you to enter negotiations with a strong hand. You also need to assess the likelihood of actually achieving an outcome that will satisfy the aims and aspirations of your support base. For people involved in social change movements there may be some things that can be compromised or bargained away and others that simply shouldn't be. Many campaigns are very long processes and are about slowly changing societal attitudes on particular issues. Examples of slow-burning social movements include the peace movement, the anti-whaling movement, animal rights, vegetarianism and anti-slavery, to name just a few. In many instances it is better for such groups to retain their identity and integrity by remaining outside of formal processes of compromise in order to continue to present a stark contrast to mainstream values. Negotiation may be possible on smaller, more specific related issues, but these will be milestones for the movement rather than a process of achieving their overall aims.

Activists need to remember that maintaining the dispute and the conflict also means maintaining the critique of mainstream practices, and this may need to be kept up for many years in order to build proper momentum for change, so choosing the right time to stand firm and the right time to compromise will always be a difficult call.

It has to be remembered that power-holders will seek to negotiate, compromise or mediate disputes only when they feel that the movement is gathering strength and that some strategic concession is needed to defuse its progress. Activists and social change advocates need to bear this in mind and make a strategic decision about whether it is appropriate or beneficial to take part in such processes at the time.

The politics of offering or refusing to negotiate can be tricky; your opponent may be trying to make you appear unreasonable if you refuse. In many cases, instead of refusing outright, you can strategically demur by insisting that a higher-order objective of your campaign remains on the table as a precondition of your participation. For example, you may say, 'We won't come and discuss a reduction in whaling unless total cessation is also on the table.' In this way you may be able to turn the tables on your opponent and reveal their unreasonableness.

Remember always that your opponent will seek an easy way out when it starts to look as if you are gaining the upper hand, and it may be better for the campaign to just play on and win if this is possible. It may in some cases be better to allow an issue to boil over in public and embarrass a government than to allow the issue to be swept under the carpet by a negotiated settlement.

In the context of public interest litigation, for example, we see again and again the way in which large industry and corporate players will defend litigation stubbornly right up until it appears likely that they may fail in court, and then they will offer substantial and confidential out-of-court settlements. This has been a feature of test cases against the tobacco giants for many years, and has now started to become common in environmental test cases as well. A win in court by a public interest advocate has one huge advantage over an out-of-court settlement – it sets a legal precedent. Insurance companies, tobacco companies and mining companies know that it's better to pay a large sum to silence a threatening litigant than to face the avalanche of indefensible claims that would follow if a legal precedent were set that confirmed their liability. In *Dagi v. BHP* [1995] 1 VR 428, a transnational mining company operating a large gold mine in Papua New Guinea offered a substantial out-of-court settlement only after many years of resisting a tort claim by villagers affected by pollution from mine waste. Such an outcome is a win for the plaintiffs at the time, but fails to assist future claimants by establishing a precedent for future cases.

There is no easy rule of thumb to decide what approach is best. In many campaigns, negotiated outcomes form the moral precedents that propel the campaign forward. This can be especially true in situations where you are pressuring corporations and businesses to change, because there may be no other clear legal or political means to pressure them. When activists are able to convince large corporations to adopt safer or more environmentally sustainable practices, it can set an important moral precedent and serve as a way of pressuring other industry players to follow suit. Examples of these kinds of action include where paper companies are convinced to stop using pulp from old-growth forests, or where concerns such as the meat industry are persuaded to adopt more humane methods, or where fishing businesses can be persuaded to exclude processes that generate too much damaging by-catch. In many cases there may not have been any other means to achieve these changes, so negotiated outcomes represent the best way forward for the campaign.

As in all its other aspects, the way forward for a campaign is always a strategic consideration. In preparing for any strategy that involves negotiation or mediation, activists and social movements should consult their whole-of-campaign strategic mapping processes, as outlined in Chapter 4.

5.0 Case study

The following case study is a good example of a public interest dispute that could have led to protracted conflict but was instead resolved through negotiation. It is a useful study partly because it reveals the power of negotiation and partly because it is unfortunately still relatively rare to see public disputes resolved in such a cooperative way.

The Paterson Hill dispute The dispute involved some real estate developers (Detala Pty Ltd) who wanted to establish a subdivision on some environmentally important lands in the world-renowned tourist mecca of Byron Bay on the east coast of Australia.

The Detala land in many ways was a developer's dream as it was situated on an easterly slope with magnificent views. Apart from the views the land seemed uninteresting, consisting essentially of low 'scrub' with a wetland at its base.

When the development application was displayed showing a fifteen-lot subdivision, local opposition focused on the density of development and its visual impact. Once the area came under scrutiny, however, it became clear just how valuable it was environmentally. Intense activity by concerned local residents was directed to identifying the flora and fauna species on the Detala land and surrounding area. This led to a successful application being made for the Byron Bay dwarf heathland to be listed under the NSW Threatened Species Conservation Act 1995 (TSCA) as an Endangered Ecological Community.

Subsequently several critically endangered species were found in the area. The presence of these species protected under the TSCA came to be very significant in the subsequent court hearings.

The development had to take place within five years of its approval.

A matter of weeks before the five years were due to elapse the developer decided to undertake 'token' work to save the application from lapsing. They dispatched an excavator to dig a foundation trench.

This work would require the removal and destruction of dwarf heathland for which no approval had been sought or given by the Byron Council under the council's Tree Preservation Order requirements. Local citizens who discovered that the excavator was on the way mustered 200 protesters within two hours and blocked the access road 300 metres before the entrance to the developer's property. This was done on the ground that the developer had not obtained the necessary approval from the council to remove protected trees.

The developer sought police support to clear the road. In the ensuing five hours sixty-four people were arrested before a council inspector appeared with a 'Stop Work' notice. (The excavator did not reach the boundary of the property and all arrest charges were subsequently dismissed by the court.)

The campaign included people who had a long history of activism and who had many contacts in government and were very familiar with lobbying and 'non-violent resistance'. The campaign (which included six court actions between the council and the developer) went through all the stages that Moyer outlines in his model of social movement life cycles.

The developer had all but run out of options for developing the land, although they did have a remaining right to appeal before the High Court of Australia. The final stage of the campaign centred on trying to find an acceptable sale price for this land. It is worth noting that early in the campaign the developer was open to a land 'swap' for other land of equal property value but not as environmentally sensitive. This fell through because the relevant government department failed to come up with any such land for consideration.

With respect to an acceptable sale price for the land the situation seemed stalled until the mayor initiated a move to personally meet the developer. In this meeting they spent several hours at a local pub getting to know each other and it concluded with the developer stating that he was prepared to sell the land for costs incurred to that date. While this was not a new offer, it was significant in that it was the first time it had been made personally to the current mayor.

The situation subsequently stalled again because the State Valuation Office took nearly a year to make their assessment of the value of the land. The mayor and the developer kept talking, however, and the activists kept talking to the mayor. The activists were then successful in persuading the Australian government to agree to contribute half the asking price of the land if the state (New South Wales) would contribute the other half.

The next major breakthrough occurred when the local action group took the initiative to meet the developer. The parties shared perspectives and discussed the price for the land. The developer concluded the meeting by saying that he appreciated being consulted and that his only regret was that it had not happened earlier. The developer was prepared to sell the land for about a quarter of the then current valuation.

The action group was delighted when the state minister for information, planning and natural resources paid a surprise visit to the site on 26 June 2003 and announced that the state government would purchase the land for inclusion in the Arakawal National Park.

In a review of the ten-year campaign with some of the main activists there was consensus that there were many occasions when the process could have failed. There was, however, agreement that a critical turning point was the decision by the activists to personally meet the developer, i.e. to put aside stereotyped views of each other, sit down together, examine issues and collaboratively agree on a strategy to bring about a mutually acceptable solution. In this case the activists established a 'negotiating team' of three people, each having special skills and experience in conflict resolution and group decision-making.

This case study is instructive. It reveals the possibilities of achieving negotiated outcomes in situations that would otherwise become protracted conflicts. What started with sixty-four arrests and earth-moving equipment moving towards threatened habitat ended in a negotiated settlement that suited all parties. This brief description of events, of course, makes it all look quicker and simpler than it was. Such a process took a lot of faith, persistence and, most of all, the wisdom and maturity to look beyond stereotypes of us and them and have the courage to hope for a shift in an opponent's position.

Of course, it also depended upon government coming up with the money to fund the purchase, but it was the rare spectacle of the community and developers agreeing to a compromise which propelled the Australian and state governments to take action. It is much easier to achieve cooperation if the path ahead is made clear for the stakeholders, and this is what the negotiation achieved.

6.0 Developing a conflict map

We have already looked at some conflict mapping tools in Chapter 4. In that chapter we were more concerned with the process of mapping and planning the strategy for emergent campaigns. Conflict mapping can also be useful in mediation and dispute resolution procedures as well, although the context is slightly different.

A conflict map can be developed by the parties during mediation, and it can be used to focus attention, reassure parties and show progress in resolving the dispute. The type of conflict map developed below is a way of analysing the dispute that can help the activist understand the conflict better.

Neighbours	Concerned locals

Needs
• Protection of unique environment
  – Dwarf heath
  – Lagoon
  – Threatened species
• Coastal development policy
• Minimum impact on infrastructure
 	
Concerns
• Environmental damage
• Visual impact
• Too much traffic
• Precedent for coastal development
	Very similar to neighbours

Developer and family	**Byron Shire Council**
Needs • Legal rights upheld • Return on investment • Minimal impact • Adequate compensation *Concerns* • Lose money • Lose land • Branded environmental vandal • Family conflict over issue • That protesters are just NIMBYs and exaggerating the environmental effects	*Needs* • To act within the law • Implement consistent policies • Satisfy community expectations *Concerns* • Council's inadequacies exposed • Councillors will lose votes • Large payout to developer • Large legal costs
State government	**Commonwealth government**
Concerns • Cost (could protect a much larger area inland for the same cost) • Hassles and cost of long-term protest • Image of local members	*Concerns* • Not wanting to help the state government out of a problem • Image of local members

11.1 Conflict map

This simple map relates to the material in the case study above. In developing a conflict map it is very important to frame needs in the most basic terms possible; doing so allows as much space as possible for the creation of options to satisfy the needs of the parties. For instance, defining one of the developer's needs as making a return on investment opens the door for land swaps and other ways of making a profit that may not involve developing the site.

One of the values of the simple conflict map provided above is that it seeks to move beyond the most obvious entrenched positions of the parties (develop the land, don't develop the land) and to go one step further by identifying the needs that have led to their respective positions. The real value of this is that if the needs can be satisfied in another way (which the parties may not have previously considered) then their positions may well change.

Conclusion

Conflict resolution is an important part of an activist's or a social change movement's toolbox. Conflict can be useful in bringing a hitherto unrecognized issue to light, but it is a risky and fairly blunt tool for finding real solutions to problems. Our study of the life cycle of social movements in Chapter 2 indicates that direct conflict is most likely to be a feature of the early stages of a campaign, but that negotiation is far more likely to be an important part of the final stages of successful campaigns. For this reason activists need to be aware of and develop skills in techniques such as strategic questioning, negotiation and mediation so that they are able to steer their particular campaigns through all the stages of the campaign cycle. Also, as we observed at the beginning of this chapter, avoiding and resolving conflict inside organizations is a vitally important skill and practice.

TWELVE | Empowerment and personal sustainability: staying active and avoiding burnout

Introduction

This chapter takes us on a journey beyond mere information and into the realms of personal experience, psychology, philosophy and even spirituality. Being an activist can be one of the most rewarding journeys in life, but it is important to be aware of the significant personal skills and awareness needed to avoid the pitfalls. As well as explaining ways to avoid personal burnout and how to survive as a lifelong campaigner, this chapter also explores ways to build sustainability into the functioning of activist groups.

> In order to be effective agents of social change, activists must first be open to the possibility that they are powerful and that their social movement might be progressing along the road to success. (Moyer 2001: 87)

1.0 The citizen activist

People become activists via many different routes, but the one thing in common is the moment when a person stops and thinks, 'This is not right and I'm going to do something about it.' The first part, 'this is not right', by itself is not especially powerful, but when it is combined with the inner call to action, an activist has been born.

Imagine a sheep paddock, with over one hundred sheep grazing contentedly. One sheep one day decides that she doesn't accept being farmed and stands up on her hind legs to see who the real power-holders are and challenge them. That one standing sheep is very obvious in a paddock of sheep on all fours; she can be seen from some distance. Not only has she found her own power, but her power is being magnified many times over by its sheer contrast with the passivity of those around her. Activists are often derided for being influential minorities. Indeed, this is the beginning of understanding the power of activism, the ability to magnify your group's influence. Historically grassroots activists and social movements have been powerful and often successful, but unfortunately many activists still fall into the trap of believing that their movement is failing. Sadly such negative thinking can be a self-fulfilling prophecy, creating a chain reaction of depression, burnout and despair, discouraging recruitment and leading to desperate tactics (ibid.: 87).

> Never doubt that a small group of thoughtful, committed citizens can change the world. Indeed, it is the only thing that ever has. (Margaret Mead, US anthropologist and popularizer of anthropology, 1901–78)

But we must be careful not to underestimate the depth of the transformations that take place as a person becomes an activist or the particular pressures and challenges that the activist's life entails. While some people seem to almost be born activists, these are relatively few; far more people are what can be called accidental activists, people who quite naively take a stand on an issue one day, sometimes not realizing how far reaching that first small step really is. Often people accidentally find themselves being anointed as local leaders simply because they did something quite natural; they took a stand.

1.1 Personal power and people power

The centralized systems of authority that modern nation-states employ encourage personal passivity. Even democratic institutions such as representative parliaments encourage us to put our faith in a government to make decisions rather than to take a direct role in political life on a day-to-day basis. In a secondary sense these structures can also distract our attention away from the important task of bringing about social change and lead us to think that lobbying politicians is the only way to achieve change. It isn't. Change usually begins to occur on the ground and in communities long before it makes an impact among power-holders. Planting the seeds of change can be done in many different ways.

The first and most important leap is to get over the idea that you can't make a difference. The story of the one sheep that takes a stand should serve to show that your efforts are magnified when you stand out from the ubiquitous passivity of the crowd. Secondly, it's important to know that you can make a difference always, even if it's only a small one.

> I act on the conviction that everyone is making a difference. Just by living our lives, consuming space and resources we are making a difference. Our choice is what kind of difference to make. (Peavey 1986)

1.2 Break the habit of passivity

Shields (1991: ch. 2) discusses at length the cultural and personal inhibitions that have built up around the idea that we are powerful and can make a difference. The habit of passivity can be broken by taking action (however small); for some it is forcibly broken by intolerable circumstances, but many take what they see as a small stand on something eminently reasonable and are surprised to become a local 'hero'. As well as overcoming the habit of passivity we must overcome other self-limiting beliefs – for example, we must overcome the self-limiting thought that we are not an 'expert', or that we don't know enough to take a stand.

As well as the habit of passivity, Moyer (2001: ch. 4) identifies three main ways in which activists often mistakenly reinforce ideas of powerlessness in themselves or in relation to their social movement. These include:

- developing rational arguments for perceiving movement failure;
- a general culture of failure (a belief system in which the strength of the opposing forces is routinely exaggerated); and even
- an aversion to success itself.

Some activists are almost afraid of recognizing success in case it will generate complacency. There is a fine balance to be struck between hubris and complacency, and it comes from maintaining a faith in the power of social movements and a measured optimism that feeds perseverance and patience.

1.3 Envisioning

Have you ever dreamed of making some changes in the world around you and later found that you have? It may be something small in your own life, such as moving to a new town and finding employment there. At first it may seem as if there is no opportunity, but because you have had the dream you have subconsciously begun to look for the opportunities that lead to its fulfilment. We have probably all heard something about the power of positive thinking. There are important ways in which positive thinking can be demonstrated to work. Many people have had the experience of deciding to buy a certain model of car. Suddenly overnight that model appears to be everywhere. There are not more of them; it's just that you have set off the 'search pattern' in your mind that will now look for opportunities to bring your vision to reality. Without getting into any magical thinking about the ability to manifest our thoughts, we need to be rationally aware that so much of our social and indeed physical space is the way it is because people before us envisioned making it this way.

This is also true of social change work – envisioning a better world will help alert you to the opportunities that exist to achieve it. This is an important lesson because some activists get very stuck on the negative mental images of an issue. While these can convey powerful emotional messages that also spur people into action, they do need to be balanced by positive messages that encourage effective and hopeful activity. I once heard an ardent animal lover tell me she wouldn't join an animal liberation group because she didn't want to get sent magazines full of pictures of suffering animals.

Envisioning a better world is a very important step, and it is also one that is much more likely to inspire other people to join you. Vision is a prerequisite of any sort of effective living, let alone effective social change. What many famous visionaries have in common is their focus upon the world they want to create, not on what they want to eliminate (Boice 1992: 23). It is so much more powerful to invite people to see the better future you are aiming for than just to talk about removing things with no clear indication of what will replace them. Merely removing one problem does not automatically bring about a changed world (ibid.: 23); it could, without an adequate vision of future change, merely allow other problems to fill the vacuum.

> The first act of imagination required of any social change activist is the vision of a better world. The next challenge is to imagine ways to convey this vision to others. (Ricketts 2006: 77)

2.0 The making of a lifelong activist

Social change is usually a David and Goliath epic. People often take on causes that have not been taken on by others or which face an uphill battle against entrenched attitudes or beliefs. It's important to be realistic about the task ahead, positive but also forgiving of oneself. You must be prepared to both forgive yourself (for perceived failures) and to congratulate yourself (for small successes). As with any long-term project you may need a little more than immediate success to sustain your enthusiasm; you need perseverance and faith to get through the long hard times.

Humility will help you to expect your path to be a long, slow one. Humility will also help you not to expect too much of yourself or to think you are the only one who cares or can do the job. Peavey (1986: 114) argues that you must fight the ego's assertion that you are saving the world: 'We all work to save little things ... When it all gets put together it makes up the big things' (ibid.: 115).

Because the campaign is likely to be a long one you need to be able to 'live on the road', so it is important not to place the rest of your life on hold while you get on with the campaign. Successful social change activists learn to be the tortoise rather than the hare. Looking after yourself and your family is important. The biggest danger is that you will decide that the campaign is just so much more important than you. This is a grave mistake and can lead to burnout, which it is important to try to avoid. Of course the campaign may be more important than you when looked at from outside, but not to you it isn't. Remember, what we want is a more sustainable world, so achieving it sustainably has to be the first step.

2.1 Awakening involves dissonance

Another important thing to bear in mind is as your awareness grows and as you explore the facts about your issue is that you may find the situation is much worse than you previously realized. Shields (1991: ch. 1) explores the idea that becoming an activist involves becoming aware of what is wrong with the world and just how deep the underlying problems may be.

In order to be able to bring about change for the better in an appropriate and targeted way we need to be able to take a good honest look at what is going on right now. It's no secret that the entire planet is in peril environmentally, so wherever you look you are going to find some signs of ill health. As an activist you may be exposed to information not available to the general public; the situation may be worse than you realized and you will need to be able to integrate this new information. You will need strategies to carry all this information around without letting it get you down.

At first you may feel a lot of despair or anger or frustration. You need to be able to acknowledge these feelings, honour them, but not let them paralyse you. The key is to find the places where you are powerful, where you are hopeful and where you have the opportunity to make a difference. You need to remember that the problems already existed in the world before you noticed them; your awakening may well be very disturbing, and your internal feelings about the problems in the world don't change it, but your actions might help to.

As well as being exposed to more information that may be disturbing to you, it's possible that you will also experience a growing awareness of the hypocrisy and apathy that exist in society and experience great frustration about the attitudes and actions of others. As an activist educator of many years' standing I have watched many people become new activists and go through this growing pain. Frequently a single issue will cause an individual to 'take a stand', at which point they do find their own power to make a difference and experience great empowerment. In a sense these are the first and second stages of becoming an activist. The third stage is often even more momentous – it is like a further episode of dissonance. Many people have spent most of their lives with some kind of benign faith in the political system. When they take on an issue and poke their head into the world of politics and power, they suddenly see power imbalances, lies and injustices in the system, or simply widespread social apathy and denial, that they hadn't really been aware of before. This can be experienced as a loss of innocence, or even as a deep sense of betrayal. In this process of transformation a person is likely to see that social change is needed at a deep structural level throughout society, and they may well significantly shift the focus of their activism from a single issue to a much deeper commitment to social justice, empowerment and participatory democracy generally. In a sense the activist moves into a 'meta' approach to social change and sees various single-issue causes as mere examples of a deeper malady that they are committed to addressing. The diagram below gives an example of a cascading process in which a person may end up orienting themselves towards a much broader picture of social change.

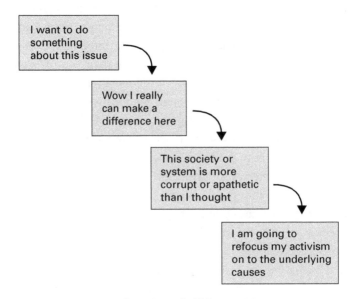

12.1 The making of a lifelong activist

3.0 What is activist burnout and how can it be avoided?

We have already discussed the idea that campaigns may be very long journeys and that activists need to develop skills of personal sustainability, or the ability to live on the road. The alternative is to work unsustainably, and this can lead to serious consequences. Burnout is the metaphor used to describe what happens to activists who obsess about their campaigns and work so hard for so long that eventually it takes an unacceptable personal toll on them.

Burnout can of course occur for people in a variety of other settings, including stressful relationships, caring for sick and dying relatives or sick children, as well as for workers in various fields, such as doctors, lawyers and social workers – in fact any situation in which a person is highly motivated out of a sense of service to other people or to situations outside of themselves. Burnout is the result of not properly balancing the different aspects of our lives, including the personal and the professional.

Burnout is very common for activists and social change workers. It is a far deeper problem than mere temporary exhaustion. It can affect every aspect of a person's life and professional work. Burnout is also a very destructive force in social change movements as it can be the cause of conflict, blame, anger, poor performance or obsession, and at worst can render an otherwise passionate and effective activist unable to continue to work for change.

Burnout in its more advanced forms is more akin to what used to be called a nervous breakdown, and during its build-up it can be characterized by depression, exhaustion, chronic fatigue, mood swings, anger, cynicism, emotional freezing and an inability to find meaning in anything (Shields 1991: 120). In the earlier stages it may be less obvious, but the danger signs include withdrawal from social life, workaholism, relationship breakdowns, neglect of family and friends and a general attitude that there is nothing more important than the campaign and no one else who can be relied upon to do it properly (ibid.: 125).

3.1 The spirituality of activism

It is difficult to seriously address the issue of burnout without delving into the spirituality of activism to some extent. This is because the prospect of burnout brings us face to face with the very things that first motivated us to become activists, the whole idea of what is meaningful or worthwhile committing oneself to, and the sometimes difficult balance between the needs of self and other.

Starting from first principles, sustainable activism proceeds from a balanced understanding of what it is to be a human in a very large and complex universe. We need to be able to see ourselves as small, but yet as capable of choice, agency and effect. Our decision to be an activist comes from a sense of ethics (however this is derived) and personal motivation to act in a way that promotes those ethics. We need to have the humility to accept the diversity of the world and its people, yet be sure enough of our position to pursue our goal with dignity and persistence. Above all we need to understand that we are a natural, valid and relevant part of the universe, just as we are, and that we have nothing to prove.

3.1.1 Moving beyond success and failure There is one very key way in which people get 'hooked in' to their campaigns in a manner that is likely to cause obsession and burnout. This is when they become personally attached to its success. Now this may sound very strange, because on one level it remains essential that all campaigners are committed to the success of the campaign, but it depends on how you commit yourself. The ego is closely focused on success and failure; but at a deeper level you are motivated by your values. The best way to commit yourself to a life of effective action is to uncover your values and commit yourself to pursuing them regardless of success or failure at any particular point in time.

If you set yourself up so that your personal well-being depends on a particular campaign outcome you have unwittingly placed yourself in great personal danger. Not only is it dangerous but surprisingly it doesn't help the campaign all that much either. OK, you passionately want to ensure that a

particular local building or natural environment is not demolished. Passion is fine. You commit yourself along with others in your community to trying to prevent its redevelopment. You pour your very best into succeeding. But what is going to happen to you if you fail? From the outset you need to find a state of mind in which you can accept the outcome, while at the same time working with all your passion for your preferred outcome. You achieve nothing by allowing yourself to be consumed by resistance and rejection of the way the world is, even if it is unjust or unsustainable; you need to accept that it is currently the way it is, and then find the determination to make changes. This is not an easy process for most people, and it usually requires some deeper personal contemplation to understand it completely. Meditation practice in this context can become a great support to action.

A simple form of meditation is simply to sit quietly and contemplate the world and the universe just as it is. What you will realize is that it is vast, complex and very much bigger than you. Your role is to contribute to change in the best way you can, not to torture yourself if you cannot overcome a particular situation.

3.1.2 Accepting failure but keeping on going Sometimes it is necessary to first accept the possibility of total failure, then to find that state of mind that will allow you still to act with hope and integrity. Ask yourself, 'If the world was ending tomorrow, would that stop me behaving responsibly towards others?'

This is where you find that part of you that finds spiritual nourishment from 'right action', 'the path with heart', independent of whether success is assured or even likely. The aim is to commit fearlessly to your values, but to be open to success and failure.

So consider an issue you are passionate about. Feel all of the passion you have for your preferred outcome. Hold that passion to one side for a moment. Now imagine just for a moment that you fail, and picture the outcome, some precious icon destroyed perhaps. Now look about and see what else in the world is still precious and alive and worthy of your respect and passion. Go back to your passion to save that precious icon and make a deal with yourself. Promise to use your passion to save that icon, all the while 'accepting' that you may not succeed.

Acceptance in this sense is not the same as despair or resignation and it's not the same as approving of something either. To accept that there is injustice in the world is actually the most important first step in organizing yourself to correct it. Accepting that there will still be injustice in the world after you have corrected some of it is also important. Acceptance is a state of simply acknowledging the way things are, and it is a great basis for committing yourself to changing them. You may have wondered how some people can live a whole lifetime among the very social conditions that they aim to change. How can a human rights worker spend years working with victims of abuse? How can an animal rights worker spend so much time dealing with scenes of cruelty? The answer has to be that they have learned to look the problem in the face without flinching (accept the existence of the problem) and then commit themselves to taking useful steps to bring about change.

One of my favourite personal sayings is: 'Accept things the way they are and then work out a resourceful way to respond'.

The world may end in catastrophe despite your efforts, but as a human you wake each day with energy, and the choice you can make is what you do with that energy (no more).

The way I am using the word acceptance here may be new to some people. Words can have many meanings, and accepting as a fact that there is injustice in the world is not the same as giving in and deciding to do nothing about it. We need to distinguish between how we internally process a fact and how we respond to that fact in our external actions. Internally it is best to simply accept that the conditions of life are as they appear to be; externally it is best to devise a constructive way to change those conditions for the better.

A successful activist should aim to minimize their internal suffering over their chosen issue in order to maximize their effective actions to bring about change. Wringing our hands and feeling bad does not change the world, but taking action can.

3.1.3 Resistance It is hard for many of us to realize that the real cause of most of our internal suffering is 'resistance'. Internally we resist the way the world is, or the way we expect it to be, and cause ourselves a lot of pain in the process (Harris 2002: 71–2). It's hard for many of us to understand that we can stop resisting something (by accepting that it is so), and yet continue to dedicate ourselves to changing it. Too often we think that feeling really bad, angry or stressed out about what's wrong with the world is part of changing it. But in truth your bad feelings don't make a difference to the outside world at all, they just hurt you; what makes a difference is the actions you take with the energy you have available. Resistance uses up the energy you could be using to promote change in the world.

These ideas about humility, acceptance, resistance and avoiding attaching our sense of self to outcomes start sounding very much like some Eastern religious tradition that we often associate with political passivity. But there is no need to become passive; quiet reflective determination is a very powerful way of being.

The Dalai Lama is a famous example of an activist who proceeds from a foundation of compassion, humility and acceptance. If this were pure passivity then the Chinese government would not be nearly so worried.

The key message here is not, however, that you have to become like the Dalai Lama or Gandhi before you can be an activist; if we waited for that there'd not be enough activists. You don't have to become perfect or enlightened first, but it is important to carry some of these messages with you. Activism will be a rocky path, and you will almost certainly find yourself needing some of these resources along the way. Activism cannot easily be separated from any other aspect of our lives – family, social life, physical health or spirituality.

The key to avoiding burnout is to develop personal habits and practices that nurture and sustain you and your loved ones internally, while taking your warrior's sword to the problem.

3.2 Preventing burnout

There are a few important rules to remember to avoid burnout. First, do not put life on hold until the campaign is won. Most campaigns take a lot longer to achieve success than you may expect and some may never be complete, so you have to be able to 'live on the road'.

The other important principle is to continue to honour and respect yourself and your body. Do not indulge in the guilt of being human, white, male or middle class; instead find inspiration in your role as a humble change agent. You need to avoid adopting a view whereby you see yourself and your needs as less important than the campaign. You need to remain ever mindful that you are just as valid a part of the universe as anything or anyone else. Your health is (at least) as important as that of every other living thing.

Covey compares the individual to a saw and observes that effectiveness depends on keeping the tool itself in good condition, sharpened (Covey 1989: 288).

> This is the single most powerful investment we can ever make in life –
> investment in ourselves, in the only instrument we have with which to deal
> with life and to contribute ... we need to recognise the importance of taking
> time to regularly sharpen the saw. (Ibid.: 289)

You should also remember to respect the needs of your family. Your family need you to be healthy and available and you ultimately need them. Family breakdown is a common consequence of burnout and is best avoided by being aware of the danger beforehand.

In essence preventing burnout is about maintaining good health, physically, mentally emotionally and spiritually (ibid.: 288).

Let go of results and find your inspiration in the quality of your experience. 'The people united sometimes win and sometimes lose' (Peavey, quoted in Shields 1991: 129) – this is a basic lesson about living in the present and cultivating the attitude of 'acceptance of what is'.

Engaging in spiritual disciplines and healthy physical disciplines such as meditation, yoga, Pilates, sport, outdoor recreation or really good sex if it's available are all great ways to get back into the present and reconnect with the vital energies of the universe.

Throughout your campaign you should learn to forgive yourself and your comrades for failure and to celebrate every success (even though you know it's not the end of the road yet). Some activists seem to fear their comrades celebrating successes and actively try to contain the celebration with more bad news or obsessively reminding everyone that it's not over yet. This comes from a fear that people are motivated only by impending disaster and that they will slack off if they are allowed to celebrate. This is wrong; we need to take a breath after each flight of stairs and celebrating small successes helps foster an optimistic and positive feeling in a campaign.

3.3 The importance of fun

The wisdom inherent in caring for and nurturing ourselves in campaigns is reflected in the overall health and effectiveness of the campaign. Many of us have probably met serious activists who have allowed themselves to fall prey to despair, anger or depression about the issue they are dealing with. Often they are also angry that other people do not join in and help enough. But if the activists themselves appear stressed, negative or overworked, it's not very tempting for others to join in. So the next big lesson is that activism needs to be made fun, and that you are not letting the side down by insisting on fun.

A fun campaign will be a sustainable, successful and growing campaign. It is always important to plan events that are political as well as social: e.g. meetings with barbecues or volleyball, meetings in nice settings, enjoyable forms of fund-raising, comical and theatrical street activities and so on. Keeping it lively and fun will inspire other people to join in and help avoid burnout. Another part of keeping it fun is to celebrate success. Make sure that all supporters in your campaign are made aware of even the smallest milestones so that 'perception of failure' does not become endemic.

Most importantly of all, make sure that your campaign group is a social group. Rarely is successful social change achieved by the mammoth sacrifice of single individuals. Building communities out of social change organizations assists both personal and group survival. The following passage about the North East Forest Alliance exemplifies this aspect.

> The social nature of the Alliance was always a key ingredient of its success, above all, blockades and NEFA meetings were fun, and provided participants with a strong sense of belonging to a large, like-minded and reciprocal social movement. Clearly in the context of battles over forests involving heroic actions, multiple arrests and common enemies, a rich sense of camaraderie was able to develop throughout the Alliance. In this way the Alliance developed a tribal function quite separate to its more formal functioning as a political campaign. (Ricketts 2003)

Because public interest campaigns are often lengthy, involve high stakes and create social, economic and political pressure they are usually also stressful. The stress created can be externally focused but, most often, it is felt and expressed internally within the campaign group. It can be manifest in short tempers, squabbles, withdrawal from the group, substance abuse, or health or relationship breakdowns. At the collective level, stress can prevent a community group from functioning well and may lead to internal division, loss of community support or the group's collapse.

The need for this stress relief may not seem great while the campaign is in full swing, or even after a busy period, but stress relief must be made a priority before the group becomes dysfunctional. Often the best time to focus on relieving stress is after a busy period, when the need for other campaign-focused activities is lessened.

Stress can be relieved through:

- games, both competitive and non-competitive;
- group activities such as going on a bush walk or for a swim;
- relaxation of previously strict rules or requirements;
- debriefings where experiences can be recounted and integrated;
- formal processes of internal feedback permitting reflection and review;
- celebrations such as shared meals, concerts and/or parties.

If individuals can feel relieved and refreshed, their commitment to the campaign can be renewed and the group focus strengthened.

4.0 Creating empowering groups

So far we have mostly concentrated on the skills and awareness needed at the personal level to engage sustainably in social change work. Now it is necessary to examine the ways in which group dynamics can sustain or destroy a campaign.

Shields (1991: 80–2) discusses the qualities of a well-functioning group. They include important values like creating an emotionally safe working environment, being inclusive of a range of different personalities and cultural backgrounds, and nurturing a sense of belonging within the group. Additionally group cohesiveness can be enhanced by keeping a clear focus on the task and involving people in decision-making as well as allowing them to choose the kind of contribution that they are best equipped to make.

Having a clear purpose helps the group's strategic work but it also helps resolve conflict, as the campaign objective becomes a touchstone against which competing ideas can be evaluated. Developing comprehensive campaign strategy maps is a key part of such planning (see Chapter 4).

As well as a clear purpose a group must have a healthy interpersonal culture; it is important to avoid having a template of the 'right kind' of person for the campaign. It's OK for meat eaters, hunters or fishermen to be part of the conservation movement, for example. While it is important to watch out for examples of real sexism or racism in a group, it is also very important not to allow your campaign to be derailed by other people's agendas in these areas. Some people may bring a significant amount of personal baggage, and it's important for the group to be able to distinguish between real oppression and the inverse where particular individuals are deliberately adopting a victim status. Often the supposed victim may actually be engaging in passive aggression.

A clear focus upon your campaign objective and goals is the best way to analyse potential internal conflict situations and resolve them by reference to your group's stated aims.

4.1 Choosing appropriate organizational forms

An important consideration is choosing an organizational form that suits your group's size and aspirations. Some kinds of structure (corporations, for example) deliberately replicate the power structures that are common in wider society, which may be inimical to the kind of horizontal cooperation your group is aiming for. You need to ask yourselves whether you need centralized control or a loosely networked (dispersed) model, or something in between, where the organization is divided into many confederated subgroups (chapters or cells) that each have local autonomy.

A common mistake is to assume that a group needs to be incorporated to be official or real. There are circumstances where having an incorporated group can be an advantage because it is able to hold property or instigate litigation in its own right, or because it may be legally able to access government funding or collect money as a charity, but unless these are real needs, there may not be a good argument for incorporation.

Incorporated organizations usually have formal decision-making structures that create a powerful executive. In larger groups that meet infrequently this is an advantage, but in smaller local and tightly networked groups it can be a waste of time and effort – and worse, it can replace a much more organic and democratic structure. Incorporated groups need to use a significant amount of their meeting time keeping their own internal structure functioning, and this can be a distraction from campaigning, and also quite boring and alienating for the membership. Another potential problem in incorporated groups is that some people focus on leadership roles or on using the internal constitutions and procedures as a means to assert their own views; this can lead to substantial distraction from the campaign.

The alliance model is one which allows groups to function with minimum formality and also to include other organizations in their network. The alliance model allows people to move in and out easily and non-formally, and it also allows other groups, whether incorporated or not, to become affiliated with the alliance. The alliance model usually has a clear campaign focus, but organizes its support base around adherence to the values and aims of the alliance rather than formal concepts such as membership. In alliance-style groups every meeting is a campaign meeting as the 'organization' effectively has no other existence apart from the campaign.

A key advantage of the fluid model of membership used in the alliance model is that membership is not a static or passive role; ongoing contribution and engagement become the sole basis of involvement in the alliance. At first it can seem odd that you cannot actually join such a group, you can merely become involved, but in practice this serves to produce a very dynamic group because there is no capacity for passive membership. A good example of a very well-functioning alliance is provided in the following extract:

NEFA [North East Forest Alliance] differed from more traditional community organisations in several key respects. It was in every sense an alliance and operated upon a basis of minimal organisational formality ...

> NEFA deliberately avoided incorporation, preferring to function as a loosely
> constructed network of committed activists. Despite conducting a highly
> successful political campaign for well over a decade, maintaining a high level
> of recognition in local and state media, and being recognised formally by
> the New South Wales government on numerous occasions, NEFA never had
> a constitution, a secretary or president, any formal voting procedures, or
> any formal process for membership. That is not to say that it was not highly
> organised. NEFA developed organically and pragmatically as a political and
> social movement and was held together by ethos, by a sense of tribalism and
> by a minimum set of agreed procedures. (Ricketts 2003)

Social movements and the groups within them can be described by
many different names which broadly reflect aspects of their organizational
structure. At the more highly structured and centralized end of the spectrum
are corporations, of which Greenpeace is a leading example, and the many
not-for-profit incorporated associations and charitable non-governmental
organizations. These include notable groups like Amnesty International, the
World Wide Fund for Nature and numerous charities and aid organizations
operating at the international level. As well as the big groups there are also
many small locally based incorporated associations that pursue social change
objectives. Cooperatives are another form of formal organization that is
used for some groups, and of course trade unions and political parties are
further examples of social change organizations. At the less formalized end
of the spectrum are numerous groups, either locally or Internet-based, that
have minimal structure and are organized according to their aims and values
and by their campaign focus. These are usually called networks, alliances,
groups or coalitions, or have names that simply reflect the campaign itself,
such as 'Lock the Gate' or 'Save Our Beaches'.

Formal and less formal groups can work together well in strategic cooperation. Formal groups can be active in broader alliances, or conversely they
can act as umbrella groups to support the work of various alliances and
networks. For example, a really strategic model for fund-raising can be to have
non-incorporated groups affiliated with more formal incorporated groups.
Many environment centres, for example, operate as incorporated groups that
can hold property, accept donations and grants and engage in litigation, but
they also actively support a range of affiliated 'alliance'-style groups running
individual campaigns. This can be a model that achieves the best of both
worlds, where unincorporated groups can fund-raise by asking donors to
contribute by directing their donation to 'Great Big Social Change Group

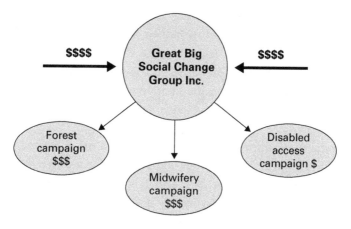

12.2 Strategic interaction of formal and less formal campaign groups

Inc.' to use in conjunction with their particular campaign. More recently Internet-based 'host organizations' such as GetUp and Move On have performed this umbrella role for numerous smaller campaigns.

4.2 Building support networks

Social change is by nature a social endeavour; there is support out there, but you need to find it, and it is important to be inclusive and to find allies, sometimes in unusual places. A useful process for uncovering potential allies is by engaging in a social mapping exercise such as that provided for the friends and foes map in Chapter 4.

Frequently people assume that in their campaign work they are on their own and it is them against the world. This is a very disempowering mistake. I have conducted many conflict mapping exercises with different groups and the most common outcome is that they are relieved to see that actually there is a lot of potential support available. When the friends and foes map is drawn up it usually reveals that the opposition is more isolated than the community-based campaign. This should not be so surprising because social change movements usually represent a campaign in the public interest against a vested interest.

One of the more useful outcomes of completing a friends and foes map is that it can open your group up to the potential for building alliances and networking with other groups. Often established groups may have some institutional knowledge about previous stages of a campaign or issue that may be useful, or other resources, links and contacts. This kind of networking is important because it can save your group from being forced to reinvent the wheel. One way of looking at this is to think of a new group as being a little like a young person, full of passion but not necessarily experience. Old groups and networks are more like the elders who may seem tired but are full of wisdom if given the time and space to impart it. Your group may be involved in a more specific or more localized issue than the group you network with, but their experience can be very useful for your more specific campaign.

One of the main impediments to working with other groups, of course, is inter-group competitiveness, or an inability to accept different approaches to a similar issue (Shields 1991: 85). This is a trap to be avoided, and again it can be avoided by a clear articulation of your group's purpose and a negotiation of the terms of any strategic partnerships.

There can be strategic political advantages to joining up with other groups. At times – for instance, where a specific issue crosses the boundaries of a whole range of different groups – groups may choose to come together with a joint media release or open letter. There have been instances, for example, where environmental groups and indigenous groups have acted together in relation to particular legislative proposals that would harm both of their interests. These kinds of coalition are seen as very powerful by power-holders (Ricketts 2006).

5.0 Group decision-making

The longevity and success of your group will depend to a large extent on how well the group is able to make decisions, particularly in situations where there are differences of opinion. There are a number of different decision-making styles, and the one you choose may depend upon your group's underlying ethics about power-sharing, the size of the group and the nature of the organization itself.

5.1 Consensus decision-making

Consensus decision-making is a well-intentioned approach that aims to allow all members to play an active part in shaping a new proposal before it gets adopted by the group. It is obviously well suited to relatively small groups that have a clearly articulated aim or goal, but it can work in larger groups – for example, many international agreements are achieved by this approach.

Consensus decision-making, as the name suggests, is an approach in which a group aims to reach decisions acceptable to the entire group. Usually this means that the proposal starts in a very 'draft' form and is worked up by the group into a form that is acceptable to all. Consensus decision-making ideally resembles a group sculpture where people are able to keep changing and modifying parts of the whole in order to make it more generally acceptable. Another pertinent metaphor is to compare consensus decision-making to the way that open-source software is developed, where a community of developers work together to continuously improve a process.

Consensus decision-making can be slow but it is not always so, and it's often surprising how initial misgivings that individuals may have about a proposal can be fixed as the proposal develops. Sometimes, where it is not possible to get complete agreement – where, for example, there are two or more equally viable courses of action – consensus can be reached by some members opting to accept an outcome that is not exactly what they wanted, provided they have no fundamental objection to it (Shields 1991: 98). This is usually called 'working consensus'.

One of the great advantages of consensus decision-making is that it frequently produces very well-rounded, very intelligent decisions. This is because the collective brainpower of the whole group has been applied to it, and different individuals have different insights, intuitions and creative abilities, and all of these are able to play a part in shaping the decision. Consensus decision-making has the potential to deliver the best available decision, particularly if all the participants are motivated by similar values, which is frequently the case within a campaign group. It can, on the other hand, lead to a lowest-common-denominator outcome, which is more likely if there is too much divergent self-interest motivating the participants. This is a problem that is particularly evident in international negotiations over environmental treaties, for example. For campaign groups, keeping a clear focus on the campaign objectives usually helps the group to move together in shaping proposals, and this is probably why consensus is such a popular style of decision-making for campaign groups.

Another key advantage of consensus decision-making for campaign groups is that a decision reached by consensus will enjoy widespread or even universal acceptance within the group.

5.2 Dealing with dissent

While consensus decision-making does have many advantages, there are some pitfalls to watch out for, particularly where there is some significant dissent within the group. If consensus cannot be reached there is a danger that dissenters will be pressured to agree or accused of blocking consensus. We need to have the maturity and wisdom to respect a diversity of opinions and accept that at times an individual will have a strong dissenting view within a group. If this dissent cannot be accommodated within the usual process of consensus decision-making it's important to find a dignified way for the person and the group to register and respect that dissent, but also to be able to move on. If consensus decision-making is taken too far there can ironically be a danger that dissenting minorities will be subjected to extraordinary pressure to agree (to not block consensus) rather than simply having their dissenting voices respected.

Some groups provide a fallback provision whereby they first aim for consensus or work back to a 'working consensus' but ultimately revert to a vote where there is entrenched dissent that needs to be noted and respected.

5.3 Majority voting

Majority voting is probably more familiar to many people than consensus styles, and it does have its advantages for very large organizations, but it is important to be aware of its serious limitations.

Pure majority rule runs the risk of alienating the substantial minority, whose views could usefully have been incorporated. In a social movement there is a need to foster a high level of group cohesion, and this is rarely achieved by ramming through majority decisions that may be unacceptable to 49 per cent of the group.

At a deeper analytical level, majority decision-making processes usually artificially create a dichotomy between complex ideas, by presenting a proposal as an either/or choice. People can be rushed into voting with or against two diametrically opposed ideas – for example, to take a particular protest action or to take no action – when in fact there may have been a number of other options not being presented. Unfortunately, when a complex situation is reduced to an either/or choice, the issue can be prematurely decided in a suboptimal way.

We have already seen how consensus decision-making can be very helpful in working up a proposal so that it enjoys the maximum possible support within the group. Some groups choose to have a deadlock provision that allows a vote to be taken if consensus cannot be achieved after a certain time, and this would allow the already heavily 'worked up' proposal to be accepted by a substantial majority (often stipulated as more than 50 per cent, possibly even two-thirds or three-quarters). This kind of method has a number of advantages:

- the proposal can be worked up to be broadly acceptable first;
- it avoids the possibility of a very small group blocking the resolution; and
- it allows dissenters to have their dissent recognized.

5.4 Weighted voting

A less well-known method of voting is to adopt a weighted voting system in which members can vote or abstain but can also attach a value to their vote. This is something which is often done with surveys, where participants are asked to rate particular propositions from strongly disagree through neutral positions to strongly agree. As a voting system it's a little complex but it can be used to weigh the depth of feeling as well as the sheer numbers of people voting for or against a proposal. This allows a strong objection to count for more than a mild misgiving. This method is sometimes used in international communities when they are choosing whether to accept a new member.

5.5 Decision-making: affinity groups

Sometimes one of the reasons why a group is having trouble making a particular decision is that it may not be necessary for the whole group to be involved. Affinity group processes are particularly effective in loosely networked activist organizations where individual affinity groups are able to split apart from the main group to undertake particular agreed action and carry with them the decision-making power over that action.

This system can be a useful way to devolve power to the individuals most concerned with a particular aspect of the campaign. So, for example, if your group has a complex campaign strategy involving publicity campaigns, litigation and digital activism, it may be possible to coordinate major aspects of the campaign through whole-of-group processes, then devolve the actual planning and implementation of particular activities to the group that will actually be performing that task, the 'litigation affinity group', the 'digital affinity group' and so on. Of course, there needs to be some basic coordination of all the affinity groups so that the campaign remains cohesive as a whole, but it is a great way to streamline the nuts-and-bolts decision-making of particular components of the campaign.

Main organization		
Litigation affinity group	Fund-raising affinity group	Digital activism affinity group

12.3 Affinity group decision-making

Frequently, when a particular action was suggested at a meeting, the individuals keen to participate would then break off into an 'affinity group' to organise the details, in this way meeting time was kept at a minimum and the affinity group was not hamstrung by an unwieldy group process. (Ricketts 2003)

Affinity group processes are very useful for complex direct action. It could be described as a devolved form of consensus decision-making. It allows the whole group to decide whether an action will go ahead, then the minute planning is delegated to the affinity group who will actually carry it out. This can avoid the active people being held back by endless debates about the finer details by people who won't be involved anyway.

The ways in which social movements have been able to explore different models of decision-making underscore their creative role in going beyond the more passive, majoritarian or representative models of modern nation-states and exploring new ways to empower participants in democratic structures and processes. In this sense the way in which an organization makes decisions is a strong indicator of its approach to democratic practice generally.

Conclusion: the joys of activism

It would be misleading to end this chapter without discussing just how fulfilling and joyful a life of activism can be. Numerous studies confirm that engagement in charity work or in causes greater than the individual self are strongly linked to overall life happiness or satisfaction (www.pbs. org/thisemotionallife/topic/altruism/altruism-happiness).

Being an activist can be a powerful antidote to feelings of powerlessness, meaninglessness, isolation and boredom with life. As an activist you will meet a lot of strong, empowered and inspiring people, and probably won't notice yourself becoming one of them as well. Some cynical people like to say that most people who work for charities and causes do so only to make themselves feel better – as if this is some kind of damning criticism. But think about it: if it makes you feel more connected and engaged with the world and gives you the satisfaction of helping bring about positive change as well, then it's the ultimate win-win, so why don't more of us wake up and join in. Go out and find yourself some old activists and ask them what the best years of their life were. Chances are they will tell you it was the height of their campaigning days.

Being an activist is about being a responsible and empowered citizen. It is about overcoming the passivity, self-doubt and resignation that hold much of the population captive to elitist power structures. Activism has the capacity not only to produce change in the world around us but also to be deeply transforming for us personally and spiritually. In many ways becoming an activist is like the completion of the process of moving from childhood to full adulthood. Instead of remaining passive and relying on the government to act as a paternal figure in their lives, activists take full personal responsibility for their place in the world and learn to accept and channel the personal political power within them. It is not surprising that it is a rocky path and that there are a number of pitfalls along the way. The risks are no reason to avoid the journey; it is an important journey for our overall collective evolution.

It is sincerely hoped that this chapter and indeed this book inspire people to have the courage and develop the skills to tackle the world's problems and to make a difference. Activists and social movements are like the immune system of the body politic – they move to the sites of dysfunction and injustice and aim to fight, repair and heal. There is no end point to history or to social evolution; there will always be a need for activists and social movements to contribute to the betterment of the world around us.

REFERENCES

1 Activism, advocacy and democracy

Kirby, The Hon. Justice Michael, AC, CMG (2002) 'Law and media – adversaries or allies in safeguarding freedom', *Southern Cross University Law Review*, 6.

2 Building social movements

Gandhi, M. K. (1951) *Non-Violent Resistance*, New York: Schocken.

Hollier, F., K. Murray and H. Cornelius (1993) *Trainers Manual 12 Skills*, Sydney: Conflict Resolution Network, sheet 30.

Iffe, J. (1995) *Community Development: Creating community alternatives – vision, analysis and practice*, Sydney: Longman Australia.

Macy, J. and M. Young Brown (1998) *Coming Back to Life – Practices to Reconnect Our Lives*, Canada: Our World New Society Publishers.

Marley, R. (1979) 'Babylon System', on *Survival*, Jamaica: Island.

Mead, M. (n.d.) *Archives 1999–2009*, Institute for Intercultural Studies, www.intercultural studies.org/, accessed 20 March 2011.

Moyer, B. (2001) *Doing Democracy: The MAP model for organizing social movements*, Philadelphia, PA: New Society Publishers.

Nash, A. (2001) *people.dot.community: A resource for effective community activism*, Geelong: Villamanta Legal Service.

Peavey, F. (2000) *Heart Politics Revisited*, Sydney: Pluto Press.

Seed, J. et al. (1988) *Thinking Like a Mountain*, Philadelphia, PA: New Society Publishers.

3 Strategy

Moyer, B. (2001) *Doing Democracy: The MAP model for organizing social movements*, Philadelphia, PA: New Society Publishers.

4 Planning and mapping your campaign

Ricketts, A. (2003) 'Om Gaia dudes. The North East Forest Alliance's old growth forest campaign', in H. Wilson (ed.), *Belonging in the Rainbow Region*, Lismore: Southern Cross University Press.

Williamson, M. (1996) *A Return to Love: Reflections on the Principles of 'A Course in Miracles'*, New York: HarperCollins.

6 Public sector activism

Inter-Parliamentary Council (1994) *Declaration on Criteria for Free and Fair Elections*, Inter-parliamentary Union 1996–2011, www.ipu. org/cnl-e/154-free.htm, accessed 20 March 2011.

Korten, D. (1995) *When Corporations Rule the World*, San Francisco, CA: Kumarian Press/ Berret Koehler Publications.

Ricketts, A. (2002) 'Freedom of association or guilt by association: Australia's new anti-terrorism laws and the retreat of political liberty', *Southern Cross University Law Review*, 6.

Tasmanian Dam case [1983] HCA 21; (1983)158 CLR 1.

US Department of State (2008) *Free and Fair Elections*, America.gov, www.america.gov/ st/democracyhr-english/2008/May/200806 09215618eaifas9.156436e-02.html, accessed 20 March 2011.

7 Corporate activism

Beilefield, S., S. Higginson, J. Jackson and A. Ricketts (2005) 'Directors' duties to the company and minority shareholder environ-mental activism', *Companies and Securities Law Journal*, 23: 28.

Crane, A. and D. Matten (2007) *Business Ethics*, 2nd edn, Oxford: Oxford University Press.

Donaldson, T. (1982) *Corporations and Morality*, New Jersey: Prentice Hall.

French, P. A., J. Nesteruk and D. Risser (1992) *Corporations in the Moral Community*, Fort Worth, TX: Harcourt Brace Jovanovich College Publishers.

Karliner, J. (1997) *The Corporate Planet: Ecology and Politics in the Age of Globalisation*, San Francisco, CA: Sierra Club.

Korten, D. (1995) *When Corporations Rule the World*, San Francisco, CA: Kumarian Press.

Manheim, J. (2000) *The Death of a Thousand Cuts: Corporate Campaigns and the Attack on the Corporation*, London: Routledge.

— (2001) 'The death of a thousand cuts', *Review*, March, www.ipa.org.au/.../Review 53-1%20The%20death%20from%201000%20cuts .pdf.

Mayer, C. J. (1990) 'Personalising the impersonal: corporations and the Bill of Rights', *Hastings Law Journal*, 41(3).

Parkinson, J. E. (2002) *Corporate Power and Responsibility: Issues in the theory of company law*, New York: Oxford University Press.

Ricketts, A. (2001) *Stretching the Metaphor: The Political Rights of the Corporate Person*, Unpublished Master's of Law thesis held at Southern Cross University Library and Queensland University of Technology Library.

Rose, J. (2001) 'Forget S11, try shareholder activism', *The Age*, 10 August.

Seidman, G. (2007) *Beyond the Boycott: Labor rights, human rights and transnational activism*, American Sociological Foundation.

8 Direct action

Cohen, I. (1997) *Green Fire*, Sydney: Angus and Robertson.

De Lint, W. (2004) *Public Order Policing in Canada: An Analysis of Operations in Recent High Stakes Events*, December.

Ricketts, A. (2002) 'Freedom of association or guilt by association: Australia's new anti-terrorism laws and the retreat of political liberty', *Southern Cross University Law Review*, 6: 133.

— (2006) 'Theatre of protest: the magnifying effects of theatre in direct action', *Journal of Australian Studies*, 89: 77–9.

Rogers, N. (1998) *Green Paradigms*, Southern Cross University Press.

9 Digital activism

Cullum, B. (2010) 'Devices: the power of mobile phones', in M. Joyce (ed.), *Digital Activism Decoded: The New Mechanics of Change*, New York and Amsterdam: International Debate Education Association, pp. 47–70.

Generation 2.0A (n.d.) 'A practical guide for using new media to recruit, organize, and mobilize young people', mobileactive.org/research/generation-2-0-practical-guide-using-new-media-recruit-organize-and-mobilize-young-people.

Joyce, M. (ed.) (2010) *Digital Activism Decoded: The New Mechanics of Change*, New York and Amsterdam: International Debate Education Association.

Radcliff, D. (2000) Network World, 29 May, www.networkworld.com/research/2000/0529feat2.html.

Ramey, C. (2007) 'Mobile phones in mass organizing: a MobileActive white paper', ed. K. Verclas, mobileactive.org/mobiles-in-mass-organizing.

Rheingold, H. (2002) *Smart Mobs: The Next Social Revolution*, New York: Basic Books, www.smartmobs.com.

Scholtz, T. (2010) 'Infrastructure: its transformations and effect on digital activism', in M. Joyce (ed.), *Digital Activism Decoded: The New Mechanics of Change*, New York and Amsterdam: International Debate Education Association, pp. 17–32.

Shultz, D. and A. Jungherr (2010) 'Applications: picking the right one in a transient world', in M. Joyce (ed.), *Digital Activism Decoded: The New Mechanics of Change*, New York and Amsterdam: International Debate Education Association, pp. 33–46.

UN News Centre (2010) 15 February, www.un.org/apps/news/story.asp?NewsID=33770&Cr=Telecom&Cr1=&Kw1=phone&Kw2=&Kw3=m, accessed 30 August 2010.

Wilhelm, A. G. (2000) *Democracy in the Digital Age: Challenges to Political Life in Cyberspace*, London: Routledge.

10 Strategic litigation

Briggs, P., J. Taberner and D. Bick (2010) 'A goldmine for environmental class actions in Australia?', Freehills, www.freehills.com.au/Print/6750.aspx, accessed 28 March 2011.

Parker, D. (2010) 'Class actions: a high stakes game', *In the Black: CPA Australia*, 80(5): 36, www.cpaaustralia.com.au/cps/rde/xchg/cpa-site/hs.xsl/intheblack-2010-june-action.html, accessed 20 March 2011.

Walters, B. (2003) *Slapping on the Writs – defamation, developers and community activism*, Sydney: University of NSW Press.

Australian Conservation Foundation v. *The Commonwealth* [1980] 146 CLR 493.

Gunn's Limited v. *Marr* [2005] VSC 251.

McDonald's Corporation, McDonald's Restaurants Limited v. *Helen Marie Steel and David Morris* [1997] EWHC QB 366.

R v. *Environment Secretary, Ex parte Rose Theatre Trust Co* [1990] 1 All ER 754.

R v. *Inspectorate of Pollution, Ex parte Greenpeace* [1994] 1 WLR 570, [1994] 4 All ER 329.

11 Social change and conflict resolution

Alexander, N. and J. Howieson (2010) *Negotiation: Strategy Style Skills*, LexisNexis Butterworths.

Boulle, L. (1996) *Mediation Principles, Process, Practice*, Sydney: Butterworths.

Fisher, R., B. Ury and B. Patton (1991) *Getting to Yes: Negotiating an agreement without giving in*, 2nd edn, London: Random House.

Hollier, F., K. Murray and H. Cornellius (1993) *Trainer's Manual: 12 Skills*, Sydney: Conflict Resolution Network (CRN).

Iffe, J. (1995) *Community Development: Creating community alternatives – vision, analysis and practice*, Sydney: Longman.

Kritek, P. (1994) *Negotiating at an Uneven Table*, San Francisco, CA: Jossey-Bass.

Moyer, B. (2001) *Doing Democracy: The MAP Model for Organizing Social Movements*, Philadelphia, PA: New Society Publishers.

Peavey, F. (1994) *By Life's Grace: Musing on the Essence of Social Change*, Philadelphia, PA: New Society Publishers.

Shields, K. (1991) *In the Tiger's Mouth: An Empowerment Guide for Social Action*, Sydney: Millennium.

12 Empowerment and personal stability

Boice, J. (1992) *The Art of Daily Activism*, Oakland, CA: Wingbrow Press.

Covey, S. R. (1989) *The 7 Habits of Highly Effective People*, New York: Simon and Schuster, republished 2000 by Information Australia.

Harris, B. (2002) *Thresholds of the Mind*, Oregon: Centerpointe Research Institute.

Moyer, B. (2001) *Doing Democracy: The MAP model for organizing social movements*, Philadelphia, PA: New Society Publishers.

Peavey, F. (1986) *Heart Politics*, Philadelphia, PA: New Society Publishers.

— (1994) *By Life's Grace: Musing on the Essence of Social Change*, Philadelphia, PA: New Society Publishers.

Ricketts, A. (2003) 'Om Gaia Dudes. The North East Forest Alliance's old growth forest campaign', in H. Wilson (ed.), *Belonging in the Rainbow Region*, Lismore: Southern Cross University Press.

— (2006) 'Theatre of protest: the magnifying effects of theatre in direct action', *Journal of Australian Studies*, 89: 77–90.

Shields, K. (1991) *In the Tiger's Mouth: An Empowerment Guide for Social Action*, Sydney: Millennium Books.

INDEX